PENGUIN BOOKS

LUSITANIA

Colin Simpson was born in 1931 and was educated
at Wellington, Oxford, Sandhurst and the University of Helsinki. At the last he read Ugro-Finnish
languages and took a doctorate for a study of the
relationship of the environment and a nation's art.
He has been a special correspondent of the *Sunday
Times* and is the co-author, with Phillip Knightley,
of *The Secret Lives of Lawrence of Arabia*. He is
married, has three children and lives in Surrey.

LUSITANIA

Colin Simpson

PENGUIN BOOKS

Penguin Books Ltd, Harmondsworth, Middlesex, England
Penguin Books, 40 West 23rd Street, New York, New York 10010, U.S.A.
Penguin Books Australia Ltd, Ringwood, Victoria, Australia
Penguin Books Canada Ltd, 2801 John Street, Markham, Ontario, Canada L3R 1B4
Penguin Books (N.Z.) Ltd, 182–190 Wairau Road, Auckland 10, New Zealand

First published by Longman 1972
Published in Penguin Books 1974
Reprinted with Epilogue 1983

Made and printed in Great Britain by
Richard Clay (The Chaucer Press) Ltd, Bungay, Suffolk
Set in Monotype Garamond

Contents

DIAGRAMS

Key to Admiralty MV Code Series 1 used in signals to and from the *Lusitania* on her last voyage.

The message is obtained by running on all the groups of letters and continuously subtracting 41513 from the number of a letter's position in the alphabet, for example:

4	1	5	1	3	4	1	5	1	3
w	v	g	n	d	v	j	s	f	v
s	u	b	m	a	r	i	n	e	s

Introduction

The Old Head of Kinsale is a steep and rocky promontory which juts aggressively into the Atlantic from the south-west coast of Ireland. On its crest are a lighthouse, a coast-guard station and the ruins of an early Celtic settlement. For two thousand years it has been a vantage point for those on shore and a familiar and essential landmark to those at sea. Behind it lies a deep and secure harbour, once the shelter of Spanish and English fleets, and the town of Kinsale, today a sleepy fishing port swollen each summer by the tourist and the yachtsman. There is little to do but talk, and any conversation eventually turns to the *Lusitania* torpedoed near by on 7 May 1915 with the loss of 1201 lives. There is a Lusitania bar, a Lusitania grill and the inevitable *Lusitania* souvenirs. Equally inevitable is the *Lusitania* legend that the great liner was loaded with bullion which is there for the taking for anyone sufficiently rich and determined to risk diving three hundred feet to the granite and current-swept bottom of the Atlantic twelve miles south and two points west of the Old Head.

There have been several attempts at salvage. Each has been abandoned, two of them ending in bankruptcy. Shortly after the end of the last war the Royal Navy salvage ship *Reclaim* moored over the wreck. Her presence was recorded in the log of the coast-guard station up on the Old Head speculation died when the *Reclaim* sailed away. In 1954 a Southampton company, Risdon Beazley Limited, moored a recovery vessel over the wreck and stayed there some days. No confirmation could be obtained by journalists that they had ever been there. The tales of bullion swelled to include a cargo of platinum and strong-rooms packed with diamonds and precious stones. There followed a series of diving ventures by an American diver, John Light, who with little money and scanty equipment made numerous descents. His most newsworthy attempt was described in the American *Sports Illustrated* on 24 December 1962. The team on the bottom included Surgeon-Commander John Aquadro of the United States Navy. Their report was inconclusive but claimed to have found evidence that previous divers had been cutting and blasting at the hulk whilst Commander Aquado stated he had seen what he thought was a gun-barrel. As a result the finance was found for an expensive series of dives. Ill-luck and differences of opinion led to the abandonment of the project and financial support was withdrawn. The ownership of the wreck and the cargo is now involved and there have not been any significant diving operations since 1965. (*See p. 18.)

I read the report in *Sports Illustrated* and at the suggestion of William Rees-Mogg, now the Editor of *The Times*, began to make my own inquiries. Since I have no taste for diving in the Atlantic, these concentrated on the archives. The story they reveal is told in this book. From the beginning my appetite was whetted by the doubts whether the ships of the Admiralty and Messrs Risdon Beazley had ever been to the wreck. Working from the Navy Lists I traced two members of the crew of the *Reclaim* and have spoken at length to them. Both freely admitted that they had been to the *Lusitania*, but they also very properly said that they could not say anything else without permission from the Admiralty, pleading in justification that they were subject to the Official Secrets Act. To this day the Admiralty deny that 'the *Reclaim* or any other Naval vessel' has been to the site or that any Royal Navy personnel have dived to the wreck. This has been their attitude for the last seven years. In January 1972 Messrs Risdon Beazley of Southampton conceded to me that they had been twice to the diving site but only 'for the fun of it'. Their managing director has asked me to state that 'no employees of this company have dived to the *Lusitania*'.

My first inquiries stemmed from the idea that here was a classic tale of sunken treasure, and because of this I accepted the undoubted reluctance of many people to discuss the matter. Nevertheless I found it a valid challenge to try and discover the facts of the story. The obvious starting point was to discover the manifest of the cargo with which the *Lusitania* sailed from New York. The files of *The Times* showed that there had been a Board of Trade inquiry into her loss six weeks after the disaster. A second inquiry took place in New York in 1918. At each, the manifest would have been a formal exhibit. The Board of Trade eventually receives copies of the manifests of all ships which are stored in the National Maritime Museum at Greenwich. If a ship sailed from New York, a further manifest should be in the archive of the New York Customs. The first three were located. All three were different. The one thing they showed in common was no mention of bullion, specie, or anything else sufficiently valuable to merit an expensive salvage operation. The Cunard Company confirmed that they too had a manifest. This was equally devoid of hints of treasure, but again it was different from the others. A detailed examination showed that all of them were copies. The problem was, where was the original? It was found amongst the private papers of the late President Franklin D. Roosevelt and I obtained a copy. That discovery and the circumstances as to how and why President Roosevelt had obtained it proved the starting point of this book. I did not tell either the Admiralty or the U.S. State Department that I had it, but asked them for access to all their records relating to the *Lusitania*. They quickly and courteously gave their permission.

The records of the Admiralty are kept secret for thirty years. They are then screened for matters affecting national security and those which pass this sieve are placed in the Public Record Office, where they are open for public inspection. In the United States a similar process is followed, the edited records being placed in the National Archives. Both sets of archives, though the *Lusitania* affair closely concerned both nations and was the first and most dramatic of the events which led to the eventual entry of the United States into the First World War, contain meagre information. There are substantial differences of fact in the two sets of papers and in many cases it is difficult to accept that the files relate to the same vessel. However, the two collections of documents both agree in their conclusions. These form the basis of the official or authorized version of the *Lusitania* affair, which was published as a small booklet by the Cunard Company in October 1915. Stripped of its bellicose statements, it accurately reflects the public beliefs of the British Admiralty and the American State Department as to what did happen and why: a belief that they share to this day. It would be unjust to both these august institutions not to quote from it.

Ever since 1840, the Cunard Steam Ship Company Limited has been intimately associated with the British Government. From time to time there have been several important agreements, not the least being that entered into in 1902, when the Company arranged to build two large steamers, to hold at the disposal of the Government the whole of its fleet, and to remain a purely British undertaking. The outcome of this agreement was the building of the world-famous ocean leviathans, the *Lusitania* and *Mauretania*.

The actual construction of the *Lusitania* was commenced in September, 1904. . . . She was launched on June 7, 1906 . . . just fourteen months, three weeks, from the laying of her keel. . . .

During the whole period of construction her progress was eagerly watched by all interested in shipping, the vessel having aroused – by reason of her size, her magnificent accommodation, her speed, and turbine engine – worldwide attention. . . .

On September 7, 1907 the *Lusitania* sailed from Liverpool to New York on her maiden voyage; and it is no exaggeration to say that never before had such widespread interest been taken in the first sailing of any liner. Fully 200,000 people witnessed her departure. . . .

The cheering of the vast crowds, supplemented by the steam whistles and sirens of all the shipping in the river at the time, as the leviathan moved from the Stage, and slowly disappeared into the darkness, made this epoch-marking event a most memorable one. These enthusiastic scenes were renewed at Queenstown, which port she left a few minutes after noon on the following day. . . . Her reception on the other side of the Atlantic was just as hearty, a whole fleet of tugs and pleasure steamers greeting her as she entered the newly dredged Ambrose Channel.

From the first, the *Lusitania* became a great favourite with Atlantic travellers, and no wonder, for in addition to her speed, she was so luxuriously appointed that her passenger accommodation was the acme of comfort, and well merited the description of a 'floating palace'.

Her decorative and architectural features compared with those of the world's finest hotels – lofty domes, fashioned and painted by expect decorators, panels prepared by skilled workers, handsome tapestries, curtains and carpets. The First Class Dining Saloon was a vision in white and gold. The style was Louis Seize, and the predominating colour was vieux rose. The magnificent mahogany sideboard, with its gilt metal ornaments, was the admiration of all who saw it, while high above towered the wonderful dome with painted panels after Boucher. The Lounge was decorated in late Georgian period, and the fine inlaid mahogany panels, richly modelled dome ceiling and marble mantelpieces constituted a luxurious ensemble. Harmony and refinement was the *motif* of the Writing Room, Library and Smoke Room. In addition to these various Public Rooms, there were Regal Suites, comprising Dining Room, Drawing Room, two Bedrooms, Bath and Toilet Rooms, with adjoining rooms for maid or valet. The accommodation for Second Class passengers was also upon a luxurious scale, and the Public Rooms included Dining Room, Smoking Room, Library and Lounge. Ample provision had also been made for those travelling Third Class. Such, in brief, is a description of the passenger appointments of the *Lusitania*. . . .

As to her achievements, and the many interesting facts concerning her two hundred and one successful trips across the Atlantic, a great deal can be written, but space will only allow of a short resume. . . . On her second westbound trip she averaged 24 knots, and reduced the passage between Liverpool and New York to well under 5 days (4 days, 19 hours, 52 minutes), and logged 617 knots for the highest day's run, incidentally bringing back to the British mercantile service the 'Blue Riband of the Atlantic', having wrested it from the German liners *Kronprinz Wilhelm*, *Kaiser Wilhelm II*, and *Kronprinzessin Cecilia*. . . .

And now we come to the last phase of her career. Although the

War broke out in August, 1914, and the British Government, according to its agreement with the Company in 1902, could have requisitioned the *Lusitania*, she was never actually in Government Service but maintained her regular place amongst Cunard sailings. In April, 1915, she left Liverpool for New York on her 101st voyage, having then crossed the Atlantic 200 times. She arrived at the American port safely, although on a previous voyage she avoided the attack of an enemy submarine. On May 1, the *Lusitania* left New York for Liverpool. . . .

Prior to the sailing, threatening statements were published in the American Press by German authorities foretelling the sinking of the liner; but in the words of Lord Mersey, who subsequently conducted the Inquiry into the loss of the vessel: 'So far from affording any excuse, the threats serve only to aggravate the crime by making it plain that the intention to commit it was deliberately formed, and the crime itself planned before the ship sailed.'

. . . On 7th May, an uneventful voyage, the Irish Coast was sighted and at 2.10 p.m. the liner was within 8 to 10 miles of the Old Head of Kinsale. Without the slightest warning, the wake of a torpedo from a German submarine was seen approaching the ship, and she was struck between the third and fourth funnels. There was evidence that a second, and perhaps a third, torpedo was fired, and the great ship sank within 20 minutes. It is impossible to satisfactorily draw a pen picture of the heart-rending scenes which followed. Men, women and children, caught like rats in a trap, were vainly fighting for their lives amongst wreckage of every description. The doomed liner's S.O.S. was answered within a few hours of the call, and 764 lives were saved. Still the Hunnish pirates had performed their task, proving to the civilized world that the whole gamut of barbarism had been exhausted in the interest of German Kultur. The Belgian atrocities, poisoning of wells, and asphyxiating gases – all these dwarfed to insignificance in the face of the foulest act of wilful murder ever committed on the high seas. The crime, which will for ever remain a blot upon the history of a civilized (?) nation, resulted in the loss of 1,198 innocent and unoffending people. . . .* As the lifeless bodies of men, women, and harmless children were brought in, the scenes were most horrifying and brought tears to the eyes of

* Cunard's figures innocently omitted three persons in the cells as explained in Chapter 9.

the most callous people. The burial of the victims took place at the Old Church Cemetery.

This appalling crime was contrary to international law and the conventions of all civilised nations, and we therefore charge the owners of the submarine, the German Emperor and the Government of Germany, under whose orders they acted, with the crime of wilful and wholesale murder.

This was the verdict of the coroner's jury at the inquest held upon the victims at Kinsale. A terrible indictment – one which will pass into history and put to shame all future generations of the German race.

This greatest outrage against humanity shocked the whole world. Yet 'WITH JOYFUL PRIDE WE CONTEMPLATE THIS LATEST DEED OF OUR NAVY' was the phrase used by the *Kölnische Volkszeitung* in an article dealing with the crime. The victory was *hailed by shouts of delight in every quarter of the German Empire*, and the school children were even granted a holiday! It was only to be expected that the enemy would attempt to justify his heinous work by proclaiming that the vessel was armed. By wireless, and through his own newspapers, the enemy made this foul and diabolical charge. This was proved to be totally unfounded. . . . Another German lie exposed!

But not satisfied with his rejoicings over such an act of treachery, the enemy had, perforce, to strike a medal with the object of keeping alive in German hearts this deed of his Navy.

When the British Press gave publicity to this morbid souvenir, its issue was at first denied by the German press. . . .

The *Kölnische Volkszeitung* was very indignant at the suggestion that German artists could ever produce such a vulgar thing; but it has had to admit that such a medal was struck, and that it was distributed throughout Germany. It was designed by Herr K. Goetz, of Munich, is $2\frac{1}{2}$ inches in diameter, made of copper-coloured metal, and is in high relief. Even the German Press Bureau now admits that the medal was privately executed. The following is a short description of the medal:

On the obverse, under the legend 'No Contraband' (Keine Bannware), there is a representation of the *Lusitania* sinking. The designer has put in guns, armoured cars and aeroplanes, but has conveniently omitted to put in the women and children which the world knew she *did* carry. On the reverse, under the legend 'Business above all' (Geschäft über alles), the figure of Death is shewn at the booking office giving out tickets to passengers who refuse to attend to the warning against submarines given by a German. This picture seeks apparently to propound the theory that if a murderer warns his victim of his intention, the guilt of the crime will rest with the victim, not with the murderer. . . .

The *Lusitania* today lies at the bottom of the sea – her name will be a lasting monument to the atrocities of a race steeped in savagery, and whose lust for blood knew no bounds.

The reference to the medal intrigued me. I quickly discovered that Herr Goetz had indeed designed one, and had circulated a total of forty-four examples. He had intended it to be satirical comment on the allegations by the German government that the *Lusitania* carried contraband. The first British publicity about the medal came in a press release from the Foreign Office to *The Times*. Checking the Foreign Office records for that date, it appears that 300,044 medals were cast, in different states and in different metals, 300,000 of them on the instructions of Captain Reginald Hall, the Director of British Naval Intelligence during the First World War. Their maker was not Herr Goetz but Mr Gordon Selfridge, the department store owner, and they had been distributed throughout the world in an effort to whip up distaste for Germany. The project presumably had a distinct propaganda value and cost the patriotic Mr Selfridge several thousand pounds.

The Foreign Office medal file contained cross references to numerous other records and these in turn produced sufficient evidence to convince me that the official version of the *Lusitania* disaster contained substantial omissions and inaccuracies. These I listed and showed to Lord Mancroft who was a member of the Bar Council, a former Parliamentary Secretary for the Ministry of Defence and Cabinet Minister, and, at the time I met him, the Deputy Chairman of the Cunard Company. Lord Mancroft in this latter capacity authorized me to search wherever I wished among Cunard's archives and instructed certain of his executives and the company's solicitors to give me every assistance. Lastly he authorized the quotation of any records that I wished to use. Without his initiative and assistance this story could not have been told.

Lord Mancroft introduced me to Messrs Hill, Dickinson and Co. of Liverpool and London and, in particular, to their senior partner, Mr Robert Leslie Adam. Messrs Hill, Dickinson have been solicitors to The Cunard Steam-Ship Co. Ltd since its formation in 1878 and to its predecessors since Mr Samuel Cunard founded the Cunard Line in 1840. Mr Adam is the son of Mr R. A. Adam, a former Superintendent Engineer of Cunard who would have sailed in the *Lusitania* on her last voyage had he not been suffering from pneumonia at the time. Mr Adam was, therefore, born and brought up in a world in which the loss of the *Lusitania* was an ever present memory. He and his firm are the custodians of many of the facts and several of the archives on which this book is based and, with the permission of the Board of Cunard Co., he has made all such facts and records available to me, and his firm has charted the course of the *Lusitania* as far as this is possible today on the available evidence and with modern charts. Sifting the accumulated archives and memories of fifty-seven years leads to error and sometimes to direct untruth. In an emotive story such as this, a degree of imbalance can creep in; which time and pride compound. To correct this account – as far as the Cunard Company are concerned – I asked Mr Adam to read a proof version of this book on the understanding that I would correct any facts which he knew to be either inaccurate or untrue. He has done this, and though in this respect my story could not have a better imprimatur, the opinions expressed and the conclusions drawn are entirely my own.

As lawyers Hill, Dickinson's main function at the time was to prepare and conduct Cunard's defence before the Board of Trade Inquiry conducted by Lord Mersey during June 1915, and later in the New York district court during 1918 before Judge Julius B. Mayer.

Both judges kept their judgment notes, together with the originals of the court shorthand writers' transcripts and many of the exhibits which were used in evidence. The present Lord Mersey has given me full access to his grandfather's papers. Certain of his grandfather's actions may appear to be unjudicial. It is important to state that this was because he had been ordered to act as he did. He was also told to return to the Admiralty all papers relating to their evidence. To his credit he eventually disobeyed his instructions and preserved his papers doubtless with the idea that one day his conduct would be explained. The papers of Judge Mayer were embargoed for fifty years and the U.S. Department of Justice released them for examination in May 1968.

The archives of both judges show that they were in close contact with many persons charged with the conduct of the war. In every case I have tried to follow up these contacts and the list of private papers and sources I have used is given in the Sources. The sum of these inquiries, added to the Cunard and Hill, Dickinson archives, was finally complemented by the discovery of the papers of the then Chairman of Cunard, Alfred Booth, and his cousin George who was Deputy Director-General of the Ministry of Munitions from 1914 to 1919.

Finally, this book does not raise the matter of the ethics of unrestricted submarine warfare. In fact it does not discuss ethics at all. However, it is relevant to recall that history tells that the first U-boat war was the brainchild of the German Admiral von Tirpitz and that deputizing for St George against the German dragon was Admiral of the Fleet Lord Fisher. It does not tell that these two men corresponded in secret. On 29 March 1916 while the recruiting posters still shrilled 'Avenge the *Lusitania*', Lord Fisher wrote to Tirpitz, 'I don't blame you for the submarine business, I'd have done exactly the same myself.'

* The ownership, and the complete series of dives carried out in the summer of 1982, together with the post-1945 'Lusitania' operation of the Royal Navy, are detailed in the Epilogue.

Lusitania

1

The *Lusitania* was the largest and fastest ship of her time. She was launched at Clydebank on 7 June 1906, an event which moved the shipping correspondent of *The Times* to such paeans that he jumbled his metaphors. 'She is', he wrote, 'a veritable greyhound of the seas . . . a worthy tribute to her illustrious lineage . . . a credit to the august and noble stable which conceived her . . .' *The Times* did not elaborate on her parentage, but adopting its idiom it may be described as 'By Naval Necessity – Out of Public Funds'. The marriage was undoubtedly one of convenience, but paradoxically it was also a shotgun wedding. The man holding the shotgun was J. P. Morgan, the American financier.

At the beginning of this century, the greater part of the North Atlantic shipping trade was in European hands. The United States by isolationist and shortsighted legislation had failed to retain the dominance, which aided by Government subsidies, her earlier steamships had gained for her. British, French and German companies monopolized the traffic, and by their own competition had in many cases reduced their individual profitability to meagre proportions. Since 1897 the two German companies, Hamburg-Amerika and Norddeutscher Lloyd, heavily subsidized by their Government, had held the Blue Riband for the fastest crossing, and their rivals were finding it difficult to raise the finance to build the ships which would provide effective yet profitable competition. Though the freight, passenger and emigrant trades were growing fast, fares and rates had been ruthlessly cut in order to obtain a share of the business, and many of the companies were barely able to pay dividends.

J. P. Morgan identified what was, in modern jargon, a classic takeover situation. He resolved to form a combine which would monopolize the North Atlantic sea routes, and thereafter adjust the rates to maximize his profits. By March 1902 Morgan's combine either controlled or held a major shareholding in every substantial shipping company on either side of the Atlantic, with the exception of the Compagnie Générale Transatlantique of France and the Cunard Company of Liverpool. The two great German lines were firmly under Morgan's aegis, and Cunard's greatest English rival, the White Star Line, was finally absorbed in December 1902. Morgan then proceeded to rationalize the shipbuilding programmes of the member companies of his combine, now called the International Mercantile Marine Co. By the end of 1902 it was the dominant and most vocal operator in the business, buttressed by a market capitalization of £25 million.

Cunard had been negotiating with shipbuilders Swan Hunter for a new fast liner and had almost finalized their plans when the Morgan combine was announced. Early in 1902 Morgan made a takeover approach to Cunard. Fortunately for them, though it caused apprehension in their Liverpool boardroom, it created consternation at the Admiralty. The Admiralty had for almost a hundred years indirectly subsidized the major passenger companies by granting them monies as mail or emigrant subsidies. In return it had the right to take up suitable vessels for employment as transports or auxiliary cruisers. Now at one swoop Morgan had deprived their Lordships of what was almost a complete auxiliary navy. To the Admiralty Morgan was then a doubtful quantity, and his connections with and reputed sympathy for German commercial interests made his motives suspect.* At the Admiralty's bidding Parliament forbade the transfer of the combine's newly-acquired ships from the British registry. Behind the scenes the Admiralty generated such pressure on the Treasury for dramatically increased naval estimates and concealed subsidies that the

* In the event, Morgan was determinedly pro-Ally. During the First World War he raised loans for the Allies of $2,396,791,777.[1]

Prime Minister, Lord Salisbury, remarked: 'We are in the face of a jingo hurricane, and driving before it under bare poles.'[2]

The Admiralty's hand was strengthened by a paper[3] prepared by H. O. Arnold-Forster, then Secretary of the Admiralty and a well-known authority on defence. He had recently visited the German bases at Kiel and Wilhelmshaven, and his views were formally accepted as official policy by the First Lord of the Admiralty, Lord Selborne, and embodied in a memorandum to the Cabinet. 'I am convinced that the great new German Navy is being carefully built up from the point of view of a war with us . . . we cannot safely ignore the malignant hatred of the German people, or the manifest design of the German Navy . . . '[4] Arnold-Forster also reported that the crack German liners were designed from the beginning to operate as armed cruisers, and their potential was such as to constitute a major threat to Britain's maritime supply routes.

The outcome was that the Admiralty decided to drop its practice of a modest annual operating allowance, and formed a committee to which were invited representatives from the Institute of Naval Architects to help formulate a set of figures which could offer guidance as to how it was to employ its funds in future. The Admiralty requirement was a ship which would achieve a constant 24½ knots in moderate weather and be capable of mounting a very substantial armament indeed. The committee arrived at its conclusions by taking the mean original costs of ships of varying tonnage and horsepower, together with the previous rates of subsidy, and extending the calculations until they achieved the required speed. The committee reported that the Admiralty specification would need 68,000 h.p.; that the construction costs would be £1,250,000 and that an annual operating subsidy of £204,000 was indicated. At that time the most powerful ship ever built was the German liner *Kaiser Wilhelm II* with engines of 38,000 h.p. which produced 23½ knots. An additional 30,000 h.p. was required to generate the extra knot or so. Armed with this brief the Admiralty began negotiations with Cunard which finally resulted in an Agreement whereby the Admiralty agreed to finance the whole of the building costs of two liners, not exceeding a total of £2,600,000, at an interest rate of 2¾ per cent, plus an annual operating subsidy of £75,000 per ship, in addition to the mail subsidy, in return for Cunard agreeing to build ships capable of maintaining a minimum average ocean speed of from 24 to 25 knots. The two ships were the *Mauretania* and the *Lusitania*.

The full terms of the agreement were embodied in two thick volumes which have never been published, as the Admiralty will still not withdraw their security classification. However, they have been briefly described as being as 'onerous as they were prolix'.[5] Those relating to the design of the ship have a direct bearing on the enormous loss of life in the ultimate tragedy. The Admiralty stipulated that Cunard should defer on all questions of design and construction; that the ships were to be built to Admiralty specifications and under Admiralty survey; that in the threat of hostilities they were to be withdrawn immediately from service so as to be fully-converted to armed cruisers, and that on the outbreak of war they were to be placed under Admiralty command. Cunard were required to guarantee that control of the company would never pass outside British hands, that in time of war they would place their entire fleet at the Admiralty's disposal, and that at all times the crews of the two liners would have a proportion of their officers and men drawn from the Royal Naval Reserve.[6] Cunard accepted all these stipulations and the formal agreement was signed by them on 30 July 1903.

The design brief which the directors presented to Leonard Peskett, their chief designer, was a formidable one. He had to fulfil the Admiralty specifications without question, and as the company had accepted an annual subsidy of only £75,000 per vessel instead of the indicated £204,000 the balance was to be earned by dramatically increased passenger accommodation. Moreover Cunard decreed that this accommodation was to be of a spaciousness and splendour hitherto unknown outside the great luxury hotels of the world. Peskett's brief may be summarized as having to devise a floating hotel with accommodation for 2300 guests and a staff of 900. The whole to cross the Atlantic at more than 24½ knots and be capable of carrying twelve six-inch guns.

The speed of a vessel is determined by a sophisticated equation in which the factors are the horsepower, the waterline length, the beam and displacement. Peskett already had the specification of 24½ knots minimum, and 68,000 h.p. He had to fit both his employers' and the Admiralty requirements into a waterline length of 760 feet and a maximum beam of 87 ft 6 in. This entailed building high; higher in fact than anyone had ever built a ship before. (The early experiments and designs were for a beam of 78 ft, but tank tests at Haslar showed the model to be so dangerously unstable that the beam was increased.)

The Admiralty also insisted that all engines, boilers, steering gear, fuel and vital controls were to be placed below the waterline, as was the standard practice in warships. The turbine rooms occupied most of the stern section, then came four vast boiler rooms, housing twenty-five boilers, which were placed in rows across the ship. The boiler rooms continued up into the taper of the bows, and forward of them were a small baggage hold and the trim tanks. The whole of the vessel was divided into eleven watertight compartments by ten transverse bulkheads, each fitted with watertight doors. Each boiler room was a separate watertight compartment, but these were too large to give the buoyancy desired, so a longitudinal watertight compartment was fitted down each side of the ship which completely flanked the boilers and machinery. To prevent collision damage, each of these vast compartments was subdivided into five sections. Engines, boilers and the two longitudinal watertight compartments totally filled the space available, and there was no place to store the 6600 tons of coal needed to drive the ship on one voyage from Liverpool to New York. To meet the Admiralty specifications, and because no one at the time knew any better, the longitudinal compartments were used to store coal. This was standard Admiralty practice and had been so since 1858. Coal, it was felt, absorbed the enemy's shot and

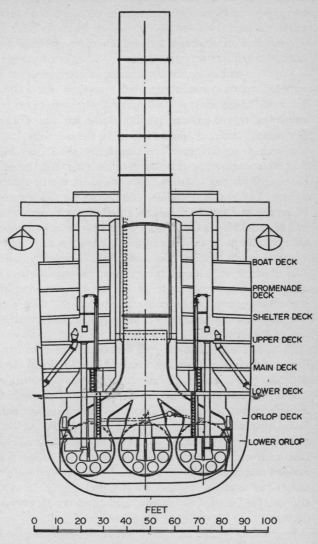

BOAT DECK

PROMENADE DECK

SHELTER DECK

UPPER DECK

MAIN DECK

LOWER DECK

ORLOP DECK

LOWER ORLOP

FEET

0 10 20 30 40 50 60 70 80 90 100

Cross-section through No. 1 boiler room.

therefore protected the boilers. No one realized that the mine and the torpedo might have a different effect. (In fairness to Peskett it must be allowed that no one had ever built boilers and engines of this size before. There is evidence that he realized that there was a risk, but probably not its degree.)[7]

With the coal stored in the watertight compartments, openings had to be cut into their bases to draw the coal out as required. These apertures were fitted with watertight hatches controlled by the stokers. Anybody who has ever drawn coal from a domestic coal bunker will know the difficulty of closing the hatch, as the weight of coal inside, plus the accumulation of dust and fine scraps of coal precludes an easy or efficient closure. With the *Lusitania*'s coal-bunkers totally destroying the effect of the longitudinal compartments she lacked both buoyancy and stability. Peskett should have realized this. He had been a designer for Cunard when the Cunarder *Oregon* sank after a collision off Fire Island, New York, on 11 March 1886. The watertight hatches could not close completely, owing to coal blocking the sills of the hatches, and though her entire complement was rescued, there was no way of saving her. At the ensuing inquiry the court ruled that the failure of the watertight bunker hatches to close was the 'prime factor' for the loss of the vessel.[8]

Even assuming that the coal access hatches could and did function perfectly, there was a second risk. Coal absorbs water and therefore increases in weight. Peskett made a series of calculations of the effect on the ship's stability if the sea entered either one, two or three of the coal-bunkers on one side. He found that with one bunker hatch open to the sea the ship would list seven degrees. With two hatches open she would take a list of at least fifteen degrees, and with more than two flooded she was unlikely to float.[9] The master's operating manual advised the captain to abandon ship if at any time she adopted and held a list of more than twenty-two degrees.[10]

By modern standards, this inherent instability would never be acceptable, but there were more compromises to be made.

Peskett had been forced to build high. On top of what may justifiably be called the 'power platform' he raised six decks. These were designated A to F, reading from top to bottom. The ship's lifeboats were suspended 8 feet above deck A, a total of 68 feet from the waterline. When they were swung out ready for lowering, they cleared the edge of the deck by 18 inches.[11] It did not apparently occur to anyone that with even a slight list it would be impossible to launch the boats on the 'high' side of the ship, short of sliding them down the ship's side. With one coal hatch flooded or a list of more than five degrees, half of the *Lusitania*'s boats were incapable of being launched. Less sinister, but equally worrying, was that the boats on the 'low' side would swing outwards from the side, and with the same degree of list the remaining lifeboats would be hanging 7 feet out from the edge of the deck, with a sheer drop of 60 feet to the water below. This fact apparently escaped Peskett. He did realize that with one bunker flooded, the sea would enter through the portholes of F deck. Therefore he caused these to be sealed up, and a set of watertight doors inserted between the boiler rooms and F deck, and again between F and E decks. These could be controlled at the touch of a switch from the bridge.[12] There was a manual over-ride mechanism which the crew below knew how to operate, but there is no record that any passengers were taught the drill, which was their only chance of escaping from what was, to all effects, the third class coffin.

Criticism with the benefit of hindsight is doubtless unfair. The *Lusitania* was in almost every way pushing the horizon of ship design and performance into what was then unknown territory. No word of reproof was ever raised, and the Board of Trade had no hesitation in granting the *Lusitania* her certificate of seaworthiness. She entered the regular Liverpool to New York service on 7 September 1907 and promptly captured the Blue Riband with a new record speed of 25.88 knots.

Her size inspired confidence from the start, and short of comparative drawings it is difficult to describe. The first impression of all contemporary observers was her immense height which seemed to minimize her length. Laid on her keel alongside the Admiralty who had fathered her, she would have dwarfed the buildings of Whitehall, while passengers on the top deck would see only the pigeons on the Admiralty roof. She was longer and higher than the complete complex of the Capitol and senate in Washington, and a stroll around the promenade deck was marginally over a quarter of a mile. This height, length and distinctive narrowness of beam, inspired the description of 'Greyhound of the Seas', which until 7 May 1915 no one realized could also be an elegant euphemism for a ship whose beam/length ratio was much like that of a canoe.

The *Lusitania* and the *Mauretania* monopolized the North Atlantic seaway, engaged in a friendly rivalry as to which could make the fastest crossing. The Blue Riband appeared to be an intership trophy for the crack liners of the Cunard Company. The first threat to this record came from the Morgan combine when the White Star Line announced their own contender, the tragic and allegedly unsinkable *Titanic*. The world knows that she sank on her maiden voyage after suffering a glancing tear from an iceberg below the waterline. This ripped a gash the length of three of her four boiler rooms. The *Titanic* was built with conventional transverse bulkheads, and she remained afloat and on an even keel for almost three hours. Formal inquiries into her loss were held in London and New York, before the same two judges who in due course were to adjudicate upon the loss of the *Lusitania*. At both the *Titanic* hearings counsel for the survivors compared construction to that of the *Lusitania*. They alleged that if the *Titanic* had been constructed with longitudinal bulkheads as were the two giant Cunarders, the gash in the side would have been contained and the *Titanic* would still be afloat. The owners of the *Titanic* attempted to refute the suggestion. Such bulkheads, they claimed in open court, were of doubtful value as far as buoyancy was concerned, and would lead to such a list that it would have been almost impossible to have launched the lifeboats.

The White Star Line did not press this defence too emphatically, as it drew attention to the boats of the *Titanic* and on this point they were vulnerable. Both inquiries were to find that the *Titanic* did not carry sufficient boats to save more than a proportion of her passengers. The plaintiffs, instead of concentrating on the alleged shortcomings of bulkhead design, seized on the emotive and much simpler argument of the boat shortage. The Board of Trade and the Admiralty appreciated the significance of both points. For the first time the Board of Trade now stipulated just how many boats a passenger liner must carry. It also *recommended* that liners with a high freeboard should adopt a form of davit which would enable the boats to be swung far enough out from the ship's side to counteract a severe list. To this recommendation they added a *suggestion* that as lifeboats had become heavier and were now designed to carry upwards of sixty persons each, a form of geared davit should be employed, as the weight of such boats fully laden would be too much for two men to lower by hand, even with the assistance of a simple arrangement of blocks and pulleys.

Cunard promptly doubled the number of boats carried by the *Lusitania* from twenty-two to forty-four. They did not double, nor did they alter the davits. They retained their simple and oldfashioned method of lowering the boats by hand: one seaman at each fall, and the falls passing through a block and pulley. The extra boats were stowed beneath the existing ones, and it would be necessary to lower the first, recover the falls, connect them to the extra boat, hoist it, swing it out and then lower it to join its fellow.

Neither the Board of Trade nor Cunard took the point about the bulkhead design, but it did not escape the Director of Naval Construction, Sir Eustace Tennyson-d'Eyncourt. He initiated a series of reports early in 1914, and all cruisers of this design were subjected to scrutiny. In August 1914 the reports were acted on. Any cruisers or battleships which had unarmoured longitudinal bunkers were on no account to be exposed to submarine attack or to play offensive roles without suitable escorts, and then only on the orders of the Admiralty War Staff.

The year 1913 began as a troublesome one for Cunard. To implement the Board of Trade orders meant withdrawing both the *Lusitania* and her consort for extensive dry-docking while the new boats were fitted. In early February Mr Alfred Booth, Cunard's chairman, received a letter from Sir William Graham Greene, Permanent Secretary of the Admiralty, which invited him to call to discuss certain modifications to the agreement that existed between the Admiralty and Cunard, and also stated that the Board of Admiralty had decided that it appeared a suitable moment to discuss the Company's obligations under the same agreement.

Alfred Booth presented himself to the Board of Admiralty at 2.30 on 19 February 1913. The First Lord, Winston Churchill, was in the chair, and characteristically he had quite a lot to say. Churchill left Alfred Booth in no doubt that there was shortly to be a war with Germany. The estimated date for its outbreak would be September 1914, when the Germans would have completed their dredging of the Kiel Canal and the European harvest had been gathered. Therefore he had decided that in the national interest it was the correct time to implement certain of the clauses by which Cunard had agreed to make their ships available to the Admiralty. He expressed a wish that the *Lusitania*, the *Mauretania*, the *Ivernia* and the *Aquitania*, then under construction, be modified forthwith so that should hostilities break out they could, without delay, take up their role as armed cruisers. He also specified a further six ships including the *Transylvania*, which were to be converted as soon as the work on the first batch of ships was completed. Booth protested, but the only concession that he managed to obtain was that the *Mauretania* was to be converted at a different time from the *Lusitania*, so as to enable Cunard to maintain some semblance of their New York service.

Under strict secrecy the *Lusitania* entered dry-dock at Liverpool on 12 May 1913. Cunard announced that she was being temporarily withdrawn from service so as to have the latest design of turbines installed, but the *New York Tribune* gave the game away on 19 June when it reported:

The reason why the crack liner *Lusitania* is so long delayed at Liverpool has been announced to be because her turbine engines are being completely replaced, but Cunard officials acknowledged to the *Tribune* correspondent today that the greyhound is being equipped with high power naval rifles in conformity with England's new policy of arming passenger boats.

The *Tribune* made one error of fact. Guns or high powered naval rifles were not actually installed, though orders for them were placed with the Royal Arsenal and they were delivered to Liverpool that November. What actually was done is well documented in the Cunard archives (all the working drawings for the alterations involved are on file at the National Maritime Museum, Greenwich).[13]

The entire length of the vessel between the shelter deck and below the upper deck – a depth of 14 ft 6 in – was double-plated and hydraulically riveted. The stringer plate of the shelter deck was also doubled. The reserve coal-bunker immediately forward of No. 1 boiler room was converted to a magazine, special shell racking was installed so that the shells rested against the bulkheads and handling lifts were installed. A second magazine was converted from part of the mail rooms at the stern of the ship and revolving gun-rings were mounted on the forecastle and on the after deck, so that each deck could mount two six-inch quick-firing guns. The teak planking which composed the floor of the shelter deck was cut into and revolving gun-rings were installed beneath it; then the sections of teak deck were replaced, in such a way that the relevant sections could be lifted off like trapdoors. The shelter deck was adapted to take four six-inch guns on either side, making a total complement of twelve guns or a broadside of six guns each firing a shell containing high explosive. A gun-ring is like a revolving wheel mounted on ball bearings and sunk flush to the deck. All that was required to complete the fitting of the armament was to lower the gun on to the ring prepared for it, and to secure twelve castellated bolts.

The *Lusitania* returned to the New York service on 21 July 1913 and on 16 March 1914 a proud Mr Churchill could announce to the House of Commons that 'some forty British Merchant ships had been defensively armed'.[14] The term 'defensive' in the case of all the Cunarders must be construed as 'politician's licence', as in each case they could mount a heavier broadside than the *Bacchante* or E class cruisers then charged with the defence of the Channel. It was, however, an extremely fortunate choice of adjective, and it must be remembered when the political arguments which followed the loss of the *Lusitania* are reviewed.

War with Germany arrived a month ahead of the Admiralty's forecast, and the *Lusitania* was about to leave New York when it was declared on 4 August 1914. Immediately on her arrival at Liverpool she was handed over to the Admiralty together with the other Cunarders designated for a cruiser role. By 8 August the *Aquitania* had had her guns installed and the *Lusitania* was moved into the Canada drydock on Merseyside to be similarly equipped.* The Admiralty gutted all the passenger accommodation on F deck, the lowest of the six decks above the boiler rooms, and enclosed a large length of the shelter deck. Her armament was installed and on 17 September she entered the Admiralty fleet register as an armed auxiliary cruiser, and was so entered on the Cunard ledgers. The *Lusitania* was ready for war.

* The speed with which the armament was installed is evidenced by the actions of the 25,000-ton liner *Carmania*, which arrived in England on 6 August. By 14 September, disguised as the German liner *Cap Trafalgar* and armed with eight 4·7 inch guns, she encountered the *Cap Trafalgar* disguised as the *Carmania* off the coast of Bahia, Brazil, in the South Atlantic. After a short engagement the *Carmania* sank the German ship by holing her longitudinal tanks. The *Cap Trafalgar* listed heavily and sank by the bow twenty minutes after receiving the *Carmania*'s first salvo.

2

On 17 September 1914 Churchill went to visit the Grand Fleet which was moored at Loch Ewe, a remote but magnificent deepwater anchorage on the coast of Ross and Cromarty in north-west Scotland. It was a remarkable visit, largely memorable for a nocturnal excursion from the wardroom of Admiral Jellicoe's flagship *Iron Duke*. The First Lord had convinced himself that the owner of a nearby house was in the habit of signalling to the Germans with a searchlight mounted on the roof of his house. The houseowner was a senile 75-year-old former Conservative M.P., Sir Arthur Bignold, and the searchlight did not work. However, commandeering pistols and ammunition from the flagship's armoury, the First Lord led an armed raid on the house, holding up the unfortunate owner and his butler at pistol point. It was an irresponsible and rather foolish adventure, possibly inspired by Admiral Jellicoe's fine brandy.* It did, however, give Churchill an opportunity for an informal conversation with Commodore Roger Keyes, one of the four officers he had impressed into his party from those present in the wardroom.

Commodore Keyes was one of the Navy's most promising officers. He was also extremely outspoken. He called the First Lord's attention to the fact that despite the Admiralty restrictions on the employment of *Bacchante* class cruisers with their

---

* Churchill's raiding party consisted of Rear-Admiral Sir Horace Hood who was later to command the escort detailed for the *Lusitania*; Vice-Admiral Henry Oliver, the Director of Naval Intelligence, whom Churchill brought in as his Naval Secretary two weeks later; Commodore Keyes; and Commodore Tyrwhitt.

unarmed longitudinal bunkers, no fewer than four of them were steadily patrolling on the Dogger Bank and had been doing so every day since the outbreak of war. They were in a most exposed and dangerous situation. Their crews were mostly young married reservists and cadets from Osborne Naval Training College. The Fleet, he informed the First Lord, had christened them 'the Livebait Squadron'. Churchill was horrified. The following day, on his return to the Admiralty he called for Tennyson-d'Eyncourt's report written as a result of the *Titanic* inquiry, and promptly ordered the patrol to be discontinued forthwith. However the Admiralty War Staff took their time to make the required dispositions and, pending the transfer of the *Bacchante* squadron, ordered three of them to patrol even nearer to the Dutch coast, in an area known as 'the broad fourteens'.

September 21 saw Churchill in Liverpool where he was to address a recruiting meeting. Before this engagement he visited the docks to inspect the Cunarders under conversion into cruisers. The *Lusitania* was alongside the dock. Churchill and Leonard Peskett, who was supervising the design modifications, stood and looked at her towering above them. Churchill mentioned the shortcomings of the *Bacchante* class and questioned Peskett closely on the Cunarder's bulkhead layout and stability. Peskett reassured him, and remarked, 'The Navy hasn't anything like her.' Churchill mumbled a reply which was to haunt him. 'We have. To me she is just another 45,000 tons of livebait.'[1]

Shortly after dawn the following day, the three *Bacchante* class cruisers, *Aboukir*, *Hogue* and *Cressy*, steamed in line ahead across their station. At 6.30 a.m. the *Aboukir* was struck by one torpedo. She capsized almost immediately and sank in twenty-five minutes. With chivalrous simplicity her consorts steamed to the scene, and both suffered immediate and similar fates: 1459 men were drowned. Many of the casualties were from Liverpool and Churchill's dockside remark had already gained a wide currency. The press were quick to discover the Navy's use of the term 'livebait', and Churchill was subjected to a venomous campaign which alleged that he knew of the danger to the cruisers and had recklessly hazarded them. As regards their loss he was undoubtedly innocent, and a secret court of inquiry cleared him and blamed the War Staff.

The immediate significance of the *Bacchante* class disaster was dramatically to reverse the Admiralty's attitude to U-boats. Hitherto, Churchill and many of the senior staff of the Admiralty had tended to disregard them. As a result, in 1914 Britain had only sixty-one operational submarines, twelve fewer than she had had in 1907. These were almost entirely employed for defensive purposes, as only seventeen were seaworthy enough to venture outside coastal waters. Germany had twenty-one operational U-boats, all capable of long-range operations.

Churchill and his advisers at the Admiralty had been almost alone in their opinions. A. J. Balfour, the former Conservative Prime Minister, in the course of a long letter to Admiral of the Fleet Lord Fisher of 6 May 1913 had identified Britain's Achilles heel as the spots where the great trade routes converged in the English Channel and the Irish Sea and added: 'The question that really troubles me is not whether *our* submarines could render the enemy's position intolerable, but whether *their* submarines could render *our* position intolerable.' Lord Fisher, who had retired from active service in 1911, replied in June 1913 with a reasoned paper which he sent to Churchill.[2] He pointed out that an enemy submarine had no alternative but to sink her victims. He went on: 'This submarine menace is a truly terrible threat for British commerce ... it is freely acknowledged to be an altogether barbarous method of warfare ... [but] the essence of war is violence, and moderation in war is imbecility.' He pointed out that neutral shipping would not be immune and remarked that 'one flag is very like another seen against the light through a periscope'.

The Sea Lords and Churchill were horrified by Fisher's paper. Churchill belatedly replied to it on 10 January 1914. He wrote that he thought in some respects the paper was both brilliant and valuable; there were some points, however, 'on which I am not convinced. Of these the greatest is the use of submarines to sink merchant vessels. I do not believe this would ever be done by a civilized power.' Prince Louis of Battenberg, the First Sea Lord, thought that Fisher's paper was marred by this suggestion. Prime Minister Asquith refused to circulate it to the Committee for Imperial Defence. Herbert Richmond, Assistant Director of the Admiralty's Operations Division, minuted that the submarine had 'the smallest value of any vessel for the direct attack upon trade', and Commodore Keyes in his autobiography confirmed that this eventuality was one that 'we had all discarded as impossible and unthinkable'. It will be seen that the arming of some merchant ships in the early spring of 1913 was not from fear of the submarine. It was from fear of the German armed liner employed as a commerce raider. Churchill's oft made autobiographical claim that he anticipated the submarine menace, and by his prompt and far-sighted action largely blunted it, has no factual foundation.

The Admiralty considered that a merchant vessel should be treated by a submarine in exactly the same way as by a marauding cruiser; in fact in the same way as the Royal Navy had operated since 1512 when Henry VIII had issued precise instructions to the Admiral of the Fleet before his expedition to Guienne. Briefly the Navy believed that it was correct practice to halt an *unarmed* ship by a shot across the bows, search it, and if it were a neutral let it go. If it were a merchant ship belonging to a belligerent, then the crew and passengers became hostages, and the cargo and ship were taken as prizes. In the event of a shortage of prize crews, or being too far from a friendly port, then ship and cargo could be destroyed. These principles, known as the Cruiser Rules, had been accepted with minor modifications by all the maritime powers. They applied however to *unarmed merchantmen*.

Churchill's action in arming British merchant ships immediately stripped them of the right to expect such treatment. In the lower echelons of the Admiralty it was realized that no submarine would ever dare to undertake the dangerous practice of

36

surfacing and ordering a heavily armed ship to halt and submit to search. Even if it did so successfully and its orders were obeyed, what was a submarine to do with the crew, passengers and prize? The submarine, as Lord Fisher from retirement and numerous junior officers forecast, had no alternative but to give those on board the opportunity to take to the boats and then sink its prize.

However, Britain had not envisaged offensive submarines, and had relied on intercepting enemy merchantmen with her surface ships. It had become plain that if a submarine could sink a cruiser, she could play havoc on our trade routes. So far no merchant ship had been sunk without fair warning, but sooner or later some merchant captain would attempt to fight it out, and this would leave the Germans no alternative but to depart from the Cruiser Rules. They would be unlikely to turn the other cheek. The direct solution was to find some method to deal with the submarine in the areas where our merchantmen were most exposed – the Channel and the seas off the south coast of Ireland. The Admiralty wrongly believed that German submarines could only reach the Irish Sea by forcing a passage through the straits of Dover. They were unaware that they had the sea-keeping qualities and endurance to circumnavigate the north of Scotland and possibly the west coast of Ireland as well. Accordingly, defensive emphasis was concentrated on the Channel, and the south coast of Ireland was very largely ignored.

Britain's first thought for submarine defence was a boom designed to stretch across the Channel, hung with nets and festooned with mines. It was a costly failure and abandoned. The only answer was intensive patrolling and the use of mines. Along the shore line and off the Irish coast a new system was devised that spoke only too eloquently of the minds of the senior staff of a navy which had not seen a general action since Trafalgar, apart from minor gunboat forays and naval bombardments in support of Pax Britannica. A coastal yacht and motor-boat patrol was established under the command of 61-year-old Admiral Sir Frederick Inglefield. However well intentioned it may have been its efforts were largely ludicrous. Only one in ten vessels was armed and then with little more than a rifle. One ship in eighty-five was equipped with a wireless. The rest depended on enthusiasm and imagination.

The imagination took some novel expression. It had been realized that though Inglefield's forces contributed a presence, they had no method of dealing with a submarine should they find one. Teams of two swimmers were organized in each motor launch. One man carried a black bag, the other a hammer. The plan was that if a periscope was sighted, the launch would cruise as near to it as possible, then the swimmers would dive in, seize the periscope, and after one man had placed the black bag over it, the other would attempt to shatter the glass with the hammer. Inglefield's other brain child was to attempt to train seagulls to defecate on periscopes, and for a short while a remote corner of Poole harbour in Dorset was littered with dummy periscopes and hopefully incontinent seagulls. Inglefield closed his distinguished career in June 1916 by volunteering to be retired in order to make room for the promotion of younger officers. His last official function was what his *Times* obituary euphemistically described as 'special service at the Admiralty'. He was the senior naval officer of the team of assessors who assisted Lord Mersey to determine the cause of the loss of the *Lusitania*, a miserable assignment with which to close an otherwise honourable career. Churchill for all his well known love of the unorthodox was among the first to diagnose that black bags, booms and seagulls were not an effective counter to the submarine. He must also have realized that sooner or later his armed merchant ships would chance on a U-boat and either one side or the other would abandon Cruiser Rules and escalate the war at sea to a degree of ruthlessness that neither Britain nor Germany had ever envisaged. He devised an ingenious and subtle strategy.

In Churchill's autobiographical account of the First World War, *The World Crisis*, he wrote: 'The distinction between politics and strategy diminishes as the point of view is raised.'[3] Churchill's viewpoint was from the summit, and the strategy he adopted for countering the *anticipated* U-boat menace was almost entirely political. There can be little doubt that at the back of his mind he wished to bring the United States into the war. To continue the *World Crisis* quotation: 'At the summit true politics and strategy are one. The manoeuvre which brings an ally into the field is as serviceable as that which wins a great battle. The manoeuvre which gains an important strategic point may be less valuable than that which placates or over-awes a dangerous neutral.' If the problem facing the Admiralty is simplified down to its essentials, it was that the only maritime power in the world of any account not engaged in the conflict was the United States, which day by day became more indispensable and a bountiful source of supply. The inward flow of war material came almost entirely from North America, and nothing must be done which would compromise this situation.

The British blockade of the North Sea had yet to be announced, but it had been minutely planned since 1907 and was in full operation. All that remained before announcing it was the necessary political excuse. In the meantime, American commercial shipping, though it had yet to be attacked by the Germans, was constantly searched and diverted by British patrols. The rumbles of protest in the U.S. Senate were causing the British Foreign Office deep concern. The neutral to be 'placated or overawed' was the United States. Churchill's strategy was to goad the Germans into a confrontation with them and by doing so the least advantages for which he hoped were to neutralize pro-German sentiment in America and to consolidate his sources of supply.

From October 1914 onwards a steady stream of inflammatory orders were issued to the masters of British merchant ships. It was made an offence to obey a U-boat's order to halt. Instead masters must immediately engage the enemy, either with their armament if they possessed it, or by ramming if they did not. Any master who surrendered his ship was to be prosecuted, and several were. *The World Crisis* again identifies both the strategy and the responsibility.

The first British countermove, made on my responsibility ... was to deter the Germans from surface attack. The submerged U-boat had to rely increasingly on underwater attack and thus ran the greater risk of mistaking neutral for British ships and of drowning neutral crews and thus embroiling Germany with other Great Powers. [4]

In order to assist the making of such a mistake, the Admiralty issued an instruction ordering all British ships to paint out their names and port of registry, and when in British waters to fly the flag of a neutral power. These orders were distributed from the Admiralty to all shipping companies, and on the copy sent to Cunard is the manuscript annotation, 'Pass the word around that the flag to use is the American.'

British naval vessels were also ordered to treat the crews of captured U-boats as felons, and not to accord them the status of prisoners of war. The introduction of 'mystery' or Q-ships – apparently unarmed merchantmen carrying concealed armament and a naval crew dressed as civilians – was planned in September 1914 by Admiral Sir Hedworth Meux, the C.-in-C. Portsmouth, when the regular steamer plying from St Malo to Southampton was so disguised. By February 1915 Churchill had endorsed the policy and 'mystery' ships were operational. He personally drafted their orders, and those that related to prisoners were symptomatic of his ruthless policy designed to escalate and inflame the war at sea. 'Survivors', wrote the ebullient First Lord, 'should be taken prisoner or shot – whichever is the most convenient.' [5]

There were other orders just as ruthless, including the notorious 'In all action, white flags should be fired upon with promptitude', [6] and they largely stemmed from two fears. The first that the Germans might win naval control, and the second the realization that the war was not after all going to be swiftly settled by one glorious fleet action, but was going to be a long-drawn-out agony of attrition. These factors called for a dramatic reappraisal of the role that the Navy had to play.

At the outbreak of war the main threat to British commerce had been the forty-two German liners which were capable of being converted into armed cruisers. To counteract this threat, Britain, outside the Royal Navy, had twenty-four armed liners and fifty-four armed cargo ships. A further forty ships were under conversion. But the German threat had largely failed to materialize. Of the forty-two potential cruisers only five were at sea when war was declared, and by the autumn of 1914 only two of these were still at large. The Admiralty planned to retain certain of the armed liners for cruiser duties in the Far East, where there was no U-boat peril, but decided that the remainder should be transferred to cargo duties as they offered a speedy method of bringing badly needed supplies from the United States and with their speed and armament should be immune from the unforeseen peril of the U-boat.

On 24 September 1914 the Admiralty officially informed Cunard that it did not propose to employ the *Lusitania* in the role originally envisaged, and requested Alfred Booth to discuss her employment at his earliest convenience. The future role of the *Lusitania* was explained to him by the Secretary of the Admiralty, Sir William Graham Greene, in the smoking room of the Reform Club on the evening of 3 October. Cunard, Booth was told, would be required to operate the *Lusitania* and run a high speed service between Liverpool and New York. All the Cunarders on that run were to hold their cargo space at the disposal of the Trade Division of the Admiralty, and on each voyage requests for accommodation in any of the ships which might come from the Admiralty, the War Office or other government departments were to be accorded priority over all other bookings. The deployment of the ships at sea was to be an Admiralty responsibility. It would inform the masters of the courses they were to follow, and Cunard was forbidden to contact them except with the permission and through the agency of the Admiralty. Any cargo space or accommodation not required by the authorities could be utilized by the Company but, in the case of eastbound cargo, only with the permission of the Admiralty staff who would be stationed in New York. It was the responsibility of Cunard to provide crews, ships and fuel. The subsidy of £75,000 p.a. would be continued and the Admiralty would pay for all cargo space it used. Insurance would be guaranteed by the Government.

Alfred Booth was flabbergasted. He was later to write to his cousin George Booth: 'In essence Sir William took me into *my own club* and ordered me to be a high grade "contrabandist" in the National Interest.'[7] He had no alternative, however, but to agree, though he protested that there was already a slump in the Atlantic passenger trade now that the war was in full swing, and that he would prefer to lay the *Lusitania* up for the remainder of the war. He argued that her original crew had been dispersed and had either joined the Navy or been found berths elsewhere. His protests went unheard, and he was instructed to prepare the *Lusitania* for sea as soon as possible and advise the Admiralty when she was ready. 'She had', said Sir William, 'a very important job to do.'[8]

3

Alfred and George Booth were cousins, members of a family which was and is one of Liverpool's phenomena. Alfred Booth and Co., the family business, accurately reflected the diverse character of its constituent members. A free-thinking Unitarian background had been matched by an equally independent and entrepreneurial business sense which had painstakingly capitalized on steam power and foreign trade. By the beginning of this century Alfred Booth and Co. owned a sizcable holding in Cunard, their own shipping line the Booth Steamship Company Limited, factories, tanneries and building enterprises in Brazil, the United States and England and were financially linked with numerous other steamship, wharfage and wholesaling concerns. The Booths' marriage ties were as diverse as they were impressive: Alfred Booth's father had married a Butler, daughter of one of Liverpool's merchant princes; George Booth's father married Mary Macaulay, the niece of the historian, and in due course became a Privy Councillor. In 1914 Alfred and George were the two most active members of the clan. The former concentrated on the shipping interests, devoting more and more of his time to the affairs of Cunard. At the age of forty-two he was Chairman.

Alfred Booth was tall and meticulously turned out, and the family independence expressed itself in him by an unwillingness to delegate and a distinct tendency to irritable autocracy. His personal letters and business correspondence show that he was rarely diverted from a course once he had made up his mind, and he liked neither advice nor instruction. Despite, or because of, these limitations he ran Cunard like clockwork.

He had a hearty contempt for the Admiralty, a contempt that he concealed from authority so successfully that a grateful government gave him a baronetcy in 1916. His main outlet for his feelings was in his letters to his father and his cousin.

George Booth was a very different man. His father, apart from running the family business, had been a radical and pioneering writer on social questions, whose monumental *Life and Labour of the People in London* had been largely responsible for reawakening the Victorian conscience as to the casualties of the materialism of the era. His friends included Henry Hobhouse, Beatrice Webb, Lord Parmoor and Daniel Meinertzhagen, the London banker. George shared both his father's sympathies and friends to the extent of marrying Meinertzhagen's daughter and introducing and maintaining a unique paternalistic social security system for his firm's employees. He was also an extremely shrewd and enterprising businessman, a fact recognized by the Bank of England, who invited him to become a director when he was only thirty-seven. In appearance he is easy to describe though he would have hated the comparison. He looked exactly like the late Humphrey Bogart.

The day after the outbreak of war George Booth took a train from Liphook in Hampshire to Waterloo. In the same carriage was Sir Hubert Llewellyn-Smith, the Permanent Secretary at the Board of Trade. Sir Hubert remarked that now the country was at war it was not going to be so easy to commute, and George Booth courteously offered him bed and breakfast at his London house on Campden Hill, Kensington. Sir Hubert accepted. Most evenings for the next few weeks the Booth house was to be the scene of a remarkable series of meetings. Dining there on 6 August 1914 Sir Hubert brought with him Walter Runciman, the President of the Board of Trade, and after dinner Runciman told those present of the first squabble in the Cabinet.

It was the Cabinet's collective opinion that the war would be over remarkably quickly, but Field-Marshal Lord Kitchener,

44

the newly-appointed Secretary of State for War, had stood out against this view. He was adamant that it would be a war of long duration, and he had closely questioned the Board of Trade as to their plans for supplying the enormous quantities of war materials that were going to be required. He had apparently also delved deep into the War Office and Admiralty plans for meeting their requirements and had been distressed to find that our stocks of munitions and supplies of all kinds were only enough for a three-month campaign. The British Army, for example, had no winter equipment, beyond its full dress parade greatcoats. 'Hitherto', he had remarked to Runciman that morning, 'equipping the army has been no more difficult than buying a straw hat in Harrods, but from now on the army, the navy and perhaps these airmen are going to need greater quantities of material than has ever been made before.'[1] He had regretted that there was no centralized buying or distribution policy and urged the Cabinet to organize something. Asquith had turned down the idea.

On Walter Runciman's initiative George Booth was now asked to form an unofficial committee of financiers, shipowners and industrialists who would help plan for the contingency Kitchener envisaged, and in the meantime assist – in a covert way – whenever there were bottlenecks or other problems in the supply or distribution of war material. By the time Alfred Booth was ordered to put the *Lusitania* back on the New York run, his cousin's committee had been formed, and was just gaining acceptance from the Cabinet. George Booth was an excellent picker of men. He chose two young accountants from the North Eastern Railway, Eric Geddes and George Beharrel, Maynard Keynes, the Cambridge economist, and Cecil Baring, the banker. F. S. Oliver from Debenham and Freebody's department store was coopted to supervise clothing supplies; and Booth's family firm was raided to obtain W. H. Tregonning, as a member of the liner requisition committee, and Austin Fletcher, who was given the task of setting up a prize court department to settle the fate of ships and cargoes caught trying to evade the British blockade. Contacts with the Government were arranged by the Board of Trade seconding U. F. Wintour from their exhibitions department as secretary to the committee (he eventually became Director of Army Contracts). Sir Frederick Black, Director of Admiralty Contracts, was detailed by the Third Sea Lord to liaise with George Booth on a daily basis.

In May 1915 after Lloyd George became Minister of Munitions Booth's committee formed the nucleus of the new Ministry. Before this date the committee was both 'officially unofficial' and secret. The members had to meet daily, but as yet they had neither premises nor formal authority. The latter point was covered by strenuous application and use of the 'old boy network'. Fortunately everyone knew everyone else. All that was needed was somewhere for them to meet. George Booth solved the problem characteristically. The meetings took place at his home on Campden Hill in the evenings, and every day at his club, the Reform in Pall Mall, which gave him a special table in the dining-room given by the committee the name of 'the Round Table'. These luncheons became the focal point around which the numerous problems of supply, shipment and finance were resolved.

Late in September 1914 Sir Frederick Black and Wintour button-holed George Booth after one of the lunches. Both had problems to be resolved which involved supplies from the United States. Eventually consignments of both the orders involved were to be shipped on the last voyage of the *Lusitania*. Sir Frederick Black wanted substantial quantities of guncotton which was needed for mines. Britain's publicly declared policy was one of antipathy to mining, and in fact the loudest voice was Churchill's, who still believed that the war would be over in a matter of weeks. The Admiralty and Foreign Office had raised a great outcry when the Germans mined the approaches to Harwich on the first day of the war, and Churchill had opposed British mining on the grounds of fouling the sea which we already commanded. Churchill was undoubtedly sincere in his beliefs, but there was a more secret reason which had hitherto denied Britain the chance to mine.

At the outbreak of the war the Admiralty's stock consisted of only 4000 mines, and their early attempts to lay them had proved a fiasco. The five-hundredweight sinkers would not hold the mines in position and they had dragged all over the place. Admiral Jellicoe had complained that 'as fast as our mines have been laid, they have drifted away, owing to our idiotic habit of using too small mooring rope'.[2] Those laid in the Channel on the outbreak of war had drifted as much as eighteen miles; and Admiral Oliver had described them as 'an infernal nuisance'. The British mines were also more dangerous to the British than to the Germans. Frequently they blew off the sterns of the minelayers, but when they did make contact with a German ship, they generally failed to explode. Numerous German ships carried a British mine mounted on their decks as a souvenir. *

There was however, a strong mining lobby in the Admiralty, and behind Churchill's back they had persuaded the Prime Minister to order him to adopt an aggressive mining policy. Asquith did so on 29 September 1914. Sir Frederick Black now wanted 1000 tons of gun-cotton to be consigned to the Director of Naval Intelligence designate, Captain Reginald Hall, who was handling the matter, as the change of policy was to be kept secret. It is likely that Hall was the prime mover of the policy switch.

For the Army Wintour had two problems. First he wanted to find a manufacturer to make up two million sets of accoutrements (leather pouches, belts and bandoliers) for the new volunteer army Kitchener was raising. This was a simple matter and a sample set would be sent to Booth. The second was a more curious tale. An American entrepreneur called Alfred Fraser had walked into the War Office carrying a sheepskin coat. He had walked out again with an order for 100,000

* The claim of the British official *History of the War* that British mines never sank a non-German ship is specious. They were, as Churchill had rightly said, a 'pollution of the seas'. Of the 9000 mines laid by January 1915, over 4000 were adrift and unaccounted for. Admiralty records confirm that as late as April 1917 over 90 per cent of British mines were too dangerous to be laid. Professor Marder covers the mining fiasco in great detail in *From the Dreadnought to Scapa Flow*, vol. ii, pp. 77–82.

of them at thirty-seven shillings each. The War Office had then been asked to pay the money in advance, but had refused to do so. Would Mr Booth check on Fraser, and if the coats existed, arrange for their purchase and immediate shipment to the U.K. There was one other small point. The American Government was being rather difficult about the shipping of military supplies and allowing Britain to incur indebtedness for war material. Wintour wondered if Booth and his family would arrange to bridge the cost of army purchases from the dollar holdings of Booth and Co. in New York. George Booth agreed to do all that he was asked.

Cecil Baring intervened to say that he thought that perhaps the Bank of Montreal could assist in this respect, and it was finally arranged that Booth would also call on the British Ambassador in Washington, Sir Cecil Spring-Rice, to discuss future funding arrangements in the event that the United States continued to be recalcitrant about the purchase and shipment of war material. Finally Sir Frederick handed Booth a written letter of introduction to Captain Guy Gaunt, then British Naval Attaché in Washington, who was in touch with the manufacturer of gun-cotton but, of course, as a diplomat, could not actually place an order or deal direct.

George Booth was impressed with the confidence shown in him. He wrote delightedly to his cousin Alfred and his father, who agreed that Booth and Co. should handle the financing of the Army purchases. Alfred asked him to make sure that Cunard got its share of the cargoes and arranged for him to have a suite aboard the *Lusitania*. George Booth sailed from Liverpool on 24 October on the liner's first voyage since the Admiralty had given instructions for her to be put back into service. He was allocated the Parlour Suite, No. B 70, but the *Lusitania* was a different ship from the one to which he was accustomed. The first point that he noticed was that the stewards were no longer as 'spry' as they used to be; the second that the ship seemed much livelier. For the first time in years of Atlantic travel he was miserably seasick. The same fate befell many of the first-class passengers, most of whom he noted in his diary were either service officers in civilian clothes or members of delegations and purchasing commissions. He raised the matter of his sickness with the master, Captain Dow, who was both an old acquaintance and notorious for being sick in all but the calmest weather. This and his native Scottish caution had earned him the nickname 'Fairweather' Dow, by which he was known throughout the merchant marine.

Captain Dow explained that the ship was lively for a very good reason. The Admiralty had gutted the lowest deck (F deck), thereby removing much of the weight in the bottom of the ship. The steel strengthening of the shelter deck (C deck) had caused an increase in her top hamper, and the area forward of No. 2 funnel on the same deck was entirely in Admiralty hands and closed off from the rest of the ship. Dow explained that the Admiralty had removed the guns mounted fore and aft, and showed Booth the concealed gun-rings in the planking of the shelter deck. He did not know whether the guns were still on board, but suspected that at least some of them were, locked up in the forward section of the deck which had been closed off. He added that the Admiralty had also closed off the whole forward passenger accommodation on all decks below C deck and that this had involved the closure of the second-class smoking-room and the third-class dining-room. Second and third-class passengers now had to feed in shifts in the second-class dining-room at the stern of the ship and the stewards were loud in their complaints. The result of gutting so much forward accommodation had made the ship light in the bow, and this was why she was 'corkscrewing as well as rolling heavily'. Dow said that he thought it would doubtless be better when that area was full of cargo on the homeward run, and Booth resolved not to disappoint him. He was to write to his cousin from New York: 'The accoutrement business goes well, which should please the War Office and settle poor Fairweather's stomach.'[3]

Booth's visit was a success. He placed orders for the accoutrements and managed to arrange for most of them to be shipped on Cunard liners as they offered the fastest service. With

Captain Gaunt he visited Dupont de Nemours and placed orders both for the gun-cotton and for the special containers in which it was to be shipped. Thirdly, with Gaunt's assistance he established that Alfred Fraser was a rogue. The sheepskin coats came from Boston, and Gaunt discovered that the Boston manufacturers were selling them to an agent in New York called Heckman at 14s each. Heckman sold them to Fraser on a 5 per cent commission basis, and even allowing for packing, shipping and insurance, Fraser was making a mammoth profit for what was really little more than an introduction. Some hard talking ensued. Gaunt appears to have been a rather unusually accomplished naval attaché. Contractual difficulties precluded the total elimination of Fraser from the bargain and he was retained on a 5 per cent commission basis for the transaction. Gaunt agreed to handle the New York end and Booth financed the purchase. Thereafter Fraser became a cypher to be used as Gaunt wished.

There was a need for cyphers. The American administration was in confusion as to whether or not to allow military materials to be shipped to belligerent powers, and eventually agreed that individuals could ship to individuals. However, it reminded its citizens that should they ship contraband, that contraband would be liable to seizure if intercepted on the high seas. In this event the American Government would not be prepared to defend the shippers' rights. It was an admirably useful neutral decision, technically giving both German and Allied nationals the right to purchase supplies and export them to their own countries. In the German case it was an abstract right because of the blockade, but the German Government accepted that it was a perfectly legal and proper decision.

The problem was to disguise the shipments so that they appeared to be an innocent transaction between one trader and another. Contraband goods were almost inevitably shipped in the names of spurious firms, and Fraser provided one such. A study of the manifests of cargoes leaving New York during the autumn of 1914 and the spring of 1915 indicates Alfred Fraser as one of the largest traders in North America, when in fact he was an undischarged bankrupt, living off the combined wits of himself and Captain Gaunt. The second reason for security was the American habit of publishing each day the details of the cargo manifests of ships which had left the day before. This provided information to Germans and Allies alike. The Allies used the manifests to discover which neutral ships carried contraband to the Germans. The Germans in their turn passed the details of British shipments to their submarines.

The British solution of this problem was to discover a loophole in the regulations of the port of New York. These stipulated that before the Collector of Customs could issue a clearance to sail, a sworn copy of the true manifest had to be deposited with him. A neat way round the regulations was found. It appeared that a passenger ship often did not know how many passengers it was going to carry on any particular voyage until shortly before sailing, and therefore, in those days before universal refrigeration, would purchase last minute provisions on the dockside. Under the health laws of New York a supplementary manifest had to be handed in after the ship sailed if additional foodstuffs had been acquired or if any last minute passengers had brought with them any dutiable luggage. It became standard British practice to obtain clearance to sail on the basis of a false manifest and false affidavit and some four or five days after sailing to turn in a supplementary manifest which gave a truer picture of the ship's cargo. This subterfuge was acquiesced in by the Collector of Customs, Dudley Field Malone, a former Treasury lawyer whom President Wilson had appointed to the near sinecure of his job as a reward for political favours. Malone knew of the ruse and countenanced it because he was determinedly pro-Ally.

The most serious problem was the absolute embargo which the State Department placed on the shipment of munitions of war upon passenger ships. Here Cunard's New York attorneys offered helpful advice. They discovered that in 1910 the Union Metallic Cartridge Co. of Bridgeport, Connecticut, which by 1915 was part of the Remington Arms Corporation, had wished to send sporting cartridges by fast passenger steamers on

American coastal routes in order to avoid interstate difficulties. They had applied to the Municipal Explosives Commission of New York City and invited them to a demonstration at which they offered to prove that cartridges would not explode if dropped or exposed to fire. The Commission accepted the invitation and the demonstration was held on 27 July 1910 at the U.M.C. testing range in Connecticut, where the company entertained the commissioners to a luncheon before setting out to the range.

The demonstration consisted of piling up a quantity of shot-gun shells in their cardboard cases, together with calibre ·22, ·38 and ·45 pistol shells, all filled with black powder. A fire was lit against the pile and kept burning for twenty-five minutes. The cartridges took fire and burned fiercely but as the gases were not confined in a gun barrel or under pressure they did not do more than throw the shot a few feet. The commissioners, who were respectively a lawyer and meat importer, were mightily impressed by this public relations exercise and granted permission for cartridges to be shipped on passenger ships and trains provided they were stamped 'Non-explosive in bulk'.

From October 1914 until they entered the war, the United States sent the Allies over half a million tons of cordite, guncotton, nitrocellulose, fulminate of mercury and other explosive substances, all franked with such a certificate, and the cooperative Malone allowed them to pass.

George Booth returned to England on the Cunarder *Orduna* early in November, well satisfied with his visit. He reported to Kitchener, the Board of Trade and Sir Frederick Black, to whom he made special mention of the immense help Captain Gaunt had been to him. He added that he felt there was an overriding need for a centralized purchasing and financial authority in New York, and suggested the name of J. P. Morgan and Co. as a suitable firm to fulfil this function. Though he had his personal loyalties to his own bankers, Baring Bros, who also favoured the setting up of such an

American organization but in conjunction with the First National Bank of New York, he was influenced by the fact that easy as it might be to arrange the financing and purchasing, the cargoes still had to be shipped. The Morgan group had substantial tonnage in their International Mercantile Marine combine, and the appointment of Morgan would help to bring this tonnage to the Allied cause.

There were other factors which influenced the British Government's decision. The attitude of the American administration did not appear to favour the Allies, and if anyone could drive a coach and horses through the mass of red tape and prohibitions established by President Wilson to support his neutrality it was J. P. Morgan Jr. In fact he had already sent a secret emissary to London to discuss the matter. This was H. P. Davidson, who told Sir George Paish at the Treasury that the house of Morgan had decided that they could not and would not remain neutral and would do all in their power to help. This so impressed Lloyd George that he decided to use Morgan's services, even though a lower rate of commission had been offered by the First National Bank. Morgan took the job and established a special department to handle the difficult matter of purchasing for Britain all the war materials she needed. Throughout the period of America's neutrality, British servicemen in civilian clothes worked at Morgan's. This great banking combine rapidly established such a labyrinthine network of false shippers, bank accounts and all the paraphernalia of smuggling that although they fooled the Germans, there were also some very serious occasions when they flummoxed the Admiralty and Cunard not to speak of the unfortunate passengers on the liners who carried the contraband.[4]

4

It is difficult to reconcile President Wilson's well publicized idealism and neutrality with his sanctioning of the Morgan operation. It is equally hard to imagine more unlikely bedfellows than the Wall Street banking establishment and Wilson's Democrat administration. Their dislike and suspicion of each other was both traditional and profound. In June 1914 J. P. Morgan Jr had privately described the administration in forthright terms: 'A greater lot of perfectly incompetent and apparently thoroughly crooked people has never, as far as I know, run or attempted to run, any first class country.'[1] Wilson had the same views about the probity of the banking community, and suspected them of trying to organize political decisions to their profitable advantage.

In 1914 America was beginning to enter a period of acute economic recession, and the bankers realized that with a European war their normal export trade would be greatly affected, but that both European power groups would have need of money and war material. The administration had hitherto indicated that it would countenance neither the lending of the first nor the provision of the latter. Two of the banks anxious to float loans for the Allies were the National City and Morgan and Co. They cooperated in a joint approach to make the President change his mind.

The operation was entrusted to Thomas B. Lamont of Morgan's and Samuel McRoberts, a vice-president of the National City. Their task was a formidable one, and it was made no easier when they realized that McAdoo, the Secretary of the Treasury, was not only almost totally ignorant of finance but held no real power.[2] His function was to supervise the implementation of the somewhat doctrinaire instructions of his President and patron Woodrow Wilson. Lamont and McRoberts realized that it was impractical to lobby the President direct, so made their first formal approach to William Jennings Bryan, the Secretary of State. They had an equally formal rejection. 'Loans by American Bankers', announced the Secretary, 'are inconsistent with the true spirit of American neutrality.'[3]

The two bankers then concentrated their approach on Bryan's deputy, the young, ambitious and urbane Counsellor to the State Department, Robert M. Lansing. Lansing was a State Department lawyer who had specialized in territorial and boundary problems. He was an expert on the ill-defined boundaries of the various trading ports on the Chinese mainland, and his legal mind had doubtless grown accustomed to the subtleties of negotiating oriental concessions. More important he had married Eleanor Foster, the daughter of John W. Foster, Secretary of State to President Harrison in 1892. The connexion had brought him into intimate contact with powerful Washington personalities. His father-in-law since his retirement had joined the boards of numerous corporations. Washington and Wall Street played at John Foster's comfortable hunting and fishing lodge at Henderson Harbour on the south-eastern shore of Lake Ontario. Robert Lansing was frequently there, with his nephews Allen and John Foster Dulles. He was a tall, well-made man, as adept with a bass rod as he was with a brief. He habitually wore tweeds and took elocution lessons to develop an 'English accent'. At this remove it is difficult to reconstruct his character, but to read his personal papers in the Library of Congress, particularly his meticulously kept desk diaries, gives the overwhelming impression of a chameleon creature, part corporation lawyer, part public relations man. Narrow as his horizons were, devious as his posthumous papers show him to have been, he stands out as someone who always did what he thought was best for the United States and Robert Lansing. He had been appointed to

55

his position in a Democrat administration as a political favour by the President to the Republican Senator for New York, Elihu Root, in return for his cooperation in forcing legislation through the Senate.

Lansing by inclination was a Republican, and had numerous personal and financial connexions with Wall Street. His nomination had been opposed by Bryan on the grounds that 'there are substantial reasons to believe Mr Lansing has been guilty of impropriety in receiving financial benefit from commercial interests' while a relatively junior State Department lawyer, but Senator Root had interceded directly with the President and Lansing was appointed. As a result he had little love for Bryan.

Bryan, for all his integrity and deepseated religious convictions, was an untidy, emotional man, incapable of subtlety and with little capacity for reasoned thought. By contrast Lansing possessed an almost pathologically tidy mind and was meticulous in his attention to detail. He had rapidly become an essential balance to Bryan's emotionalism and Bryan had been content to delegate to him both the drafting of diplomatic correspondence and the preparation of the memoranda upon which the President and Bryan could base their policy decisions. From the Lansing papers in the Library of Congress it is evident that Lansing enjoyed finding flaws in Bryan's policies, possibly never more so than after Bryan had publicly pronounced them. He must have taken considerable relish in informing Bryan in a memorandum on 13 October 1914 that 'the President of the United States possessed no legal authority to interfere in any way with the trade between the people of the United States and the nationals of belligerent countries'.[4] Bryan realized that he had to tarnish the true spirit of neutrality. However the bankers very naturally wanted the President's blessing upon their plans, so they used Lansing as their envoy.

Samuel McRoberts of the National City Bank prepared a long letter to Lansing setting out the grave dangers to the United States economy if America's normal trade and international finance were absorbed by countries such as Canada,

Australia and Argentina. McRoberts composed the letter at the bank on the morning of 23 October. Lansing was present and then took the letter back to the State Department and prepared a 'memorandum for a policy decision', which was almost word for word identical to McRoberts' letter except that he changed such phrases as 'the bank feels' to 'I feel'.[5] By the time he had finished it was almost 8 p.m. and Secretary Bryan had long since left for home. Lansing took the memorandum over to the White House that night, and within half an hour had the President's agreement. The next day he informed Morgan and Co. at a meeting of the Metropolitan Club in New York that the President would not object to their floating credits for the Allies. Bryan learnt the news from the *New York Times*.

Lansing's actions went a long way towards changing America's publicly stated policy of 'strict neutrality' to one of 'strict legality' and when that legality was in doubt he constituted himself as the arbiter of what was just. Fortunately for the Allies his opinions favoured them. If his inclinations had favoured the Germans, he would undoubtedly have eventually been convicted of high treason. Within a month of securing the President's acquiescence to the bankers' plans he was to render Britain an even greater service – this time at the expense of his own countrymen.

Germany had laid mines opposite British ports in the North Sea on the first day of the war. They had informed all neutral powers that they had done so, and given them routes so that they could steer clear of them. In reply Britain had informed the United States that though Britain had not laid any mines in the North Sea she reserved the right to do so. All the mines that Britain had had in stock at the outbreak of the war had been laid in the Channel on 8 August to cover the passage of the British army to France.

Asquith's order to the Admiralty to commence a vigorous mining policy led to the establishment of major British minefields in the North Sea, and on 2 October the United States was informed that 'because of German mine-laying activities the whole of the North Sea must be considered a military area'.

There were no directions as to how to avoid them, and Britain required, in the interests of safety, every ship making passage in those waters to report to a British port in order to receive either pilot or up-to-the-minute avoiding instructions. Any ship that did not do so would be stopped on the high seas and ordered into the nearest British port. All ships, whether they reported as requested or were stopped at sea, were then subjected to search, and numerous cargoes were either delayed or detained. At the same time Britain declared almost every category of cargo to be contraband, and contraband was confiscated as a matter of course.

There was a storm of protest, mainly from American commercial interests who saw their trade being eroded before their eyes, and also from liberal opinion which correctly recognized the British action as a form of speculative capture, designed to ease the lot of the patrolling Royal Navy. The Navy claimed they could not search at sea as the Cruiser Rules stipulated, because of the danger of German submarines.

There was dissension within the American cabinet, and the Secretary of the Interior reported to Counsellor Lansing in order to help him formulate his diplomatic notes to Great Britain. 'England makes a fool of herself by antagonizing American opinion, insisting upon rights of search which she has never acknowledged to herself.'[6] Lansing managed partially to satisfy public opinion in the United States by adopting a show of belligerence which did not fool the British Foreign Office. In fact it was never intended to. He explained why in his memoirs: 'In dealing with the British Government there was always in my mind the conviction that we would ultimately become an ally of Great Britain, and that it would not do, therefore, to let our controversies reach a point where diplomatic correspondence gave place to action.'[7] He concentrated on writing notes of protest that would delay any positive action by the United States, and admitted it quite frankly: 'The notes that were sent were long and exhaustive treatises which opened up new subjects for discussion rather than closing those in controversy. . . . It was done with deliberate purpose. It ensured continuance of the controversies and left the questions unsettled.'[8]

With these thoughts influencing him, Lansing committed the United States to tacit acceptance of Britain's doctrine of an almost total blockade and her declaration that the North Sea was out of bounds to the world's shipping without the express permission of the Royal Navy. This supine acceptance has been hailed as a triumph of British diplomacy, but in reality it was the triumph of Lansing's undermining of the beliefs of his own Secretary of State and of the unanimous opinions of the Solicitors to the State Department, who had held that the British actions were contrary to International Law.

With such valuable support from the State Department, and from a man on whom the President was tending to rely to an increasing degree, Morgan's had little difficulty in commencing their purchasing operation. It was a vast enterprise. In the first year of operations alone, Morgan's purchased war material worth $1,100,453,950 and earned themselves a purchasing commission of well over $11 million. Such turnover dictated the necessity for sound management and Morgan had brought in Edward Stettinius, then President of the Diamond Match Co., to head the operation. Stettinius was made a full partner of Morgan and remained in charge of the complete operation throughout the war. He was assisted by British staff sent over from the Treasury and a considerable number of naval and military ordnance officers who wore civilian clothes and were attached to the staff of the British Consulate in New York. The senior British officials in New York were Tom Catto (who as Lord Catto was to become Governor of the Bank of England) and Sam (later Sir Hardman) Lever.

Morgan handled the negotiations for, and the financing of, the purchases, and after inspection the goods ordered were consigned to G. K. Sheldon and Co., the Admiralty forwarding agents. False names were used to prevent the true identity of shippers and manufacturers being discovered by the German intelligence service, the security side being handled by Captain Gaunt. His other responsibilities included the allocation of precious or vital cargoes to the faster ships, and keeping the Admiralty informed as to which ships carried what cargo, and of their destination and estimated date of arrival.

So far as security matters were concerned, Gaunt was assisted by the British Consul, General Sir Courtenay Bennett, who directed the British counter-intelligence operation in New York. Sir Courtenay was also responsible for screening would-be passengers to England and this function was eased by centralizing ticket issues in one office, no matter which ship a passenger wished to sail on. The office chosen was Cunard's which had the largest facilities in New York.

The Cunard piers were also the scene where most of the contraband ships were loaded. Gaunt had his own desk in the Cunard general manager's office. In addition to operating its own fleet, Cunard was also charged by the British Admiralty with the port administration and dispatch of numerous other ships, which were under direct Admiralty charter, but for security reasons cleared from New York as under charter to Cunard. The manager of the Cunard operation in New York was Charles P. Sumner, a tall outspoken Bostonian, known and respected throughout the east coast of the United States as 'a good steamship man'. Sumner had little time for politicians or the activities of Morgan and Co., Captain Gaunt and Sir Courtenay Bennett. He had no time at all for false manifests and legal subtleties and their acceptance by Collector of Customs Dudley Field Malone. When these were explained to him by Sir Courtenay and Gaunt he reacted violently.

There is no precise record of exactly what he did say. On 30 October 1914 Sir Courtenay was to telegraph Sir Eyre Crowe, the Assistant Under-Secretary of State at the Foreign Office and the titular head of the Intelligence Services, that Sumner 'must be in the pay of the Germans' as he had been 'very offensive and extremely lewd in his refusal to ship munitions in any Cunard passenger ship'. Sir Courtenay went on: 'He sees neither the logic nor the necessity of shipping Government supplies in bottoms of British registry, even when those bottoms are under contract to the Admiralty.'[9] It is not difficult to imagine Sumner's reply to the Consul-General. As a result of Sumner's stand, the *Lusitania* sailed home on 4 November with a mixed cargo of a general nature. It was the only voyage she was to make without a cargo of munitions.

Sir Eyre Crowe had a quiet word with Alfred Booth. Sumner's salary was doubled to £5000 a year and, hard-headed businessman or possibly conscientious Cunard servant that he was, he withdrew his objections and took the money.

Though Sumner had withdrawn his objections, he had made a serious enemy of the Consul-General, and from then on Sir Courtenay's agents delved deep into the Cunard line, shadowing their employees and producing a series of inflammatory and not very accurate reports of which the following are some samples.

German Influence in the Cunard Company

... The position of the Cunard Company ... is aggravated by the fact that all shipping companies in the United States advertise in the foreign language press of the United States through the Association of Foreign Language Newspapers, Woolworth Building, New York, the President of which is Mr Louis Hammerling, a German agent. The Association is practically owned and directed by the German shipping lines and by German interests in such large corporations as the Standard Oil and the St Louis Breweries ... it is politically powerful and exercises great influence especially in immigration matters, and hence its use by the shipping companies as a means of advertising transatlantic services for immigrants.

There is ample reason for supposing that Hammerling is actively working in German interests both by propaganda and by spying. He was responsible for the recent manifesto of the foreign language press against the export of arms. His influence over the Polish and other Slav, as well as the Jewish and Italian, elements in the United States has recently led the Foreign Office to consider how his activities might be counteracted ...

The organization established by the German Shipping lines, and especially the Norddeutscher Lloyd in the United States has been built up for years and we cannot hope to counteract it by any improvised organization during the war. It is probable that the only way in which safety can be secured for the enormous shipping business about to be carried on in the next few months from the United States for the Government is to provide for the supervision of all matters connected with Government service in the shipping offices in America by Admiralty officials in those offices themselves.[10]

At the head of the [Cunard] office here is a Boston man, Mr Charles P. Sumner, who in Boston was always considered to be anti-British, and since his removal here some years ago has been careful not to identify himself with anything of English tendency, and lives and makes his home at a club well known for its German and Jewish propensities, and is indeed there just as popular as he is unpopular outside, both with the public, shippers and his associates connected with the English lines.

. . . Mr Herman Winter, who is a sort of assistant manager, is a German by birth [actually born in Baltimore] and opinion.[11] [He] is well-known in German Circles. . . . He is a member of [clubs] . . . mainly composed of Germans. It is stated that he holds a considerable quantity of stock in the Hamburg American company, and that he has strong and influential German connections numbering amongst his friends such rabid Germans as . . .[12]

There is no doubt whatever that every vessel of the Cunard Company whilst in the port of New York, is kept under the closest possible observation by German agents from the time she arrives to the moment she sails. . . . Even longshoremen that work about the piers have noticed and commented upon the fact that men of unmistakable German appearance have been on the docks at different times, whilst steamers including the 'Lusitania' have been tied up.[13]

Coming to the Cunard Dock we find an Irishman named Mallon, a discharged member from the New York Police Force, in charge of the Police of the dock. Mallon is on very friendly terms with . . . the Detective Agency which is sending men to Canada to blow up bridges, etc., and which also, in concert with men from Pinkertons Agency are guarding the Hamburg American Docks. He was heard recently to qualify Irishmen who had enlisted in our Army, as 'd——d' fools to fight for any Country that had kept them down all their lives' . . . [He] has a private office . . . in the Vincent Building, 302 Broadway . . . full of German Jews.[14]

Sir Courtenay Bennett kept up a steady flow of similar reports; his final one sent two days after the *Lusitania* sailed on her voyage was no. 183. Of all his allegations the most serious was that Cunard continued to pay the salary of a German-born employee called Farenheim although they had banned him from the office. Cunard replied somewhat stiffly that Farenheim was an American citizen who had been in their employ for eleven years, and that in the national interest they had suspended him for the duration of the war on full pay. Under the American labour laws they had no alternative but to continue to pay him or offer him substantial compensation. Perhaps, Alfred Booth icily inquired of the Foreign Office, public funds would meet this expense? His letter terminated the correspondence.

5

The port of New York provided an appropriate background for the operation of the British and German intelligence services. The concentrated and cosmopolitan character of the city, the presence of large and vocal German and Irish communities initially favoured the German service, headed by Captain Franz von Papen, military attaché at the German Embassy (whose later career took him briefly to the German Chancellorship), and his colleague the naval attaché, Captain Boy-Ed. Their policies, which were essentially within the unspoken rules of diplomatic espionage, were eventually to prove too subtle to appeal to their superiors in Berlin, while the arrogance of both men made them increasingly unpopular with the Americans. It was an unpopularity based both on their physical appearance and on their almost incredible snobbishness. Both were tall, urbane, monocled military men, the epitome of the cartoon Prussian officers whom the pro-Ally press liked to depict as approving the rape of Belgian nuns, or using children for bayonet practice.

Von Papen himself regarded the Americans as impossibly uncouth, motivated entirely by the profit motive, and contended that their greatest shortcoming was that it was impossible to obtain either decent service or properly decanted claret in any native American restaurant. He held the view that the average American was not long out of the trees, was wont to speculate publicly 'that he was unable to understand how they had made the transition from walking on four legs to two', and would then offer his own answer that 'probably someone had indicated there was more money to be made by walking that way.' He was also revolted by the public acceptance of political corruption and financial malpractice within the local political power groups, which he interpreted as 'a national ability to fall into decadence without the customary intervening and uplifting period of civilization'.

In his private letters to his wife and his published memoirs, von Papen gives a detailed account of his activities at this time, and also takes the credit for inspiring certain acts of direct sabotage such as blowing up sections of the Canadian railway lines and at a later date placing time bombs aboard British merchantmen in New York Harbour. However, German archives show that these overt paramilitary acts were neither von Papen's idea nor his responsibility. They sprang from the activities of fringe immigrant Irish and German fanatics. Von Papen's methods, though they did not endear him to his superiors who tended to favour the more direct and indiscreet efforts of militant immigrants, did have both sublety and humour. Neither characteristic endeared him to the British contingent in New York or to the American authorities.

His reaction to the visits of George Booth and similar purchasing delegations was correctly to divine their requirements. These he attempted to finesse. His first move was to register an arms manufacturing company in the name of an American businessman of German sympathies and advance him the money with which to construct a vast factory. This company then ordered the requisite machine tools, presses and other machinery required for the manufacture of munitions in such quantities that it filled the order books of most of the American machinery manufacturers for months to come. This operation caused severe delays in the meeting of British orders. The second operation was more insolent. Again using the names of German sympathizers, von Papen formed numerous small companies which existed on paper only, and which bore irreproachably English-sounding names. These companies then offered their non-existent wares to the British and succeeded in obtaining numerous contracts, with, in several cases, substantial payments in advance. It was only when Morgan took over and coordinated the British purchasing efforts that his successes came to light.

Two relatively minor operations of von Papen had a direct influence on the fate of the *Lusitania* and the political argument that followed. Firstly, in January 1915 he contracted to purchase through one of his dummy companies the entire forward capacity for almost two years of the special cases in which gun-cotton was packed for shipment. These were the speciality of a subsidiary company of Dupont de Nemours. Von Papen took delivery and paid in advance. The suppliers had no idea that they were dealing with the Germans. Secondly, he established a network of agents who reported to him exactly what was going on in and around the Cunard Dock. Sir Courtenay Bennett was accurate when he stated that the Germans knew exactly what was going on, but he was looking in the wrong direction. Von Papen's main success was to infiltrate a German agent called Curt Thummel, who on 29 January 1915, under the name of Charles Thorne, secured employment as a steward aboard the Cunard liner *Transylvania*.[1]

British Intelligence overseas was largely dominated by the Navy, and the personality of the Director of Naval Intelligence, Captain Reginald Hall. He had taken over the position in October 1914 from Churchill's companion in the abortive midnight spy hunt at Loch Ewe, Admiral Oliver, who had been promoted to Chief of the Naval War Staff. Hall was a remarkable sailor and his intelligence gifts were only discovered when ill-health forced him to relinquish command of the battle-cruiser *Queen Mary* and transfer to a desk job. In a hidebound age he was unconventional to the point of eccentricity. His habit of screwing up his eyes as he talked earned him the nickname 'Blinker'. An excellent contemporary judgment of him is to be found in the correspondence of Walter Hines Page, the American Ambassador to London, who on 17 March 1917 wrote to President Wilson:

Hall is one genius that the war has developed. Neither in fiction nor in fact can you find any such man to match him. Of the wonderful things that I know he has done, there are several that would take a volume to tell. The man is a genius – a clear case of genius. All other secret service men are amateurs by comparison. . . . For Hall can look through you and see the very muscular movements of your immortal soul while he is talking to you. Such eyes the man has! My Lord! I do study these men here most diligently who have this vast and appalling War-Job. There are most uncommon creatures amongst them – men whom our grandchildren will read about in their school histories; but of them all, the most extraordinary is this naval officer – of whom probably, they'll never hear. He locks up certain documents 'not to be opened till twenty years after this date'. I've made up my mind to live twenty years more. I shall be present at the opening of that safe.[2]

The bulk of Hall's information came from an entirely unofficial censorship of the mail which he had induced the Post Office to set up shortly after his appointment. At that time most Atlantic mail from Europe came through London, and Hall's initiative in censoring it led to many clues as to where Germany was arranging to purchase her war requirements. It was this flood of information which led to the increase in the stopping of neutral steamers bound for continental ports, and which indirectly led to the British strict control of neutral traffic in the North Sea. Hall's intelligence had meant far too large a 'search load' for an already grievously stretched navy to achieve while at sea.

Hall's second piece of luck was the wireless intercept information provided by the Marconi Company and a team of amateur British radio hams. This had been expanded by his predecessor Admiral Oliver; by December 1914 Naval Intelligence was intercepting almost every German signal and a staff of experts under Sir Alfred Ewing was analysing them. A stroke of good fortune had provided the Admiralty with the official German naval codes and by the end of February 1915 Marconi had perfected a method of radio direction finding.

By the end of January 1915, Hall was able to advise the

Admiralty of the departure of each U-boat as it left for patrol, as it was German practice to test their ship to shore radio when about fifty miles from their base but before commencing their patrol. Hall's main priority was to keep a permanent listening watch in case the German fleet put to sea, but his two personal preoccupations were the exploitation of commercial and political intelligence which he garnered from the radio and the mail and also, since Britain owned the transatlantic and Pacific cables, from censorship of all cables. He circulated the information made available to him as he saw fit, and there is no doubt that he used it to develop a personal power base from which his activities extended far beyond those of any previous Director of Naval Intelligence. As the war progressed Hall became one of the most powerful men charged with the conduct of the war, and possibly, where its direction was concerned, the most powerful of all. The two main areas in which he exploited his information were the south coast of Ireland and the United States. His interest in the former lay in his determination to crush the Sinn Fein movement. It was Hall's information that led to the capture of Sir Roger Casement and it was Hall who leaked the existence of the notorious 'Casement Diaries' to the press in order to stifle sympathy for the condemned man and to destroy any chances for his appeal then pending.

The United States however was his main operational area and to facilitate his aims he went to extraordinary lengths to achieve an accurate picture of what was going on there. In London, for example, a cypher clerk of the United States Embassy was an Englishman on Hall's payroll, and every message between the State Department and its European embassies was deciphered and read by Naval Intelligence probably before it reached its recipient. This accurate background material proved invaluable to Hall's deputy in America, Captain Gaunt.

The British Intelligence operation in America was divided into two sections. The gathering of military and commercial intelligence was the work of the Embassy attachés, dominated by Gaunt. Civilian counter-intelligence, which included the screening of passengers wishing to travel to Europe was controlled by Sir Courtenay Bennett. Both men were the opposite to their German counterparts. Both were gregarious, and Gaunt obviously liked the Americans, who in return thought the world of him. His views and his interpretations of American policy were widely sought, and because he was astonishingly well briefed he acquired a reputation as a man who was both wise to and understanding of the American point of view. He was especially intimate with Counsellor Lansing, and the two men liked nothing more than to take a leisurely Saturday lunch together and thence to go off together to a football game. He also fascinated Lansing's two nephews, Allen and J. Foster Dulles, and was probably the inspiration of the former's lifelong interest in security work, as possibly Counsellor Lansing's taste for power and brinkmanship was to the latter. Through Lansing, Gaunt met many of the members of the American security services and became a close friend of Special Agent Bruce Bielaski, the senior operative of the Department of Justice. It was to prove an opportune and profitable relationship.

Like von Papen, Gaunt established a comprehensive network of informants. Many of these were drawn from Englishmen resident in the United States, notably from the members of an organization called The League of Patriotic Britons Overseas. However, he spread his net wider than this small cross section, and one of his recruits who is relevant to the story was a nervous and emotional little Hungarian-born chemist, Dr E. W. Ritter von Rettegh, who by the outbreak of the war had become an American citizen. A well-known expert on explosives, he had invented and patented a process for making liquid petroleum from natural gas, and because of his birth the Austro-Hungarian Embassy had asked him to work for them. Gaunt had made a similar approach and persuaded von Rettegh to accept the Austro-Hungarian offer, but at the same time to accept a modest 'retainer' for technical advice on subjects which 'did not conflict with his other employment'. Gaunt paid him by cheque, and rapidly established the standard espionage convention of a 'blackmail hold' over his double agent.[3]

Gaunt reported directly to the Admiralty. Sir Courtenay's reports were channelled through the Foreign Office. The two men's duties naturally overlapped in many respects, but in one area this overlap mattered. The Admiralty's confidential instructions to the masters of merchant ships were formulated by the Trade Division of the Admiralty under Captain Richard Webb. The instructions were then submitted to the Intelligence and Operations staffs and once cleared were dispatched to officers in every port, known as Senior Naval Officers (S.N.O.), to brief each departing captain on his route, speed etc, together with up-to-the-minute information on U-boat activity and details of the wireless call signs and codes in force for that voyage. There was, of course, no S.N.O. in any neutral port, so in New York Sir Courtenay was given this function.

The system could and did lead to confusion. Sir Courtenay would brief the outgoing captain, who was forbidden to depart from his instructions. However, Captain Gaunt had to advise the Admiralty as to the date and place of arrival of each ship and the details of their cargoes, so that suitable escorts or unloading facilities could be arranged. Bennett was based on New York, Gaunt on Washington. Over 1100 ships a month were clearing from North American ports for Britain, and unless Gaunt was immediately told the speed and destination of each ship, there was frequently too little time to inform the Admiralty in time for them to arrange an escort and for that escort to steam to the rendezvous. On 20 May 1915 when the Admiralty conducted their own secret inquiry into the *Lusitania* disaster, Vice-Admiral Oliver, Chief of the Naval War Staff, pinpointed the problem:

It happens sometimes that large numbers of Canadian troops come in ordinary passenger ships or that valuable heavy guns or mountings come in merchant ships and have to be met and escorted. It also frequently happens that the ship has sailed before it is known [at the Admiralty] that troops or valuable government warlike stores are on board.[4]

Apart from the admission that ordinary passenger steamers were being simultaneously employed as troopships, a fact which successive Admiralty spokesmen have categorically denied for fifty-seven years, it is obvious that the arrangements for escorts were not as efficient as they should have been. The other contributory reason for this was that the Admiralty still believed that in order to operate in the waters off the south coast of Ireland U-boats had to force a passage through the heavily mined and diligently patrolled English Channel.

On 30 January 1915 the U-21 appeared off Liverpool and in one afternoon sank three unarmed merchant ships. No lives were lost as in each case the U-21 followed the Cruiser Rules. She surfaced, challenged the ships, gave the crew ample time to take to their boats and then destroyed her captives by placing bombs on board. On board her first victim, the 3000-ton *Ben Cruachan* of the Ben Line of Edinburgh, she captured a complete set of Churchill's inflammatory orders, including the instructions to ram and to fly a neutral flag.

The Admiralty reacted speedily. They anticipated that the U-21 would return the way they believed she had come down through the Irish Sea, around Land's End and thence home via the Channel. Admiral Oliver immediately sent an urgent cypher signal to the Naval Base at Queenstown (now Cobh).

Cypher D.   From: Admiralty
84 Urgent.   To: Vice-Admiral Queenstown
                                   30.1.15.

The Cunard Steamers *Transylvania* due off Fastnet Sunday night January 31st. and *Ausonia* due off Fastnet Wednesday night February 3rd., both having valuable cargo, are to be ordered into Queenstown and berthed safe from submarine attack.

Both ships have M.V. Code.

Written across the signal in Admiral Oliver's handwriting is the notation: 'Deflected into Queenstown on account of 2 seventy-ton guns on board for R.N.'[5]

The background to this is both curious and illuminating. The guns were two of a series of four pairs of 14 inch guns complete with turrets which the Bethlehem Steel Co. had been constructing for the Greek battleship *Salamis*. Churchill heard about them and persuaded Mr Schwab, the President of Bethlehem Steel, to sell them to the Royal Navy. Equally curious, but not unexpected, neither ship's clearance nor supplementary manifests handed in at New York mention them, which is indicative of either the inefficiency or the pro-British sympathies of the neutrality officials inspecting all outgoing steamers, and the attitude of Collector of Customs Malone. In each case, the turrets with their guns mounted were carried on the Cunarders' foredecks.

Both liners were duly warned by Queenstown, and as soon as they docked all passengers were held incommunicado. The scare lasted two days, and four indignant American passengers' complaints eventually percolated back to the State Department. All four complaints specifically mentioned the guns, but, though each one is initialled by Counsellor Lansing, they do not appear to have been forwarded to either the Secretary of State or the neutrality officials of New York Harbour.

Behind the two Cunarders which had been diverted into Queenstown was a steady procession of cargo and passenger ships, each bringing its complement of supplies and each following the same track, aiming to make its landfall at the Fastnet rock, before discharging at either Avonmouth or Liverpool. The commander of the U-21 reported to the German Admiralty: 'Having only one torpedo left for the return voyage, I was forced to decide not to mount a surface attack on forty-one merchant vessels which as I was able to ascertain from my annuals were armed.'[6] The annuals referred to were two British publications, *Jane's Fighting Ships 1914* and *The Naval Annual 1914*. Both publications were standard issue to each U-boat. One ship which escaped thanks to the U-21's reluctance was the *Lusitania*, which cleared the Fastnet at dawn on 5 January. Both British naval publications listed her as armed, *Jane's* as an auxiliary cruiser, *The Naval Annual* as an armed merchantman. On this voyage as before she was commanded by Captain 'Fairweather' Dow, and amongst the passengers was Colonel Edward House of Houston, Texas.

House was the personal representative and confidential adviser of President Wilson. His mission was a secret, for he brought with him the President's proposals for a peace initiative that he was to place in turn before the Allies and the Kaiser. His diary of his visit to Europe survives in the archives of Yale University:

Feb. 5th
... the first two days we had summer seas, but just after passing the Banks a gale came shrieking down.... It lasted for twenty-four hours and the *Lusitania*, big as she is, tossed about like a cork in the rapids. This afternoon, as we approached the Irish Coast the American flag was raised. It created such excitement, and comment and speculation ranged in every direction ...

Feb. 6th
I found from Mr Beresford, Lord Decies' brother, who crossed with us, that Captain Dow had been greatly alarmed the night before and had asked him, Beresford, to remain with him on the bridge all night. He expected to be torpedoed, and that was the reason for raising the American flag. I can see many possible complications arising from this incident. Every newspaper in London has asked me about it, but fortunately I was not an eye witness to it and have been able to say that I only knew it from hearsay. The alarm of the Captain for the safety of his boat caused him to map out a complete programme for the saving of passengers, the launching of lifeboats, etc. He told Beresford that if the boilers were not struck by the torpedoes, the boat could remain afloat for at least an hour, and in that time he would endeavour to save the passengers.

Captain Dow, it would seem, did not share the views of the owners, designer and builders of the *Lusitania*, and was only too aware of the vulnerability of the longitudinal bulkheads. He had yet, however, even to sight a submarine, and no ship of any character had ever challenged him. So far no merchant ship had been attacked without warning, but several submarines had narrowly escaped disaster from attempts to ram and feelings amongst the U-boat commanders were running hot.

In Germany the effects of the British blockade were beginning to be felt and rationing of cereals, milk and flour had been introduced the previous week. The formal British declaration of the North Sea as a prohibited area was the final signal to the Germans that they must speedily introduce such counter measures as would relieve a situation which threatened to undermine the economic structure of the country and through this collapse lead to military defeat. It was exactly the result the British war plans had envisaged, but these plans had not envisaged the submarine. Lord Fisher had done so, but as has been already explained, his views had been spurned. Now sitting in the First Sea Lord's office in Whitehall he anticipated the German solution and recorded it for his memoirs. 'If dear old Tirpitz is only far seeing enough, those damned Germans will multiply means of "dishing" the blockade by making the life of surface ships . . . a burden to them by submarines.'[7] As usual, he was to be proved correct.

6

The British proclamation of the North Sea as a war zone, in November 1914, and the realization by the operational officers of the German Navy that not only were a great many Allied merchant ships armed, but that all had instructions to disregard the Cruiser Rules and immediately to attack any submarine sparked an immediate backlash. The German officers prepared a memorandum addressed to the Chief of Naval Staff, Vice-Admiral von Pohl, urging that U-boats should also abandon the Cruiser Rules and attack all Allied merchantmen without warning. Neutral ships, they suggested, should be warned not to sail into British ports, unless they had previously furnished the German Admiralty through consular channels with a description both of the ship and of its cargo which must not be war material. Their proposal was, in fact, a counter blockade.

Von Pohl liked their argument and put it before the German War Staff, where Admiral von Tirpitz opposed it. He had doubts about the international legality of a submarine blockade and foresaw trouble with neutrals. The increasing use by the British of neutral flags was bound to lead to mistakes. Von Pohl agreed to drop the word blockade and suggested the retaliatory measure of declaring the waters off the British and Irish coasts a war zone. Von Tirpitz replied: 'This . . . is more far-reaching in its effect on materials than a regular blockade and is thus considerably more dangerous politically. . . . The reference to the measures taken by the English in designating the North Sea as dangerous does not seem to be apt.'[1] He went on to explain that the British justification for their war zone had been the allegation that the Germans had laid mines there; an allegation which he said was false, as the only German mines laid had been offensive fields limited to the approaches to East Coast ports.

At this point the German Foreign Office entered the argument stating that they preferred the idea of a war zone, as declaration of a blockade would weaken their own protests that total blockade was illegal. German public and press opinion also demanded retaliation against the British measures and the announcement of a war zone operative from 18 February was formally made by the Kaiser on 5 February 1915. The same day he addressed the U-boat commanders at Wilhelmshaven. Towards the end of his speech he mentioned that by sinking enemy merchant ships without warning there would be undoubted loss of life amongst the crews. At this point he paused, and then said: 'If it is possible for you to save the crews of the merchant ships, do it.' After a further pause, he added: 'If you cannot save them, then it cannot be helped.'[2]

Some U-boat commanders went off on patrol, but on 15 February the Kaiser had second thoughts, for he telegraphed every U-boat commander at sea ordering them 'on no account to attack ships flying neutral flags unless they were recognized with positive certainty as being enemy ships in disguise'.[3] The Kaiser's telegram was motivated by the reaction of the United States.

The German proclamation of a war zone together with an accompanying 'memorial' of explanation was presented to the State Department on 5 February by the German Ambassador Count Bernstorff. Secretary Bryan was away in the West on a speaking trip, and the German note was received in his absence by Counsellor Lansing. The text of the note is important.

The waters surrounding Great Britain and Ireland including the whole English Channel to be a war zone. On and after the 18th of February 1915 every enemy merchant ship found in the said war zone will be destroyed without it being always possible to avert the dangers threatening the crews and passengers on that account. Even neutral ships are exposed to dangers in the war zone, as in view of the misuse of neutral flags ordered on January 31st by the

British Government and of the accidents of naval war, mistakes will not always be avoided and they may be struck by attacks directed at enemy ships.[4]

The proclamation went on to list safe zones in which neutral ships could travel without danger, though none of these zones led to an English port. The memorial which accompanied the proclamation went into an elaborate justification of the German decision. It stressed that the British had been the first to declare such a war zone and finished by asking the United States and all neutral powers to take such steps as they thought necessary to warn their nationals not to sail as passengers or to entrust their cargoes to enemy ships.

Lansing read the proclamation at first without consulting the memorial and the same day in Bryan's absence he drafted a note of protest to Germany which he submitted to the President at 7 p.m. the same evening. It was a menacing and belligerent epistle describing the proclamation as a 'wanton act unparalleled in naval warfare'.[5] However, after reading the memorial and conferring with the Solicitors to the State Department, he submitted a further memorandum two days later stating that the advisability 'of any protest at all' was 'open to question'.[6] By February Lansing's belligerency had returned, and he produced a draft note which the President accepted. This draft entirely ignored the suggestion that the American Government should warn Americans not to seek passage on Allied ships, and Bryan, now returned, protested angrily at this omission to the President, who countered by asking Lansing to prepare him a brief as to the precise legal situation regarding passengers on belligerent merchant ships, with particular reference to cases where such merchant ships were armed. It was at this juncture that Lansing committed the United States to the path that was to lead to war.

The outstanding case law on the subject is contained in the judgment of an action called 'The *Nereide* case' in which Chief Justice Marshall of the Supreme Court had opined that an armed merchant ship 'is an open and declared belligerent, claiming all the rights and subject to all the dangers of the belligerent character'. The *Nereide* was a British merchant vessel which was captured by the American privateer *The Governor Tomkins* on 19 December 1813. Ship and cargo were confiscated by the American authorities in the United States' role as an ally of France. A Spanish passenger, Manuel Pinto, owned part of its cargo. He claimed it back on the grounds that he was a neutral and did not know the *Nereide* was armed or that she had orders to resist attack. He lost his case. The appeal went to the Supreme Court on 6 March 1815.[7]

Lansing, a distinguished lawyer, quoted several of the arguments from the *Nereide* case in support of his views. These so impressed the President that later when Congress was attacking him for appearing to drag the United States into the war he asked Lansing to enlarge on his summary of the *Nereide* precedent for the benefit of those congressmen who were to speak on behalf of the administration. On both occasions Lansing omitted the vital sentence of the judgment quoted above. At this remove the only charitable explanation is that Lansing's 'opinion' to both President and Congress was bad in law. But there is some justification for thinking it may have been a deliberate omission. Twenty-one years later a Senate Committee on Foreign Relations examined the matter. Evidence was given that: 'Of Marshall's opinion a garbled version was got out ... a version so false as to constitute practically a forgery; but it was widely disseminated and it was used in speeches even in Congress.'[8]

Bad law or bad faith, Lansing's opinions were accepted by the President, and diplomatic honour was outwardly maintained by sending simultaneously with the note to Germany a sharp note to Great Britain complaining of the use of the American flag, and trusting that 'no explicit sanction had been given to this procedure by either the British Admiralty or the Foreign Office'. Unfortunately President Wilson sent a private telegram to Colonel House then in London which 'regretted the necessity of sending the note, but sooner or later it could not be avoided'.[9] The telegram of course was deciphered and read before House even received it, and the British Foreign Office blandly replied to the American Government:

The German proclamation of February 5th of sinking British merchantmen at sight without giving any opportunity of making any provision for saving the lives of non-combatants, crews, and passengers had led to the master of the *Lusitania* hoisting the American flag as a defence measure and it had only been hoisted at the request of American passengers in order to ensure their safety.

The note went on to confirm that neither the Government nor the Admiralty had sanctioned such action. This was the diplomatic lie direct, and Lansing must have known it as the German memorial had enclosed photographs of the Admiralty instructions they had captured. He had ignored them and had not mentioned them to either Bryan or the President.

The American note to Germany possessed what Lord Morley, a former cabinet minister and close friend of Churchill, described at the time as 'an air of senseless animosity'.[10] After first condemning any departure from the Cruiser Rules as unprecedented in naval warfare, it carried the ultimate threat that was to bring the United States into the war. 'In the event that German submarines should destroy on the high seas an American vessel or the lives of American citizens, it would be difficult for the Government of the United States to view the action in any other light than as an indefensible violation of neutral rights.'[11] It added that if such a situation should arise the German Government would be held to 'a strict accountability'.

The view that the presence of any American citizen on any Allied ship, even if that ship was an armed munitions carrier, was in fact a warning to Germany that she attacked it at the risk of war with the United States, astounded the Germans as much as it delighted the British. The German Government began to backpedal. Germany promptly offered to drop the offending instructions to her submarines and to observe the standard Cruiser Rules, provided in return that England would permit foodstuffs to enter Germany and cease arming merchant ships. She also suggested that if the United States would inform her of any American vessels sailing to English ports, together with their routes and destinations, and preferably if she would arrange to paint the Stars and Stripes on the ships' sides, she would guarantee their immunity from attack. These concessions made sense to President Wilson, but from England the American Ambassador reported that there was not 'a ray of hope of any agreement between Germany and England whereby England will permit food to enter Germany under any condition'.[12]

Churchill's policy of arming merchant ships and ordering them to ignore Cruiser Rules had been designed to embroil Germany with neutral powers. Now it was so obviously doing so, he was not prepared to abandon it. Germany's protests at Britain's arming of merchant ships had also received cavalier treatment from Lansing who had tacitly allowed them to use American ports. He had stipulated that while in port their armament must not be mounted, and without consultation with Bryan, came to an informal understanding with the British Embassy that they would inform him which ships did carry guns. Of the known 1319 armed ships in the merchant marine which frequently used American ports from September 1914 until the United States' entry into the war, the State Department was informed of only seventeen. One case came to the notice of Secretary Bryan, and it is indicative as to how seriously Britain took America's reservations.

On 1 September 1914 the steamer *Merion* entered New York displaying an armament of six 6-inch guns. The German Embassy informed the State Department. Bryan approached the British Ambassador who gave an assurance that the armament would be dismounted immediately. Three days later the British Embassy asked the State Department if there would be any objection if the dismounted guns were subsequently shipped to Britain as cargo on another ship since guns as cargo were against the U.S. law. Bryan's reply speaks for itself: 'Replying to your note of September 4th it seems unnecessary to answer the query as to the shipment of the *Merion*'s guns to England as cargo in another vessel, for the reason that the Department is informed that notwithstanding the assurances of your Government, the *Merion* sailed with her guns and ammunition.'[13]

At the British Ambassador's request the last sentence was withdrawn from the official record by Lansing, as it reflected on the honour of the British Government. Nor did Lansing pass the correspondence to the archives, but retained it amongst his own papers.

The arming of merchant ships had been only one of Britain's attempts to prepare for a submarine offensive, for the German announcement of a blockade had been long expected and in some Admiralty quarters accepted as legal. This acceptance had surfaced publicly in *The Times* on 16 July 1914 when Admiral Sir Percy Scott wrote with reference to the anticipated proclamation of a war zone:

Such a proclamation would, in my opinion, be perfectly in order, and once it had been made, if any British or neutral ships disregarded it, they could not be held to be engaged in ... peaceful avocations ... and if they were sunk in the attempt it could not be described as a relapse into savagery or piracy in its blackest form. ... Look up the accounts of what happened to blockade runners into Charleston during the civil war in America ... the blockading cruisers seldom had any scruples about firing into the vessels they were chasing ... the submarine torpedo will be a newer deterrent.[14]

Sir Percy's opinions were shared by the Chief of Staff of the French Mediterranean Fleet who expressed his opinion that submarine warfare as announced by the Germans was justified'.[15]

News of the dialogue within the German Navy and of the pressure for a submarine blockade had reached the Admiralty by mid-November. There is evidence from Commander J. M. Kenworthy, a member of Naval Intelligence staff (Political Section) that it was actually hoped for at the time that Britain made her declaration about the North Sea. The defensive measures to counter such a threat had been finalized by early December 1914.

The waters around the coasts of England and Ireland were divided into twenty-three areas, each patrolled by a new force called an 'Auxiliary Patrol'. These units incorporated the coastal motorboat operation commanded by Admiral Sir Frederick Inglefield, but not his seagulls. Each area was designated with a number. The south coast of Ireland was area 21, under the overall command of Vice-Admiral Sir Charles Coke, whose headquarters were at Queenstown, Cork. His defences consisted of four torpedo boats and four small units of the new Auxiliary Patrol, each containing one armed yacht, four motor fishing boats, and one motor boat. Their task was to provide effective submarine protection for 285 miles of coastline. Under standing Admiralty Instructions of 1910 the torpedo boats' duties were to be confined to sweeping the approaches to Queenstown harbour and these had never been altered. This left the Auxiliary Patrol to carry the entire defensive burden. Between them they had five wireless sets and a motley collection of armament, the heaviest calibre weapon being a 12-pounder mounted on the yacht *Scadaun*. By the middle of April 1915 wear and tear had reduced the strength of the Auxiliary Patrol to a total of seventeen small vessels, and allowing for rest and maintenance it was impractical to have more than eleven at sea at the same time. The fastest ship was capable of making 11 knots, and the patrol area of each ship encompassed 300 square miles. This absurdly small force was the main protection for the area which was Britain's most vital supply route, and the focal point for all shipping heading for the British Isles from North America.

Further out in the Atlantic off the Irish coast was a patrol cruiser from No. 11 Cruiser Squadron, known as E for signal purposes, also based on Queenstown. These were old ships of 5600 tons, carrying eleven 6-inch guns; a slightly smaller armament than that which the *Lusitania* had been designed to carry. Their age, and the fact that they belonged to the class of cruiser with unarmoured longitudinal bulkheads not to be exposed to submarine attack, meant that they were of dubious value. The only useful ships in the western area were a flotilla of five destroyers based on Milford Haven some three hundred miles away. These were kept exclusively for escort duty to ships carrying valuable cargo.

The German submarine offensive was to be mounted by a total fleet of only twenty-one submarines, but maintenance and repairs meant that in practice never more than seven could be at sea, and in the waters around the Irish coast and the English west coast ports, there were rarely more than two U-boats present at any one time. However, it was in these areas that 80 per cent of the effects of the German proclamation was felt. From February, when the German war zone came into force, until 28 March 1915, twenty-five merchants ships were sunk by German submarines. Sixteen of these were torpedoed without warning, and from these sixteen fifty-two crew members out of a total of 712 were killed. Thirty-eight of this total were lost when the *Tangistan* loaded with nitrates blew up off Flamborough Head. On the twenty-five ships sunk there were 3072 passengers, and not one of these lost their lives. Twenty of the twenty-five ships sunk suffered no loss of life whatsoever.

On 28 March this not altogether discreditable record in what history has designated 'total warfare' was blotted. Thirty-eight miles west of the Smalls lighthouse and shortly after 2 p.m. the U-28 ordered the 5000-ton cargo and passenger liner *Falaba* to halt by firing a shot across her bows. The *Falaba* refused. Eventually the U-28 forced her to a halt and gave her master ten minutes to abandon ship. The *Falaba* continued to send out wireless messages for assistance, and as disembarkation was still in progress the U-28 extended the period by another ten minutes. A third extension of three minutes was granted and shortly after this an armed British trawler came to the scene. The U-28 promptly put a torpedo into the stern of the *Falaba* and her cargo which included thirteen tons of high explosive exploded. Amongst the casualties was an American citizen, Leon C. Thresher.

The fury with which the American press reacted was to bind the President politically even closer to his acceptance of Lansing's doctrine of 'strict accountability'. At the time the public version of events was that little or no warning had been given, that the torpedoing had been a cold-blooded and wanton act of destruction. The true nature of the cargo was vigorously denied (the manifest and the statements of the ship's officers were not released *in full* until 1965). The inevitable showdown with Germany was delayed because the battle of ideals between Lansing and Bryan was now in full swing.

Lansing insisted that Germany wanted war with the United States and that a hard line should be taken. Bryan diligently acquired a reasonably accurate account of the *Falaba* story from the American Consul in Plymouth who had interviewed several survivors. At last the President appeared to favour Bryan's viewpoint and admitted that perhaps a hard line was the wrong course, and wrote to him that 'Perhaps it is not necessary to make formal representations in the matter at all.' The President was still in this indecisive mood a month later.

Both the German community in New York and the Foreign Ministry in Berlin could see the writing on the wall. Should there be any further escalation of the crisis, there was little doubt that the United States would embark upon a European war on the side of the Allies. The Berlin view was that it would make very little difference, as to all intents and purposes America was already so industrially and financially committed to the Allies, and this opinion was shared by many Americans of importance. Colonel House reported from London that 'the sooner America entered the war the better', as he felt that the Allies found America's peace proposals 'futile' and 'possibly offensive'. He advised the President to take a sharp line with Germany and darkly hinted, 'a more serious breach may at any time occur'.[16]

The possibility of a further and more serious breach was worrying the German community of New York, and on 20 April a group of them met to see if they could do anything to avert it. The meeting was convened by George Vierick, the editor of the German-owned American newspaper *The Father-land*, and among those present were a Dr Bernhard Dernburg and a Dr Karl Fuehr. The meeting reviewed the situation and Vierick remarked, 'Sooner or later some big passenger boat with Americans on board will be sunk by a submarine, then there will be hell to pay.'[17]

Others present argued that they were on the wrong track. It would be better to concentrate on making Americans aware of the immorality of the British blockade and the fact that merchantmen were being instructed to disobey instructions to halt. Dr Fuehr suggested that if any emotional emphasis was due it should be given to details of the starving children of Germany. But Dr Dernburg's counter-argument carried the meeting. 'The American people cannot visualize the spectacle of a 100,000, even a million German children starving by slow degrees as a result of the British blockade, but they can visualize the pitiful face of a little child drowning amidst the wreckage caused by a German torpedo.'

Dernburg's graphic picture prompted Dr Fuehr to ask the date of departure of the next great English passenger liner to England. It transpired it was the *Lusitania* due to sail in ten days' time on 1 May. Vierick shouted: 'Then publish a warning before the *Lusitania* sails.'

7

Throughout the winter of 1914 and into the following spring, the *Lusitania* made the monthly round voyage from Liverpool to New York and home again. She no longer made her previous record times because in November 1914 the Board of Cunard took an unpopular and possibly unwise decision. They reduced her speed.

Alfred Booth kept a keen eye on his company finances. On 16 November the accounts department informed him that the operation of the *Lusitania* was losing the company £2000 a trip. The reasons were the increase in the price of coal and the falling off of passenger revenue. The accountants considered that there was really no justification for operating a passenger service at all. The existing American liners had sufficient surplus capacity to meet the demand. To give added emphasis to their point, they produced figures to show that in the first ten months of 1914 the *Lusitania* by reason of her reduced passenger load and the time she had spent in the Admiralty dockyards had lost them £24,591. They suggested that if the passenger service were not stopped completely, at least it should be suspended for the winter. Booth, and his Board of Directors, more probably after pressure from the Admiralty, refused to agree to either suggestion. They decided to cut their overheads. They reduced the crew by 258, thereby saving £1325 per trip in wages. The engine room lost eighty-three men, so that it was only possible to fire three of the four boiler rooms. This led to a coal saving of 1600 tons a trip and the joint economies more than cancelled out the indicated loss. It meant, however, that the maximum speed available under emergency conditions was

21 instead of 26 knots, and the cruising speed was reduced from 24 knots to 18.

It was an unpopular decision with the staff. On the first westbound voyage under these conditions, twenty-five of the seventy-seven able seamen refused to sign on. In New York forty-five stewards jumped ship and Charles Sumner, the New York manager, cabled his chairman in some dismay. He thought at first that the decision to cut a boiler room and reduce the intake of coal was due to some more sinister motive – possibly sabotage: 'was reduced quantity coal intentional or result "alleged" error in loading. Rush answer.'[1] Booth confirmed that the reductions of coal and crew had been intentional, so Sumner wrote a personal letter explaining his questions and delicately suggesting that it would be better to carry a full supply:

About the time I received your cable confirming the quantity of coal aboard the *Lusitania*, I thought there seemed to be very strong evidence that there were two people at least aboard the steamer who were not friendly to our interests. Thinking this matter over carefully it occurred to me that possibly the short supply of coal might be the result of crookedness on the part of one of the so-called spies in the engine room. I was much relieved however to find that the reduced quantity was the result of premeditation and that it would be explained in your letter of November 18th.

It occurs to me that it would be prudent in view of the somewhat unsettled conditions of things on the North Atlantic at the moment to have a full supply of coal on board, even though you restricted its consumption except in emergency cases.[2]

Sumner's suggestion was turned down. Booth contended correctly that it would take twenty hours to relight the boilers which had been shut down, and in any case there would have been insufficient stokers to man the furnaces. He replied that whilst he appreciated Sumner's anxieties he 'did not know what the possibilities are to which you refer . . . with our knowledge of the German methods of warfare we do not think that they would wait until volunteers on the *Lusitania* have got up a sufficient amount of steam by lighting the extra section of boilers before they came to the attack.'[3]

However, Sumner got his coal. Captain Dow, after Sumner had explained the situation to him, categorically refused to make the eastbound voyage without full bunkers, and on his return to Liverpool shortly before Christmas 1914 took his case direct to the chairman, who finally acceded to his point of view. It was not Fairweather Dow's bluff eloquence that won the point, but a memorandum from the accounts department that coal was cheaper in New York, and therefore it was in the Company's interest to buy it there travelling westbound with a reduced load and returning home full. Booth's instructions to Sumner allowing this contained yet another minor caveat against unnecessary expense. 'If Captain and Engineer desire you may arrange give Lusitania full bunkers reducing fresh water much as possible.'[4]

Captain Dow's caution, though legendary, was not misplaced. The following trip the *Lusitania* narrowly avoided the German raider *Karlsruhe* in the mists off the Grand Banks, and on the next there was a submarine scare. He took the *Lusitania* out of Liverpool on 20 February 1915. From the start of this penultimate voyage the danger of submarines began to materialize. On the first day two nearby merchant ships were attacked and sunk by the U-30 within ten miles of the *Lusitania*'s track and on the homeward trip the U-20 torpedoed the cargo ship *Bengrove* just as the *Lusitania* entered St George's Channel. Captain Dow had had enough. On 8 March he informed Alfred Booth that though he did not mind commanding a merchant vessel in these waters, he refused to carry the responsibility of mixing passengers with munitions or contraband. Possibly he was influenced in his thinking by the fact that on his final voyage the enterprising Captain Gaunt had loaded the double bottom of the *Lusitania* with 100,000 gallons of diesel oil, which had not improved either Dow's peace of mind or his sea-sickness-prone stomach. Alfred Booth decided that Dow was suffering from severe strain and looked around his staff for another master. He chose Captain William Thomas Turner.

'Bowler Bill', as Turner was known because of his habit of wearing a bowler hat at all times except when on the bridge, was a martinet who first went to sea before the mast. His first command had been a square-rigged ship. He had joined Cunard in 1883, and had captained both the *Lusitania* and the *Mauretania* since becoming a Cunard captain in 1907. At the outbreak of war he was in command of the *Aquitania,* now an armed cruiser.* He was immensely broad, chunky-faced and notoriously taciturn. It had been for this reason that Captain Dow had been preferred to him, as Turner lacked the polish that Cunard expected of its masters. He was however an extremely capable seaman with a legendary reputation for personal strength and ability. He loathed the social side of a captain's life and deliberately took most of his meals on the bridge, so as to avoid the passengers who clamoured to sit at his table. In Captain Turner's book, passengers tended to be, as his housekeeper Miss Every recalls, 'a lot of bloody monkeys'. By modern standards a tame description, but one which sounded apposite enough when expressed in Bowler Bill's pungent Liverpool accent. To redress the social balance the Board of Directors nominated Captain John C. Anderson as second or Staff Captain to undertake any socializing that was required. Captain Turner inspected the *Lusitania* from stem to stern on 10 March 1915, and had quite a lot of fault to find. He deplored the standard of crew, he found faults with the boats and the trim tanks, and by the time his demands had been met it was 20 March before he made his first voyage. When he returned to Liverpool on 11 April, Miss Every remembers him as both an angry and a worried man. By her account he handed in a blistering report to Booth complaining about the standard of seamanship, the state of the lifesaving equipment and the performance of the turbines. Not content with reporting to Cunard, he complained directly to the Board of Trade Surveyor for Liverpool.[5]

There was little Cunard could do about the standard of the

* The *Aquitania* sailed on 8 August and was an armed cruiser for only four days when she was in collision. She was dismantled at the end of September and refitted. From May to August 1915 she was a troop ship and, thereafter, a hospital ship for a time. In 1918 she carried American troops to Europe.

crew. The war had made severe inroads on their more experienced men, who had been called to the Royal Navy, and crews were having to be scratched up on the Liverpool dockside. Stokers and able seamen were signed on for the round trip, but stewards were only recruited for a single voyage, and the number required depended on bookings. Many stewards who sailed outwards only did so as a free way of emigrating to the United States. Turner's other complaints were dealt with promptly. All life-saving equipment was inspected by the Liverpool Emigration Officer, Captain Barrand, who had every defective item replaced, including three of the lifeboats. Mr Laslett of the Board of Trade inspected the machinery and found a fault in the valves of the low pressure turbine which would possibly fail if put on full astern under a high steam pressure. However, the low pressure turbines were customarily only used for manoeuvring in and out of the berths, so it was not a matter which was regarded as needing immediate attention. The Chief Engineer Officer and Captain Turner were warned that application of full astern to the low pressure turbine might well create complications, probably what is called 'steam feedback' which in simple terms would mean that the steam unable to escape by driving the turbine would build up immense pressure and probably blow out a main steam pipe. A simple analogy is suddenly to block the spout of a boiling kettle. The lid will blow off.

This defect apart, the *Lusitania* sailed on 17 April 1915 in first rate order. Her name and port of registry on the stern were obliterated and she flew no ensign. Miss Every watched her leave and recalls that Staff Captain Anderson took her out from the berth, while Captain Turner stood up in the forecastle grunting at the bosun and his windlass crew. She noted with pleasure that 'Thomas was wearing a new bowler hat'. It was an uneventful voyage and the *Lusitania* docked in New York on 24 April. During that last westbound crossing events in New York, London and Wilhelmshaven were taking a course and a sequence that were to decide her destiny.

George Vierick left the meeting of the New York German community authorized to insert a suitable warning in any fifty newspapers of his choice. It had been decided to place the advertisement on the shipping or travel pages which were a Friday feature in most of the East Coast papers. He planned to run it to appear on Friday 23 April, so as to give it at least a week's exposure before the *Lusitania* sailed. Seven days' publicity and debate he believed, would give any intending passenger ample notice to change his mind. He drafted the wording in his office and when he had finished telephoned von Papen to explain its import and ask if he approved the text. Von Papen did approve, but he unofficially suggested that instead of signing it 'The German Committee of New York' it should be signed 'The Imperial German Embassy'. He justified this course by saying that the German Foreign Office had asked the Embassy to take steps to warn Americans not to travel but it had been unable to do so, because of the diplomatic and legal niceties involved. He explained that under American law the advertiser could be liable for damages for libel and causing loss of custom to British shipping companies, but if the Embassy could deny that it was the author, then all would be well. According to Vierick, von Papen also stipulated that Vierick should ask for the advertisement to be placed as near to the Cunard sailing notices as possible. The advertisement department of *The Fatherland* dispatched the 'copy' of the advertisement, together with an appropriate cheque, to each of the fifty papers Vierick had selected. Those addressed to the New York papers were delivered by hand the same night, so that there would be no question of missing the deadline for Friday 23 April. The advertisement ran as shown on page 92.

The advertisement reached the *New York Sun* shortly before midnight, and as the advertisement department was closed the envelope marked urgent was brought up to the night news editor. Scenting a story, he telephoned to Charles Sumner at the residential club where he lived for a comment, and to the night duty officer of the State Department for advice. Sumner

NOTICE!

TRAVELLERS intending to embark on the Atlantic voyage are reminded that a state of war exists between Germany and her allies and Great Britain and her allies; that the zone of war includes the waters adjacent to the British Isles; that, in accordance with formal notice given by the Imperial German Government, vessels flying the flag of Great Britain, or of any of her allies, are liable to destruction in those waters and that travellers sailing in the war zone on ships of Great Britain or her allies do so at their own risk.

IMPERIAL GERMAN EMBASSY
WASHINGTON, D. C., APRIL 22, 1915.

replied that the *Lusitania* was faster than any submarine launched and probably went back to bed. The duty officer of the State Department replied that it would be highly dangerous to run the advertisement as it could be construed as libellous and suggested that they verify the text with the German Embassy the next morning. The night editor decided to adopt this course, and possibly so that his rivals should not scoop him, put what is called a 'black' on the advertisement throughout the United States by telephoning United Press and asking them to circularize all newspapers subscribing to their service that the State Department had contacted the *Sun* and ordered that no advertisement should be carried by any publication for any belligerent embassy without the authorization of the State Department or its attorneys. Of Vierick's original fifty selections, only the *Des Moines Register* carried the advertisement on 23 April.[6] In the meantime the advertisement became a talking point amongst many American journalists. Captain Gaunt heard about it sometime before 10 a.m. New York time on 21 April, at which time he cabled the text to Captain Hall at Naval Intelligence in Whitehall, who in turn drew it to the attention of the War Staff at the noon meeting on 22 April.

Hall immediately decided that the Germans had planned a trap for the *Lusitania*, and arranged to warn Admiral Bacon of the Dover Patrol and also sent orders to the 'mystery' ship *Lyons* stationed off the Scilly Isles. His message to the 'mystery' ship specified the *Lusitania* as the target. The signal to Admiral Bacon merely warned that submarine attacks were to be expected on very large transports in the Channel and off the West Coast and urged extra vigilance. At this time the *Lusitania* was still at sea on her way to New York, and Hall's belief was that the attempt would be made on this voyage. Similar signals were also sent to the Senior Naval Officers at Liverpool and Dartmouth, and a copy to the Vice-Admiral in command of Queenstown.

Somehow the German Admiralty heard of these moves, and early on the morning of 24 April Fregattenkapitän Bauer, commander of the third submarine flotilla, was summoned to the flagship in Wilhelmshaven. The source of the German Admiralty's information is unknown. Possibly it was an intercept, but at that time the German deciphering was not so efficient as to get the message so quickly. In the German archives the information is in the form of an order based on intelligence docket KZ 7927 and the source is listed as 'untried'. Fregattenkapitän Bauer's war diary tells the story.

25 April 1915

U-30 puts to sea from the Ems to the west coast. U-9 after completion of repairs goes from Wilhelmshaven to Heligoland. As a result of KZ 7927 the naval staff after discussion on the flagship decided that three stations be occupied as quickly as possible for interception of troop transport ships in front of Dartmouth, Bristol Channel, and Liverpool. U-30 pursuant to following radiotelegraphic message is ordered to Dartmouth via Norddeich, Borkum and Heligoland. 'Await large English troop transports coming out from west and south coasts of England. Head via the most rapid route around Scotland for the English Channel. Take position in front of Dartmouth. Attack transports merchant vessels warships. Keep position occupied for as long as supplies allow. U-20 and U-27 to Irish Sea and Bristol Channel. Ends.'*

U-30 is scheduled for Dartmouth for the reason that this is the least important of the three stations and the transmission of the order to the U-30 is the safest for if she does not get the order at all or it gets garbled, there is first eliminated the occupation of the particular port which presumably comes least into consideration . . . ascertained that communication U-30 exists so assumed U-30 has received order.[7]

Bauer also ordered the U-20 and the U-27 to prepare for sea. The U-20 needed attention to the watertight seal of her periscope housing, so she left four days later than the others, and was able to remain on her patrol beat in the Irish Sea some days longer than her consorts.

* This signal to the U-30 would almost certainly have been picked up and deciphered by the British who monitored all U-boat signals. If it was, no copy was sent to Queenstown.

Vice-Admiral Bacon had only just assumed command of the Dover Patrol. His predecessor Vice-Admiral Hood had fallen foul of Lord Fisher's temper. To Fisher's reasoning, the appearance of U-boats in the Irish Sea could only mean that they were slipping past the Dover defences. Hood had been peremptorily relieved of his command and was transferred to Queenstown where he hoisted his flag in the ancient cruiser *Juno* which was engaged in the lonely Atlantic patrol west of the Fastnet Rock. His immediate superior was Vice-Admiral Sir Charles Coke who was in overall command of Area 21 which stretched the length of the southern coast of Ireland. Coke's communication with the Admiralty was by direct telephone line and shortwave radio. All Admiralty messages concerning Area 21 came first to Coke, and from his headquarters they were telephoned to wireless transmission stations at Crookhaven and Valentia in the south-west of Ireland. As the majority of the ships at Coke's disposal did not have wireless, his messages were signalled to them visually from the shore by flag or signal light. There were five such shore signal stations on the 160 miles of coast between Queenstown and the Fastnet.

If ships at sea wished to communicate with Coke and were out of range of the shore stations, they had to come ashore and find the nearest telephone. There was no difficulty in signalling to the *Juno* which carried comprehensive wireless equipment.

Admiral Coke was bitterly aware how tenuous his defences were. Throughout his period of command he made repeated requests for extra ships, preferably destroyers, but the Admiralty refused to sanction them as they still regarded the waters to the west of England and the south of Ireland as the lowest priority for anti-submarine defence. The Admiralty War Staff were influenced by statistics, which could be expressed in two ways. Seen from one angle, the German U-boat campaign had so far only succeeded in sinking less than 0·5 per cent of the ships using the western ports of England. From another viewpoint, during the first four months of 1915, forty-nine merchant ships had been sunk in British home waters by submarine attack.

Of these thirty-seven were in the waters to the west. The War Staff preferred the first and more palatable view.

The morning of 26 April had been an irritating one for Captain Guy Gaunt in Washington. He had received a disturbing phone call from Mr Stettinius at Morgan and Co. informing him that he had discovered that the special containers for the packing of gun-cotton were unobtainable. The concern which made them had apparently sold their entire stocks and forward supplies to a company hostile to the Allied interests. There would be a considerable delay before alternative sources of supply could be arranged. Gaunt was being pressed by Dupont de Nemours, the manufacturers of the gun-cotton, for particulars of the packing and shipping of their latest consignments. He had this problem on his mind when he had a brief interview with the agent he had persuaded to work for the Austro-Hungarian Embassy, Dr Ritter von Rettegh. Von Rettegh's affidavit of that interview is in the archives of the investigation department of the Department of Justice. On Mr Lansing's orders it has never been published.

On April 26th 1915, I visited him [Gaunt] at his office at his request. During the conversation we talked about explosives and he asked me to give him a statement of the character of the fuel used by the German Government in its submarines. After some little conversation he asked me what effect, if any, sea water coming in contact with gun cotton would have. I inquired of him why he wanted to know this. He said 'We are required to send by one of our fastest steamers in the next day or so about six hundred tons of gun cotton, which we have purchased from the Du Pont Powder Company.' I told him there were two kinds of gun cotton. One is the trinitro cellulose, made from the fibres of pine; that this gun cotton would not be affected by sea water, because it is non-hydroscopic. That the other called pyroxyline, made from cotton and highly hygroscopic, by the law of capillarity, absorbs water and moisture, especially when warm and in a loose condition. That under such circumstances if sea water comes into contact with the gun cotton immediately a chemical change takes place. The free sulphuric acid in the latter will be chemically attacked by the bromine and iodine salts and also common salts contained in the sea-water, raising the temperature and causing sudden explosion. He asked me what to do to prevent this, and I said keep it in a dry place.

During this visit he sent several telegrams. These were dictated in the next room, but loud enough so that I could overhear some of the things that were said, and these telegrams related to the subject of our conversation.

He asked me in this conversation whether or not I thought gun cotton explosion caused the sudden sinking of the *Audacious* and *Courbet*.* I said it was possible. Whilst we were talking and near the close of the conversation, the first secretary of the British Embassy came in and handed Captain Gaunt a telegram, and said, 'Captain, finish with the Doctor, because you will have to hurry down'. At this meeting Captain Gaunt gave me two cheques as a personal loan – one for fifteen and one for twenty-five dollars. I gave him a paper marked I.O.U. and with my signature.[8]

The truth of von Rettegh's statement cannot be proved or disproved fifty-six years after the event. However, on 28 April Captain Gaunt did file a memorandum on characteristics of diesel fuel as used in German submarines. On 26 April he went down to New York staying in the Gotham Hotel overnight. The following day he visited the plant of Dupont de Nemours at Christfield, New Jersey, which manufactured pyroxyline, and on 27/28 Dupont shipped some 600 tons of this explosive to the order of Morgan and Co. which were delivered to the Cunard wharf.

---

* The *Audacious*, one of Britain's latest dreadnoughts, struck a mine off the Irish coast on 27 October 1914. Her crew were evacuated safely and though she was low in the water she was taken in tow. Three hours later she suddenly exploded, capsized and sank. The official inquiry never established the cause of the explosion but unanimously agreed that it had been internal. Her captain did proffer the theory that the contents of the magazine might in some unexplained manner have been ignited by the boilers. It is not known if she carried any pyroxyline aboard. It was not used as a propellant by the Royal Navy though it was used as an explosive filling for depth charges and high explosive shells. The *Courbet* also exploded in mysterious circumstances.

George Vierick spent 26 April asking the State Department why his advertisement had not been published. Eventually he managed to obtain an interview with Bryan and pointed out to him that on all but one of her wartime voyages the *Lusitania* had carried munitions. He produced copies of her supplementary manifests which were open to public inspection at the collector's office. More important, he informed Bryan, no fewer than six million rounds of ammunition were due to be shipped on the *Lusitania* the following Friday and could be seen at that moment being loaded on Pier 54. Bryan picked up the telephone and cleared the publication of the advertisement. He promised Vierick that he would endeavour to persuade the President publicly to warn Americans not to travel. No such warning was issued by the President, but there can be no doubt that President Wilson was told of the character of the cargo destined for the *Lusitania*. He did nothing, but was to concede on the day he was told of her sinking that this foreknowledge had given him many sleepless hours.

8

One of the first crewmen off the *Lusitania* was the steward Charles Thorne (Curt Thummel) whom von Papen had infiltrated aboard the Cunarder *Transylvania*, and who after a profitable three months' garnering information in Liverpool had shipped back to the United States aboard the *Lusitania*. He took the precaution of having his discharge book signed by Staff Captain Anderson, in case he should ever need to use the identity of Thorne again. The address he gave in his discharge papers was 20 Leroy Street, N.Y.C.

It is a brief but essential departure from the narrative to record that by 26 April Thummel had become Chester Williams of Kingsland, New Jersey, and on Monday 3 May he commenced employment at the Freight Terminal operated by the Leigh Valley Company in Lower New York Harbour. After a seven months' stint he transferred to the Kingsland Assembly Plant on the grounds that it was not so far to travel to work. At each firm he was employed as a staff or labour officer, and his function was to locate and hire unskilled labour. Both firms were engaged in crating and dispatching items purchased by Morgan for the British war effort. Leigh Valley handled the shipments of the Remington Company's non-explosive ammunition. On 29 July 1916 Chester Williams and two others set fire to the Leigh Valley complex. The resultant bang shook even the acquiescent explosive commissioners of New York. Thirty-seven loaded freight trains, several warehouses, twelve cargo barges, the loading piers and a complete rail terminal went up in one mammoth explosion. The Kingsland plant caught fire on 11 January 1917 and FBI records show Chester

Williams as one of the incendiaries. The complete installation was shattered by the blast and the 'goods in transit' destroyed were valued for insurance at seventeen million dollars. Chester Williams' role and previous identities were only revealed in February 1930 by the wartime Director of British Naval Intelligence, by then Rear-Admiral Sir Reginald Hall, who had been invited by the American lawyer Amos Peaselee to assist him unravel the two cases after twelve years' fruitless inquiries by the FBI. Hall's contribution clinched the case and on 15 July 1939 Franz von Papen advised Adolf Hitler to settle with the American insurance companies concerned for 55 million dollars. Hitler accepted the advice and it can be conjectured that possibly Hitler's decision was influenced by von Papen's personal recollection of the matter.

Staff Captain Anderson needed to find more than one steward, for the 1 May eastbound crossing looked like being a busy one. He was therefore delighted to accept a young man called Neil J. Leach, who had never been to sea in his life before except as a passenger. The recommendation came from Leach's uncle, a provisions importer who lived in New York and who was slightly acquainted with Anderson on a social basis. Both Leach and Anderson were lost when the *Lusitania* went down, but a detailed dossier on the former was compiled at Lansing's request by Chief Agent Bruce Bielaski.

Leach was the son of an English lawyer then in practice in the West Indies. He had been studying modern languages at Cambridge and in the long vacation of 1914 he went to Germany to take up a temporary post as tutor to the son of a German industrialist. When the war broke out Leach was interned, but eventually released on giving his parole to return to the West Indies and not engage in hostilities. He travelled via Holland to the United States and on the ship he met a German steward called Gustav Stahl. Stahl left the ship in New York and as Leach had very little money he agreed to take rooms with Stahl at a small boarding house to which Stahl had had an introduction. It was the already familiar 20 Leroy Street. They arrived on 15 April 1915 and Leach booked a room until 30 April, on which date he told Miss Gertrude Weir, his landlady, he would be sailing to England. Why he did not go direct to his uncle or continue his trip home according to the parole that he had given, is a matter for conjecture. On 26 April Stahl invited Leach for a midday meal with two German girls who also lived in the house, Misses Bunker and Masser. They were joined at the meal by another man from the boarding house called Hans Hardenburg and his room-mate Curt Thummel (Chester Williams). They talked of money and their lack of it and at Hardenburg's suggestion, Leach agreed to go with him and Curt to the German consulate at 11 Broadway.

Under the guise of a 'commercial adviser' Captain Boy-Ed, the German naval attaché, had a room there and the German archives show that on this date Curt Thummel made a statement at 11 Broadway to the effect that he had seen four guns on the *Lusitania*, of which he gave precise details, including their hiding places. Boy-Ed minuted on the report that he had instructed Hardenburg and another man to obtain photographs of them, and authorized Paul Koenig, also known as Stemler, to control the operation. Koenig was the security chief of the Hamburg-Amerika line and in charge of the German liners then interned in New York Harbour.*

The same evening Neil Leach saw his uncle and told him that he was trying to raise the money to travel to England to enlist. His uncle arranged with Staff Captain Anderson for him to work his passage as a steward and gave him twenty-five dollars to help him on his way. Leach joined the *Lusitania* on 29 April, and was put immediately to work on cleaning ship. On 30 April he wrote to his mother telling her he was filling in time between catching the next boat to Jamaica by doing a trip

---

* They were interned on the grounds that they were auxiliary cruisers of the German Navy and there has never been a satisfactory explanation why the American authorities did not give the same treatment to the *Lusitania*. German sources have, perhaps uncharitably, claimed that it was because Morgan and Co., who owned a large part of the equity the German liners represented, did not wish to expose their investments to the attentions of the British Navy which constantly patrolled the mouth of the Hudson River.

as a steward on the *Lusitania* which was 'very highly-paid as they find it so difficult·to get good men in these dangerous times'. He added that she was not to worry as the *Lusitania* was 'exceptionally fast and carried several copper-coloured cannon'.

Nothing further is known of Leach except that he went down with the ship and that he probably intended to return to New York, as he left his cabin trunk behind him and travelled only with a small case. It is a reasonable assumption that he made this trip as a result of pressure or financial inducement from the Germans. He does not appear to have been strictly truthful to his family or honest in his money dealings. The cheque drawn on his Cambridge bank with which he paid his two weeks' rent in New York was dishonoured as there were insufficient funds to meet it. The reason why he appears in the narrative at all is because his very existence and Agent Bielaski's dossier on him go a small part of the way to substantiating allegations that were to be made at a later date by Gustav Stahl. It was almost four years before the British Consulate and Cunard confirmed to his parents that he sailed on the *Lusitania* at all, which could possibly indicate that they were embarrassed by his letter to her. His written evidence that the *Lusitania* carried 'cannon' must be taken as inconclusive, as he does not say that he had physically seen them and he could well have been told about them by the versatile Curt Thummel.[1]

Staff Captain Anderson had more worries than finding the odd replacement steward. The *Lusitania* had to be coaled, the cargo loaded and the ship provisioned. There were to be far more passengers than was usual for a wartime voyage, and the volume of cargo was larger than it had been for several previous trips. His main problem was in hiring sufficient able seamen to work the ship: he required seventy-seven, but when she sailed, she only carried forty-one. This was a ratio of just under one able seaman per lifeboat, so that Anderson had to make up boat crews from the stewards and stokers. Many of the former had little or no seagoing experience, and the latter were fully occupied in coaling the ship.

The *Lusitania* was berthed with her starboard side against

Pier 54. The coal and cargo lighters clustered against the port side. The coal was 'hand shovelled' on to elevators which raised it from the lighters to the loading apertures in the ship's sides. Once aboard it had to be distributed evenly between the longitudinal bunkers stretching down each side of the ship. Working day and night the last coal barges did not leave the ship until 9 p.m. the night before she sailed.

Anderson was drowned, so he cannot be questioned, but undoubtedly he did allocate a crew to each boat and saw that each man knew his boat station and particular duty, though how well that duty was performed is an open question. What is difficult to accept is the truth of the signed certificate which Anderson rendered to the Pier Superintendent before the *Lusitania* sailed that all the boats had been lowered down 'into the water' and the boat crews practised in 'unshipping the oars, getting under way, recovery of man overboard at sea and davit drill'. Circumstantially it appears unlikely that any lifeboats were actually lowered to the water or that the boat crews practised either raising or lowering the boats upon the davits. The coaling lighters had drawn alongside within two hours of the *Lusitania*'s arrival and left after dusk the night before she sailed. The quay on the starboard side and the lighters on the port would have precluded the lowering of the boats and at least seven of the able seamen who helped make up the total of forty-one aboard were only transferred to the *Lusitania* at 6 p.m. on the night of 30 April from the S.S. *Queen Margaret* which was berthed nearby. Three of these men, Leslie Morton, his brother John and Henry Thomason, survived and were later to give key evidence at the inquiries in London and New York.

Staff Captain Anderson handed his certificate to the Assistant Pier Superintendent Captain Chalmers, who endorsed it. Anderson's and Chalmers' main preoccupation was loading and storing the cargo. They were assisted in the paperwork by the Cunard shore staff, but the internal distribution of the cargo was very largely Anderson's responsibility; faulty cargo planning could materially affect the trim of the ship. In making a stowage plan he was guided by three factors. Firstly weight was all important. The object was to get the heavier items stowed in the lower holds, and within each hold the heavier cases had to be placed at the bottom of the stack. The second factor was the nature of the cargo. Barrels of oysters, pickled herring and other pungent items had to be placed well away from bolts of cloth or similar articles which might be affected by spillage or smell. The third factor was the storage life of the goods consigned. Perishable items including meat, butter, fresh fish were usually placed in the refrigerated hold or, if stowed elsewhere, at the top of each stack to ensure adequate ventilation, and as far away from the boilers as possible.

The *Lusitania* had not been designed as a cargo ship and she carried only a small refrigerated compartment on F deck and two small cargo holds below this deck known as the orlop and lower orlop. The latter two holds were below the waterline and were situated in the space between the foremost boiler room No. 1 and the bow. However, since her conversion all the decks immediately above the orlop holds had been converted to cargo carrying so that, viewed in elevation, the entire area from the keel to the anchor winches and forward from the first funnel to the bows was cargo space. The problem was that there were no hatch or handling facilities available on any but the fore and orlop decks, so the actual cargo had to be manhandled if it was destined for any of the temporary holds.

There was a formidable amount to load, much of it priority government shipments. In these cases special note had to be taken so that any item likely to offend the Collector of Customs would be left off the 'loading manifest' on which sailing clearance would be given, and then subsequently entered on the supplementary manifest which would be handed in once the *Lusitania* was safely on the high seas. On this trip almost the entire cargo was to be contraband. The lower orlop hold starting from the aft end nearest the boilers was loaded with a strange and possibly sinister mixture of goods. It included 1639 ingot bars of copper which were very properly spread over the entire floor of the deck, which was in fact the very bottom of

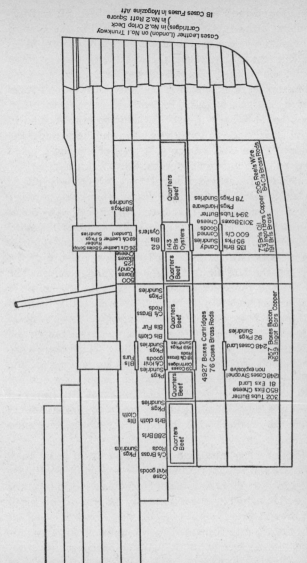

Disposition of cargo and baggage leaving New York 1 May 1915.
Re-drawn from Triplicate No. 1.

the ship. Above these were 1248 cases of shrapnel, and this consignment is the first that needs scrutiny. On the Cunard waybill it is simply described as shrapnel – small pieces of metal with which to load shrapnel shells. However, the shipping note of the Bethlehem Steel Co. which supplied it to Morgan's order is more precise. It specifies '1248 cases of 3 inch Shrapnel shells filled; 4 shells to each case and 250 cases to each lot; weight of the lot being 51 tons'. The shipping note is dated 28 April 1915 and the consignment was No. 23 of a total under the same order of 214 consignments. It was, of course, franked according to the regulations 'non-explosive in bulk'.

In addition to this fairly lethal load, which was placed directly adjacent to the bulkhead leading into No. 1 boiler room, were placed seventy-four barrels of fuel oil; 3863 boxes of cheese each weighing a shade over 40 lb; 600 cases of canned goods; 696 tubs of butter; several hundred packages of sundries and 329 cases of lard. With understandable coyness, only the sundries and the lard figured in the clearance manifest. The reasons for the omission of the copper and the shells are obvious, but the omission of the food is significant. It is worth noting that the cheese and butter were consigned to a box number in Liverpool, unlike the modest shipments of butter and cheese also shipped and stowed elsewhere which were consigned to such innocent and obvious destinations as the Cooperative Wholesale Society. The Liverpool box number was that of the Superintendent of the Naval Experimental Establishment at Shoeburyness. There is no other direct evidence as to whether or not the butter and cheese were what they were stated to be.

This load of mixed cargo wholly filled the lower orlop hold. The main orlop hold was devoted to seventy-six cases of brass rods consigned to Thomas Firth of Sheffield and 4927 boxes of cartridges. These had been consigned by the Remington Small Arms Co. and were addressed to the Royal Arsenal at Woolwich. Each case contained 1000 rounds of ·303 ammunition, and the net weight of the consignment was 173 tons. Each cartridge was fitted with a fulminate of mercury cap, and the weight of explosives in this consignment was marginally over ten and a half tons.

Above the orlop was F deck divided into a small refrigerated compartment and an area of passenger accommodation which had been opened out for storage or carrying troops. The refrigerated compartment was filled with sides of beef and barrels of oysters. The remaining area is marked as empty on the stowage plan maintained in the Cunard archives. In March 1918 it was established from a member of the crew that the two forward sections of F deck had been filled with cargo. However, the exact nature of that cargo has never been disclosed. There is no doubt that it was ammunition. The evidence for this is a cable sent by Sumner to Alfred Booth two days after the disaster in answer to Booth's cabled inquiry as to where the ammunition had been stored. Sumner replied that it had completely filled the lower orlop and orlop holds together with the trunkways and passages of F deck.

E deck held more brass rods, sixty-two barrels of oysters and innumerable sundries, while the deck above was loaded with the Cooperative Wholesale Society's cheese and lard. Unlike the similarly described cargo in the lower orlop hold where each package weighed 40 lb, the Co-op's cargo was in hogsheads weighing approximately 320 lb each. In addition to these were 500 cases of candy and 184 cases of accoutrements for Booth and Co., which were the haversacks, pouches, etc., the purchase of which George Booth had organized on his early trip. Lastly there was a mystifying 323 bales of raw furs shipped by Booth's undischarged bankrupt entrepreneurial acquaintance of the saga of the sheepskin coats, Alfred Fraser.

Fraser's shipment is still largely unexplained. Three clues exist to show that it was not what it purported to be. Firstly it was insured for 150,000 dollars but no claim was ever made on the insurers. Secondly, the shipping documents show that it came by barge from Rheaboat, Maryland and by railcar from the Hopewell freight station of the Pennsylvania Railway. Neither Rheaboat nor Hopewell were fur storage depots, both had branches of Dupont de Nemours. Thirdly, it was all consigned to Messrs B. F. Babcock and Co. of Liverpool.

Benjamin Franklin Babcock was an Anglo-American dealer in the cotton trade, with a thriving business in importing cotton from the southern states. During the war he was purchasing raw cotton for the Allies for the manufacture of gun-cotton, and whilst so engaged allowed the Liverpool end of his business to diminish so that it dealt on a very minor scale and then only in piece goods. B. F. Babcock Ltd are still in business in Liverpool, and their records, which they have checked for me, show firstly that they never had any business with Alfred Fraser, secondly that they have never dealt in or imported furs, treated or otherwise, and thirdly that in 1915 they imported nothing at all. The furs, the butter and the cheese have not been publicly explained to this day, though Fraser's activities were later to occupy a great deal of Lansing's and Chief Agent Bielaski's time. All these unexplained consignments had one more factor in common. They were shipped at the rate specially agreed between Cunard and the British government and no insurance was ever claimed on them.[2]

The loading of this cargo and the coaling were almost completed by dusk on 30 April, when Captain Gaunt sprung a surprise on the overworked Sumner and Captain Anderson. He wished to transfer seventy passengers and just under 200 tons of cargo from S.S. *Queen Margaret* to the *Lusitania*. At this remove the reason for the transfer cannot be ascertained, but Sumner and Anderson agreed – the latter on the condition that he was given seven of the *Queen Margaret*'s crew as well. The passengers comprised sixty-seven men and two women, one of them with a baby. They were accommodated on E deck and none of them appear to have survived. The couples were allotted vacant saloon cabins in the name of Mr and Mrs R. Matthews and Mr and Mrs Palmer. Mr Matthews endeared himself to Sumner by calling for volunteers from the transferred passengers to help shift the cargo between the two ships, which was hoisted out of the *Queen Margaret*, lowered down to a lighter and then lifted from the lighter by the *Lusitania*'s cargo boom. It is evident that at least a part of this cargo was ammunition, because the archives of Remington include a letter from their traffic manager to their agent, E. H. Wilson of the New England Steamship Co. asking him to load 2000 cases of small arms ammunition on to the *Queen Margaret* berthed at Pier 54. Coupled to this letter is a Cunard receipt for 2000 cases of ·303 ammunition marked with the serial N.E. 101 and with the name *Queen Margaret* cancelled and *Lusitania* written across it.

The identity of Mr Matthews and his volunteers may be reasonably assumed from the report of a body washed up on the rocks of the Old Head of Kinsale on 8 May, and the list of effects which were found on it: 'Male body identified as Lt T[emporary]/Capt. R. Matthews of the 6th Winnipeg Rifles by certificates and papers found in his pockets.'[3] The papers included steamer warrants for himself, his two dependants and a draft of volunteers from the 6th Rifles. Amongst the wholly personal memorabilia was a slip of paper attached to a badge of the *Lusitania* marked 'First prize Ladies Potato Race: Mrs Matthews'. The Kinsale coroner's report is franked with the remark: 'body requested by the military and buried CORK city May 10th.'

The *Lusitania* completed loading shortly after 9 p.m. on Friday 30 April. The loading manifest totalled twenty-four closely written pages, but clearance to sail was applied for on a manifest which filled one page, listing assorted items. They were not the first items loaded, but carefully selected to satisfy the somewhat somnolent eye of Collector Dudley Field Malone. The affidavit that accompanied the manifest was sworn at 4 p.m. on 30 April and a clearance was granted to sail at 10 a.m. the following morning. So automatic had been the entire procedure that it was issued in the name of Captain Dow.[4]

9

At 8 a.m. on 1 May the two masters-at-arms of the *Lusitania*, Peter Smith and Billy Williams, took up their places at the head of the main gangway. Behind them was a small bevy of the ship's staff. The pursers, the chief steward, the senior stewards of each deck and John Lewis, the Senior Third Officer. They were there ready to welcome the passengers in the traditional manner, but there were few passengers to be seen. Those who did arrive were heavily outnumbered by reporters and a cinema newsreel team complete with naphtha lights. John Lewis's first reaction was that some very famous person indeed was about to embark, and he whispered behind his hand to the purser in his soft Welsh accent, 'Who's the quality travelling with us then?'[1] And the purser replied with the bored condescension peculiar to pursers and hotel managers everywhere: 'We have no quality booked, just monied people.' The crowd of reporters were quickly explained when one of them came up the gangway and showed Lewis the morning edition of the *New York Tribune*, folded open to show the German warning. He asked to see the captain, but, sensibly, Lewis refused and arranged for someone to telephone Charles Sumner to come down to the pier and speak to the press. Sumner arrived shortly after nine o'clock.

He cast scorn on the threat apparent in the warning. The *Lusitania*, he claimed, was the fastest ship on the Atlantic – if not in the world, and there was no German warship or submarine afloat that could catch her. The reporters were far from satisfied. As each embarking passenger approached they clustered round and tried to obtain a reaction or a quotable remark.

Sumner remonstrated with them jocularly but quietly gave orders that on no account were any of them to be allowed aboard. Shortly before 10 a.m. the first telegrams began to arrive. The *Lusitania* was linked to the shore telephone service and also had a direct link with Western Union. Telegrams were phoned straight through to the Marconi room where telegraphist Robert Leith received them and after entering them in his log sent them down to the purser's office for distribution. Leith knew from which office the telegrams were sent, though he rarely put it on the delivery form. The first telegram was addressed to Alfred Vanderbilt, undoubtedly the richest passenger, and it warned him not to sail. The second, almost identical, was addressed to the well-known theatrical producer Carl Frohman. The third, fourth and fifth were also addressed to socialites though Leith could not recall their names and his log book went down with the ship. A total of nine were received altogether. Leith held on to them, and asked Sumner what he should do. Sumner told him to try and find out where they had been handed in and if possible who was sending them. This took him nearly an hour but he was able to establish that five had been sent from the same Western Union office, almost next door to the editorial offices of the *Providence Journal*,* and that the young man who had brought them in was employed by John Rathom, the editor of that paper.

Sumner instructed that none of the telegrams were to be distributed, but that did not stop several enterprising journa lists quoting them word for word in their articles. When Alfred Vanderbilt and his party had arrived he had been asked by the *New York Sun* reporter if he was going to take any notice of his telegram. Sumner noted that Vanderbilt had joined the ship some twenty minutes before Leith had received it and he realized that the telegrams were nothing more than a

* The *Providence Journal* established a reputation for anti-German 'scoops' which dramatically increased its circulation and authority. The complete run for the war of the *Providence Journal* urgently needs re-examination and should be seen in the light of the substantial payments made to Mr Rathom by Captain Gaunt on behalf of British Naval Intelligence.

journalistic stunt in the worst possible taste. He immediately had the pier cleared of reporters with the exception of two press agency representatives and the newsreel crew. The eye-witness accounts of the *Lusitania*'s departure which dominated much of the American press the next morning were as fictitious as the telegrams which became one of the recurrent themes of the *Lusitania* story. Charles Sumner kept the telegrams and Captain Turner was able to state perfectly truthfully, in answer to Alfred Booth's later inquiry, that '*no passenger* received a warning telegram'.

Many of the passengers boarding the ship that morning had not seen the papers with the German warning, but nevertheless it was not long before news of it spread throughout the ship. Third Officer Lewis remembered that there was a nervous atmosphere everywhere which he himself found infectious. A group of travellers stood expectantly around the purser's office eyeing each other and saying nothing. There was none of the party spirit which usually went with a sailing, and Lewis recalled the stewards's whispering to him that many of the passengers had asked the cabin staff not to unpack their clothes. He felt that everyone was waiting for someone else to have the solitary courage to decide to cancel their passage. Shortly before noon, and within minutes of sailing time, Captain Turner appeared and without even doffing his bowler hat stalked down the gangway in a determined hurry. For a moment Lewis felt that he would be followed by a flood of passengers who had surged near the gangway in order to speak to him. Fortunately they never got within speaking distance as at that moment there occurred a scene of low comedy, which probably defused the situation.

A large family party had just come up the gangway. It comprised Mr Paul Crompton, a partner in Alfred Booth and Co., his wife and six children, plus a bevy of porters, and the Cromptons' coloured children's nurse who had come to see the children off. As the children were ushered on to the deck, they broke loose with whoops of delight, two started fighting and the nurse burst into tears. Captain Turner made his exit amidst the hubbub and the incident Lewis remembered above the din was a determined squeal from one of the children of 'Potty, potty'.

Captain Turner was on his way to collect his sailing orders from Sir Courtenay Bennett, who performed the function of S.N.O. for New York. Normally one of Sir Courtenay's staff would have brought them to the ship but this time Turner had received an urgent telephone call asking him to come at once. He connected the call with the German warning and long afterwards confided that he expected the sailing to be either delayed or cancelled. He knew that that same day the American liner *America* was also sailing to Liverpool with her passenger space almost empty and before calling on Sir Courtenay he went into the Pier Superintendent's office and phoned up to check on *America*'s vacant passenger accommodation. However, the thought apparently never crossed Sir Courtenay's mind.

When Turner arrived he asked for his course instructions and was told that none had been received, therefore he was to take the same course as last time. He was informed that elements of Cruiser Squadron E would rendezvous with him ten miles south and within forty miles west of the Fastnet; from the recognition signals given him, it transpired it was to be the cruiser *Juno*. He was instructed which Naval Code was to be employed on that trip and told to use No. 1 edition of the Merchant Vessel Code. He was also handed the *Lusitania*'s radio call signs, CQ for routine transmissions and MFA for signals of an operational nature. Apart from this Sir Courtenay had two further items to discuss. Firstly, he handed to Turner a sealed and lead-weighted canvas bag which contained despatches from the Embassy for the Foreign Office and formally read out to him the instructions that in the event of a German attack the bag must be thrown overboard at once. Secondly, he told Turner that reports were just coming in that an American ship was being attacked by a U-boat in the Irish Sea.[2] Taking the bag and the wireless instructions, Turner returned to his ship. As he boarded her, one of the passengers, Mr. C. T. Hill of

Richmond, Virginia, accosted him and asked the question that was on everyone's lips: 'Is there any danger? And if so, what is being done about it?' Turner replied emphatically: 'There is always a danger but the best guarantees of your safety are the *Lusitania* herself and the fact that wherever there is danger your safety is in the hands of the Royal Navy.'

The *Lusitania* sailed shortly after noon, hoisting her ensign and her house flags, together with a bevy of other flags which were her identification signal to the British cruisers which blockaded the three-mile limit at the mouth of the Hudson River. As she nosed her way out into the stream the two masters at arms inspected the decks to ensure that there were no passengers' guests or stowaways left aboard. Just forward of the children's nursery on the shelter deck in the port side stewards' pantry they discovered three men and a camera. Williams locked them in the pantry while Smith hurried off to report to Staff Captain Anderson who was still discussing Captain Turner's remarks with Mr Hill, a regular and popular passenger and a director of the British American Tobacco Co. As such his queries were not to be evaded.

Anderson went forward and found that the three men were Germans. They were taken down to the cells and Anderson confiscated the camera and a bundle of plates. Hill watched at a distance, but was unable to see whatever it was the men had been photographing. Anderson reported to the captain, who hauled the *Lusitania* over to the blockading cruiser, the *Caronia*, and stopped engines. The two ships rolled gently opposite each other about three hundred yards apart whilst Marconi operator Robert Leith operated the signal light. A party from the *Caronia* rowed over carrying the crew's mail for home and took back with them the camera, plates and a brief report written by Captain Turner and addressed to Gaunt in New York, which the *Caronia* was to hand to the next inward-bound British ship. Hill wondered why the three prisoners were not transferred and when he questioned Anderson, he was told that they were to be taken to England for interrogation. Anderson intimated to Hill that it was not the first time that the *Lusitania* had carried unofficial and suspicious passengers, and remarked jokingly that the Cunard Company's cells were the most comfortable in the trade. The identity of the men is a mystery but there is little doubt that they were the photographic party ordered by Captain Boyd-Ed and organized by Paul Koenig. The steward allocated to the port side pantry was Neil J. Leach. Presumably the men's task was to locate and photograph the guns which von Papen's agent Curt Thummel claimed to have seen. The *Lusitania* hauled down all her flags, and gathering way headed out into the Atlantic towards her rendezvous with Cruiser Squadron E.

Fregattenkapitän Bauer's half flotilla of U-boats were obeying their instructions. The U-27 had had to turn back with jammed bow planes. The U-20 after having her periscope packing repaired sailed on 30 April and tested her radio with a wireless trial to the Borkum and Ancona stations at 1 p.m. This was picked up by the British intercept service and on 1 May Captain Hall informed the Admiralty War Staff and all relevant coastal stations that three submarines were heading for the Irish Sea. A copy of the signal was seen and initialled by both Churchill and Fisher. Apart from Hall's warning, 1 May was to provide more direct evidence of Bauer's operation. The U-30 commanded by Captain von Rosenberg-Gruszczynski had left earlier on 24 April and had been diverted by Bauer to take up a station opposite Dartmouth. On his way von Rosenberg played havoc on the trade routes leading to England's west coast ports. The Admiralty official history of the war at sea, *Naval Operations* by Sir Julian Corbett, originally attributed the U-30's successes to a 'whole pack of U-boats who were presumably lying in wait for the *Lusitania*'.* In fact the U-30 was the only U-boat in the area, and she was relieved on 4 May by the U-20.

On 28 April the U-30 stopped the 1950-ton collier *Mobile*, allowed the crew to escape and sank her by gunfire. On 29 April she meted out identical treatment to the 3200-ton *Cherbourg* and the following day ordered S.S. *Fulgent* to halt. The *Fulgent* attempted to escape, so von Rosenberg put a shot into the

* First edition only.

bridge killing the captain and the quartermaster. The remainder of the crew were allowed to take to the boats. The crew of the U-30 boarded the prize and after helping themselves to fresh food and her papers, sank her with an explosive charge on the keel. The same afternoon the 3100-ton *Svorono* was stopped and sunk, and the following morning the *Edale*, loaded with grain, and the French merchantman *Europe* were both stopped and destroyed. The only lives lost in these six sinkings were the two on the *Fulgent*.

At noon the U-30 stopped a Dutch steamer some forty-five miles north-west of the Scilly Isles and after inspecting her papers allowed her to proceed. While making this interception the U-30 was observed by the steam drifter, *Clara Alice*. This ship contacted the naval patrol vessels *Filey* and *Iago* which set off to search for the U-30. On their way to her last reported position they stopped the American tanker *Gulflight* twenty days out of Port Arthur, Texas, with a cargo of oil bound for Rouen. The commanders of the patrol boats were not satisfied with the *Gulflight* papers and suspected her of illicitly fuelling the marauding U-boat, so they abandoned their search and ordered the tanker to accompany them into the nearest port, St Mary's in the Scilly Isles. The *Filey* took up a station ahead of the *Gulflight*, the *Iago* on her flank.

Shortly before 1 p.m. von Rosenberg surfaced ahead of them and ordered the little convoy to stop. The *Filey* was flying the white ensign and von Rosenberg justifiably took the tanker to be British and under convoy. The *Filey* attempted to ram him, so he crash-dived and a few minutes later fired a torpedo into the *Gulflight*. The torpedo exploded but caused only superficial damage. There was no fire or loss of life. According to von Rosenberg's log he then saw the American flag flying from the stern of the *Gulflight* and abandoned his attack. No more torpedoes were fired. However, after being hit, two members of the *Gulflight*'s crew panicked, jumped overboard and were drowned. Later that night as the *Gulflight* approached St Mary's still under convoy, her master had a heart attack and died. For the second time American citizens had died as a result of

U-boat attack, and the *Gulflight* incident served to sharpen the duel between Lansing and Bryan and to impale President Wilson further on Lansing's thorny doctrine of 'strict accountability'.

Predictably, conflicting versions of the incident were published. Britain concentrated on the diplomatic advantages to be gained, and quietly interred the findings of the Admiralty inquiry which came down heavily in favour of the U-30. The Admiralty concluded that the U-30 had behaved most properly and that the reason for the attack was the action of the two patrol vessels taking the *Gulflight* into protective custody. They also decided that if the patrol boats had not forced the American ship to slow down to match their slower speed, it was highly doubtful if the U-30 could have manœvrued into position for attack. Understandably there was little political advantage to be gained from conceding that von Rosenberg's actions had throughout been in accordance with the Cruiser Rules, and the version published for public consumption in both Great Britain and the United States was that of a murderous and unprovoked piratical attack. Equally predictable was Lansing's reaction. Secretary Bryan was promptly given a memorandum urging immediate and vigorous protest. According to Lansing the *Gulflight* incident indicated that the German government was hell-bent on a policy of 'wanton and indiscriminate destruction of vessels regardless of nationality'.[3] He concluded that Germany was making 'a determined effort to affront the United States', and thereby force an 'open rupture of diplomatic relations'. The essence of Lansing's memorandum was that Germany wanted and was prepared for 'open hostilities' with the United States.

Any student of Lansing is immediately struck by the ambivalent character of the man. His public utterances and the advice he proffered did not always accord either with his conscience or, if a subtle comparison be made, with his convictions. In his own mind he was far from convinced that Germany wanted war with the United States, and he certainly showed in his private papers that he appreciated the German point of view.

117

On the same day that he tendered his belligerent advice to Bryan and Wilson his legal training got the better of him and he wrote out both sides of the question. He came to a personal conclusion very far removed from that which he handed to his masters. He embodied his thoughts in a memorandum which is in the custody of his nephew Allen W. Dulles, part of which Mr Dulles allowed to be published in the *New York Times Magazine* on 31 January 1937.[4] This memorandum reveals a conciliatory spirit and appreciation of the German position which if it had been reflected in his official advice would have led the United States towards a policy of forbidding the supply of arms to either side in the European conflict, a policy which would have taken America on a path that led directly away from the collision course to war on which he had placed it.

Perhaps Lansing had a talent or lust for brinkmanship. Perhaps it was that he could see that the United States plus the Allies were bound to be victorious, whereas United States nuetrality would lead to a European peace very largely dictated by the Germans, with correspondingly enormous financial losses to such companies as Morgan and Co. His motives will probably never be clearly divined but the two most likely reasons are either that rigid legalist as he was he felt bound to continue to support the policy that he had advised earlier, or, less charitably, that he wanted Bryan's job, and the only way to get it was to oppose Bryan's conciliatory and liberal viewpoint; to the immediate benefit of his political and commercial patrons, and ultimately to the satisfaction of his ambition.

The *Gulflight* incident completed the laying of the powder train which was to explode when the *Lusitania* encountered the U-20 already pushing southwards around the west coast of Scotland. The sign was plain to all who cared to read it, and perhaps the most sagacious of those who did were the editor of the *New York Times*, who expressed grave fears for 'the *Lusitania* now heading for the danger area', and his counterpart on the *Tribune* who took more direct action. He cabled his London correspondent Vance Pitney and ordered him to proceed at once to Queenstown to cover the *Lusitania*'s arrival. The *Tribune* shared a common belief that if there was any danger to the *Lusitania*, then a watchful Admiralty would promptly escort her into Queenstown until such danger was passed, in much the same manner as a few weeks earlier had been done with the *Transylvania* and the *Ausonia*. Pitney left for Queenstown on the evening of 4 May, and unknown to him the signs were that the Admiralty was taking steps to cover the *Lusitania*'s approach. Admiral Hood aboard the ancient cruiser *Juno* was steaming just south of the Fastnet rock and about to enter his patrol station where he was to meet her.

Hood had been informed that there was a serious submarine threat as the Admiralty radio direction finding stations had picked up the signals of Bauer's half flotilla. These had been deciphered and certainly both Naval Intelligence and the Admiralty War Staff knew not only of the U-boats' presence, but also of their mission, for Bauer's message to the U-30 had been explicit. However it had not occurred to anybody to send a warning to the *Lusitania*.

The auxiliary patrol at Queenstown was feeling the effects of working at understrength and for too long hours. Of Admiral Coke's twenty-four small ships, eight were unable to go to their patrol stations owing to the need to rest the crews or carry out essential repairs. Coke would have liked to utilize the four motor torpedo boats which were in Queenstown harbour to strengthen his defences, but the Admiralty had laid down that they were only to be used for mine sweeping duties within the approaches to Queenstown harbour, and though the instruction was dated 1910, nobody was prepared to vary it.

That same evening of 4 May the U-30 was heading northwards and home towards Germany and at 8.30 p.m. was just off the entrance to Galway Bay. At the same time in the U-20 Kapitän-Leutnant Walter Schwieger noted in his log that he had sighted the north-west coast of Ireland on his port bow as he commenced the long run on the surface southwards down the west coast towards the Fastnet light.[5] There is little in the survivors' statements to say what was happening aboard the

Lusitania at that time except that deck sports had been held on the after promenade deck and a peacetime atmosphere had been enjoyed by all concerned. The only definite fact known about that afternoon aboard the *Lusitania* was that Mrs Matthews won the Ladies' Potato Race.

10

On Wednesday 5 May Churchill had an unusually early breakfast and by 8 a.m. was closeted in the Admiralty with Fisher, his First Sea Lord. By now their working relationship had soured and each felt that the other was impeding and confusing naval policy. Churchill saw his role in an untraditional way, and unlike previous First Lords he was not content to leave the day to day operations of the Navy to the professionals. He had a finger in every pie, and whilst his vigour and vision had done much to shake up what can only be described as the 'somnolent service', his actions were deeply and publicly resented and had earned him both enemies and a reputation for irresponsible meddling.

The post had first attracted him because of the possibilities it offered him of achieving personal glory. Like most Englishmen he had accepted the Navy's conviction that the war with Germany, when it came, would be decided quickly and decisively at sea. If there was to be another Armada or Trafalgar, Churchill was determined that history woulds how him to have been the architect. He had now reluctantly realized that the war had developed into one of attrition in which the Navy had a largely passive role. He was looking for a graceful exit from his naval cul-de-sac, preferably an exit on to the path to the glory which he sought. Twice in the previous few months, he had intimated his willingness to resign or be transferred. His ambitions at this time were directed at a senior command on the field. To achieve this he had built up a strong personal relationship with Field-Marshal Sir John French, the Commander-in-Chief of the British Expeditionary Force in

France. This relationship was bitterly resented by Kitchener, the Secretary for War, who suspected that the two men were intriguing against his interests.

The contact with French necessitated frequent visits by Churchill to the sixty-three-year-old Field-Marshal's headquarters in the field. The King, Kitchener, the Prime Minister and Churchill's wife, Clementine, had all remonstrated with him about these frequent and unofficial absences from the Admiralty and on the occasions when Churchill did go, the visits had to be either clandestine or cloaked by some pretext. Among his staff his hankering after the Field-Marshal's company and possibly his baton were unkindly described as 'trips to the French mistress'. Lord Fisher characteristically misconstrued this 'in' joke and was shortly to wound Clementine Churchill deeply by referring to it.*

A major reason why Fisher and Churchill had managed to work together for so long, without a dramatic and disastrous clash, was the complete dissimilarity in their working habits. The old Admiral, nearing seventy-five, rose at dawn, worked until 2 p.m. then tended to rest in the afternoon, attended the 6 p.m. meeting with Churchill and went early to bed. The strain of events, the eternal disputes over the Dardanelles campaign which had been launched the previous March by the Navy and which already looked like being the costly failure it became, together with his age, had taken a heavy toll on the old sailor, and there were increasing signs that he was losing

* Martin Gilbert, official biographer of Winston Churchill, recounts the following story in *Churchill 1914–16*, iii, 419: 'When Churchill had left for France on 5 May the responsibility of the daily conduct of Admiralty affairs had fallen automatically upon Fisher's shoulders. The responsibility agitated him. In an effort to soothe him, Clementine Churchill invited him to luncheon at Admiralty House. All went well and the Admiral departed in a cheerful mood. But some moments later, when she herself was leaving she found him still lurking in the corridor. 'What is it?' she asked. 'You are a foolish woman,' he replied. 'All the time you think Winston's with Sir John French he is in Paris with his mistress.' Clementine Churchill was stunned by such a wounding remark. It was for her a sure sign that Fisher's mind was unbalanced. She reported all this to her husband on his return, fearing that Fisher might break down. The Admiral, she later recalled, was 'as nervous as a kitten'.

his judgment, if not his reason. Churchill habitually rose late, worked in bed at his papers, and usually timed his appearance at the Admiralty around luncheon. The political side of his life dictated his later movements and he was wont to return to the Admiralty after dinner in the evening, or when the House of Commons rose for the night, and then work until the small hours. There was little liaison between the two men at this time, and to smooth the operation of the Admiralty Churchill had formed and trained what he called the War Staff. In *The World Crisis* he concedes that for this staff to have reached the pitch of efficiency required would have taken fifteen years' training, for the human material he had at his disposal was in the main composed of kindly, dedicated men who honoured the Empire and their wives in that order and who had no personal war experience whatsoever.

Every minor request and piece of paperwork from the fleet had first to be approved by the Admiralty, and the action tray on the desk of a Sea Lord was as likely to contain a request from the master of a minesweeper asking for permission to spend two shillings on lime juice for a sick seaman, as it was to contain the latest intelligence of the German fleet. The Admiralty was one enormous bureaucratic anthill stultified by a century of peace and the well-meaning ignorance this had engendered.

During the first winter of the war the twin energies of Churchill and Fisher had provided the Admiralty's main impetus and the most important naval decisions had been taken by an inner war staff consisting of Churchill, Fisher, Admiral Oliver, the Chief of Naval Staff, and a seventy-three-year-old veteran of the Crimea, and former First Sea Lord, Admiral of the Fleet Sir Arthur K. Wilson, whom Churchill had brought out of retirement and into the Admiralty without any formal position in order to assuage public criticism of his own immaturity and irresponsibility. 'Tug', as he was popularly called, was a public folk hero who had won the Victoria Cross in 1884, by knocking down a series of dervishes with his fists after the British square had broken at Tamai in the Sudan.

He worked for Churchill without pay. Of this inner staff or war group as it was called, Fisher had left the best picture in a memo he wrote to Churchill on 23 March 1915: 'AKW and dear Oliver are mules . . . besides they divert for days on some side issue . . . Oliver so over-burdens himself he is twenty-four hours behind with his basket of papers.'[1]

Fisher's comments on the Admiralty staff are equally illuminating, even if at times they are unfair. If his balance or sense of proportion were in error, he at least recognized the basic situation and pinpointed it in two letters to Admiral Sir John Jellicoe: 'We have a regular menagerie of charity Admirals totally unfitted for the work they are employed on as the Admiralty is quite full of young naval officers who ought to be at sea – doing simply clerks' work. The corridors are crowded with them.'[2] His second letter to Jellicoe was more astringent and showed his concern at Churchill's insistence on dabbling in everything simultaneously. The letter was franked: 'Please burn at once.' 'Winston has so monopolised all initiative in the Admiralty and fires off such a multitude of purely departmental memos (*his power of work is absolutely amazing*) that my colleagues are no longer *superintending Lords* but only *the First Lord's registry*! I told Winston this yesterday and he did not like it at all, but it is true! And the consequence is that the Sea Lords are atrophied and their departments are really run by the private office . . .'[3]

However, there were other eyes which viewed Fisher and Churchill and their relationship with concern. Prime Minister Asquith had written to his wife that 'Winston is devoured with vanity',[4] whilst Clementine Churchill had her worries over Fisher, and hoped that 'he was not like the curate's egg'.[5] Admiral Beatty discerned the real cleft between the two men and prophesied that the split would shortly come. 'The situation is curious, two very strong and clever men, one old, wily and of vast experience, one young, self assertive, with a great self satisfaction, but unstable. They cannot work together, they cannot both run the show.'[6] Beatty was right. On the morning of 5 May 1915 Fisher was too tired to run it, and

Churchill's mind was elsewhere and he was in a hurry. He had a train to catch to Paris. The discussions were brief and, as a result, the decisions were faulty.

The *Gulflight* was the first item on the agenda. The Foreign Office had to be informed of the Admiralty's inquiry. More pressing from an immediate and tactical point of view was the realization that U-boats were entering the western approaches around the north of Scotland and the west coast of Ireland. As a result Churchill graciously conceded that Admiral Hood had been unfairly relieved of his command of the Dover Patrol and minuted a note to make amends as soon as possible. Most serious of all – particularly to a man to whom the word 'live-bait' was a cruel jibe – was the fact that several of the cruisers patrolling the western approaches were not suitable for exposure to submarine attack. There had to be an immediate revision of the cruiser dispositions if another *Bacchantes* disaster was to be avoided.

Churchill, Fisher and with them Admiral Oliver went down to the great map room of the Admiralty to study the plot. Captain Hall, the D.N.I., was ordered to attend and to bring with him Commander Joseph Kenworthy, then working in the political section of Naval Intelligence. One side of the room was and is covered by a great map of the world, measuring some 30 ft by 20 ft. Being a marine map only the physical characteristics of the oceans are charted, whilst the land masses stand empty except for the location of signal or cable stations and routes. At that time the entire surface was covered with a grid which had been copied from one found amongst papers trawled up from a sunken German ship by an English fishing boat on the Dogger Bank. This was the German Admiralty grid used throughout the war to indicate with ease the precise whereabouts of their forces. A U-boat reporting its position did not signal a set of coordinates but merely wirelessed 'located south east section Square T 14' or whatever was appropriate.

Since September 1914 the Admiralty had been in possession of the German naval cyphers and from February 1915 a chain of interception and direction-finding stations established around the English and Irish coasts, had enabled Naval Intelligence not only to read almost every German naval signal but also to pinpoint from where it came. Marked on the great map, and changing as each fresh signal was intercepted, located and decoded, were the approximate positions of almost every unit of the German Navy, together with the ships of the Allied navies. This was known as the plot.

Each ship, whether friendly or enemy, was marked by a pin with a circular head. The diameter of the circle corresponded to the field of view from the highest vantage point of the ship in question. There were two exceptions. U-boats were marked with a red square which covered an area thirty-two miles square, together with an arrow indicating the direction in which they were believed to be heading. Secondly, the areas covered by the auxiliary patrol service were not marked with pins representing each individual motor boat or armed yacht; the patrol area was merely hatched in. Lastly, the map contained red squares slashed with a white diagonal which represented a suspected or unconfirmed sighting of a U-boat, usually from shore watchers. Regarded with hindsight this system had two built-in errors that could produce a wrong decision. The squares representing a U-boat were based on a submarine's underwater speed and endurance over a period of four hours. In that time a U-boat could cover some eighty miles on the surface. Secondly, the boldly hatched patrol areas gave an overall and misleading illusion of strong defences, when in real terms the auxiliary service was almost powerless.

The responsibility for marking the map with the up-to-date positions of hostile forces was that of Naval Intelligence. Admiral Oliver's war staff marked the position of Allied warships, and Captain Webb, the Director of the Trade Division, had to maintain the pins charting the movements of all merchant ships under government contract, armed merchantmen and those carrying important government supplies. At a glance then, the plot would show the precise and reasonably up-to-date position in any sector of the world's oceans, and upon its accuracy and regular maintenance depended the operational decisions of the Admiralty. Churchill with a train to catch had to ensure that Fisher, who would be carrying the responsibility in his absence, knew exactly what was going on. Fisher did not want the responsibility. He chided Churchill for going at all, and Clementine Churchill herself had tried to dissuade her husband, telling him that the septuagenarian Admiral would not be able to bear the strain. Churchill heeded neither the requests of the Admiral nor the entreaties of his wife. It was therefore a somewhat sullen Fisher who had been at his desk since dawn and now had to listen to Admiral Oliver's briefing on the plot and the decisions of a First Lord of the Admiralty thirty-five years his junior who characteristically was instructing him on how to conduct a navy at war.

Admiral Oliver dealt with each operational area in turn. When he came to the western approaches he pointed out the red squares marking the U-30 and the U-20: the former heading north and by now well to the north of Ireland, and the latter sighted shortly at 9 a.m. a few miles to the north-west of Fastnet. He explained that the War Staff had on their own initiative altered the disposition of some of the cruisers as a result of the U-20's activities. The *Orion*'s departure from Devonport had been cancelled and the *Colossus* out on station in the North Atlantic had had her recall cancelled as she would have been likely to have crossed the path of either of the two U-boats then to the west of Ireland. Both these decisions were approved. However, looming large on the map in the area of Fastnet were the red square denoting the U-20, the large disc of the cruiser *Juno* and the largest disc of all which represented the tallest ship on the seas, the *Lusitania*, which was then well out to the west and closing Fastnet at upwards of twenty knots. If the U-20 remained stationary the two would meet at dawn the following morning, with the *Juno* in the area close by. If the U-20 turned west, then the rendezvous would be even sooner. Admiral Oliver drew to Churchill's attention the fact that the *Juno* was unsuitable for exposure to submarine attack without escort, and suggested that elements of the destroyer flotilla from Milford Haven should be sent forthwith to her assistance.

At this juncture the Admiralty War Diary stops short, perhaps understandably as it was here that the decision was taken that was to be the direct cause of the disaster. No one alive today knows who took it, but Churchill and Fisher must share the responsibility. Shortly after noon on 5 May the Admiralty signalled the *Juno* to abandon her escort mission and return to Queenstown. She was to travel south-east overnight so as to clear the Fastnet by some fifty miles and under cover of darkness. The *Lusitania* was not informed that she was now alone, and closing every minute to the U-20. Admiral Coke at Queenstown was informed of the order and instructed to protect the *Lusitania* as best he could. Coke in his turn did not warn the *Lusitania*.

Captain Hall queried the decision, but with whom it is impossible to state positively. The morning's discussion on the *Gulflight* had reminded everyone present that there were grave dangers threatening the *Lusitania*, and the papers in London had been full of the German warning which had been universally construed as being directed at her. It was an incredible decision by any standards and can only be explained on two grounds. Firstly, that both Churchill and Fisher were so preoccupied with the Dardanelles and their personal problems that they failed to appreciate it; or secondly, that it was the pinnacle of Churchill's higher strategy of embroiling the U-boats with a neutral power.

Commander Kenworthy, who was not called on to speak in such august company, was wondering why he had been summoned in the first place. His only previous contact with Churchill had been when he had submitted a paper at Churchill's request on the political results of an ocean liner being sunk with American passengers on board. He did not know if Churchill had even read it, but had naturally supposed that in the turmoil caused by the torpedoing of the *Gulflight* this was why he was required for the conference. What was said will never be known, but Kenworthy left that meeting in the map room disgusted by the cynicism of his superiors. In 1927 he gave a hint of what did transpire in his book *The Freedom of the Seas*. 'The *Lusitania*', he wrote, 'was sent at considerably reduced speed into an area where a U-boat was known to be waiting and with her escorts withdrawn.'[7]* Their Lordships, he concluded, had obviously decided to let the international legality and success of the German U-boat offensive be tested in the court of public opinion. Kenworthy's is the only eye-witness account of that morning in the map room, and if responsibility is to be apportioned, then at this stage it must be the reader's decision. Churchill had an early lunch with Clementine at Admiralty House and caught the train to Paris.

On 5 May Captain Turner took his lunch on the bridge as was his custom, and irritated Third Officer Lewis by gnawing noisily on a chicken bone. Turner was preoccupied as on the following day he would be entering the danger zone, and the German warning was uppermost in his mind. The sea was calm, with intermittent patches of fog, and he reasoned that if the weather remained foggy as he drew near the Irish coast, he would have to reduce speed in case of collision. His course was heading him directly for Fastnet, the point where the North Atlantic steamer routes converged and where the first submarine threat would present itself. He retired to his day cabin to work out his plans. Two were required – a fair-weather plan, and a contingency one in case the fog persisted. Reduced to military terms, Turner's aim was simple. It was to bring the *Lusitania* to the bar which fronted the River Mersey at Liverpool as soon as there was sufficient water to allow him to cross it. He had been authorized to come up the Mersey without a pilot and this was infinitely preferable to awaiting a pilot for an hour or so and in doing so presenting a sitting target to any U-boat in the vicinity. The first suitable period of high water at the bar was at 4.30 a.m. on 8 May, his scheduled day of arrival. He took 4.30 a.m. as his deadline for

* The original manuscript stated 'was *deliberately* sent'. The word 'deliberately' was deleted after representations from the Admiralty to Messrs Hutchinson, the publishers.

crossing the bar, and worked backwards to his estimated position.

The first factor to his advantage was that he would come through the narrow St George's Channel between Ireland and Wales during the hours of darkness. The entrance to the channel was marked by a lightship called the Coningbeg light, and here and at the Mersey Bar were the two most likely areas of submarine attack. The safest part of the channel was in the middle, but the entrance was only twenty-four miles wide, and after any natural error which might have grown into his navigation across the Atlantic he would need to establish his position some time on 7 May before setting course for the channel entrance. With the fog which looked like lasting, he decided to give the Fastnet a wide berth and set a course some twenty miles south of the Irish coast and endeavour to obtain a precise fix during the morning of the seventh from one of the several prominent landmarks on that shore. There were several: Galley Head, the Bull Rock, Brow Head, Mizen Head, and the Old Head of Kinsale. All should, if the weather was clear, be visible from twenty miles out, and also he would be visible to the auxiliary patrols whose area extended ten miles out to sea.

To guide him in taking his decisions he had recourse to the instructions to masters issued by Cunard. These laid down precise details of the procedure to be followed in making a landfall in all weathers. In addition he had two large bundles of Admiralty Instructions and Admiralty Advices. The former were obligatory and could not be departed from. The latter were precisely what their name said and were there for his guidance, nothing more. On this trip he had no special instructions. Sir Courtenay Bennett had suggested that he adopt those issued for his previous trip. These were simple and to the point. He was advised to keep off the normal steamer track when near the coast, maintain strict wireless silence, attempt to make his landfall and destination at dawn and give all headlands a wide berth. On the previous trip he had done just this. Usually the *Lusitania* cleared the Fastnet by a mile or so and then followed a parallel course along the south Irish coast about a couple of

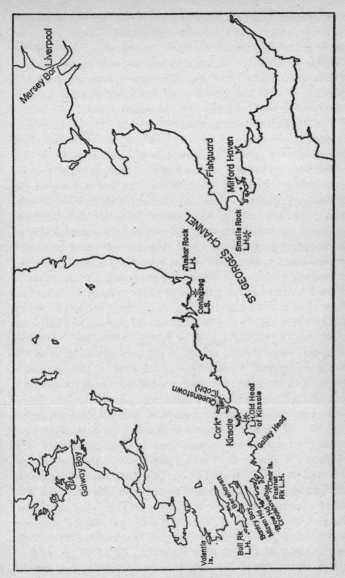

St George's Channel and its approaches

miles off shore. On his last trip Turner had cleared the Fastnet by twelve miles, and thereafter maintained an even ten miles between the shore and the ship. The threat of fog and the U-boats clinched his decision to widen his margin of safety, which also obviated any risk of collision with the *Juno*. His decision to clear the Fastnet and the Irish coast by at least twenty miles was both prudent and seamanlike.

The Admiralty Advices to mariners were a motley collection of documents, many of them contradictory. One stated there was no serious danger from torpedoes. Another told him that submarines rarely operated in sight of land. A third warned him against coming too close inshore as that was where the submarines operated. These instructions were mostly the product of Fisher's 'menagerie of charity admirals' and there was no one in the Admiralty who had ever had the responsibility of manœuvring a 45,000 ton ocean liner at high speed in hostile waters. Turner, like most of his breed of merchant captains, treated the Admiralty Advices with contempt. The momentum of the *Lusitania* was such that many of the evasive tactics recommended to him were a physical impossibility, whilst to execute a high-speed ninety degree turn would probably cause some thousands of pounds' worth of damage to the interior of the ship, and cause serious injury to the passengers. Most of the Advices appeared to be written for nothing larger than a frigate, and were totally impractical for what in effect was little less than a high-speed floating six-storey hotel.

At 5.30 p.m. Turner accompanied Staff Captain Anderson on a tour of the ship. It was a time when the passengers were resting, writing letters or preparing to dress for dinner. The May sun had lost its warmth and the decks were almost deserted. It was the time Turner liked best, for it seemed as if he had the great ship he loved to command almost entirely to himself. He planned to turn in early, as on Tuesday night custom decreed that he attended the first class passengers' smoking room concert, and he intended to spend the night of the seventh on the bridge during the last dangerous leg of his journey.

Kapitän-Leutnant Schwieger in the U-20 logged that he

cleared south-east from Fastnet shortly after 2 p.m. and he then set a course some twenty miles parallel to the coast almost identical to the one Captain Turner had planned for the *Lusitania*'s passage through these waters on the morning of the seventh. Towards evening he closed towards the land and at 5.30 p.m. he sighted the sailing schooner *Earl of Lathom*,.99 tons and bound from Liverpool to Limerick, in ballast. He surfaced, ordered her to stop through his speaking trumpet and told the crew to abandon ship and bring him the ship's papers. This they did, and Schwieger then sank her by placing grenades on the keel. This took place twelve miles south and slightly west of the Old Head of Kinsale, in full view of several Kinsale fishing smacks and a small steamer. One of the fishing smacks approached him thinking he was a British submarine and only realized its mistake when the grenades aboard the *Earl of Lathom* exploded. Then the fog which had also been troubling Captain Turner closed down and when it cleared shortly before dusk the U-20 attacked another steamer some twelve miles east of Kinsale. The steamer escaped into the fog and Schwieger retired out to sea to spend the night on the surface away from the patrol areas and the customary steamer traffic lanes.

Both attacks were promptly reported to Admiral Coke at Queenstown and relayed by him to the Admiralty. No action was taken.

Mr Churchill arrived in Paris shortly after 9 p.m. and for reasons known only to himself booked into the Ritz Hotel under the name of Spencer. Admiral Fisher went to bed about the same time and the Admiralty appeared to enter into a slumber from which, in Churchill's absence, only the nightmare of Schwieger's torpedo was to awaken it.

11

Churchill's trip to Paris was ostensibly to take part in the naval convention the Allies were to sign with Italy, whom they had succeeded in bribing into entering the war on their side. Churchill's biographers have stated that these delicate negotiations took three full days, but this was not the case. Churchill's part in the negotiations was completed by late afternoon on Thursday 6 May, and there was no valid reason for his not returning to the Admiralty. Instead he went straight to the Pas de Calais where he joined Sir John French. It is probable that he was involved with French in an effort to discredit Kitchener by revealing to *The Times* correspondent the desperate shell shortage on the Western Front, but this charge of intrigue is not fully proved. What is known is that in the company of Repington, *The Times* correspondent, he drove to the Pas de Calais and that he neglected his duties at the Admiralty and stayed from Friday till Monday at St Omer near Calais with the ostensible object of watching Sir John's costly failure of an attack upon the Aubers Ridge which was to be launched on 9 May.

It was a strange divertissement for him considering his knowledge of Fisher's state of health and the crisis that had developed in the Irish Sea and on the beaches of Gallipoli. It would appear to be an unjustifiable decision, and a minor result of it was that his private office when they learnt of it had to rush a note round to the American Ambassador regretfully cancelling Churchill's acceptance of a dinner engagement there on the evening of Friday, 7 May. The dinner was being given in honour of Colonel E. M. House, whose abortive mission as President

Wilson's confidential peace emissary was drawing to a close, and Ambassador Walter Hines Page had made sure that though the Colonel was to return empty-handed, he would have as fine a send-off as London's emasculated society could offer. Other guests included Sir Edward Grey, Wickham Steed, the foreign editor of *The Times*, and a bevy of notables including George Booth, Captain Reginald Hall and, especially at House's request, Lord Mersey, the Wreck Commissioner for the United Kingdom and F. E. Smith, who had just been appointed Solicitor-General and knighted.

House's mission had foundered when he introduced a concept into his proposals called 'The Freedom of the Seas'. Briefly this was an idea that the merchant shipping of all nations should be free from attack or interference. It meant that both Germany and England could trade as and where they wished and the entire concept of blockade would be dropped. The navies of each country would then concentrate on fighting each other, instead of blockading and hampering the world's trade. It was a startling proposal which, if it had been honestly observed, would have forced a European armistice in a matter of weeks, besides enriching the neutral suppliers of war material who could then literally auction their wares to whichever customer, assured the safe passage home, would pay the most. The Germans warmly endorsed the concept; so did President Wilson.

In Britain, Sir Edward Grey, the Foreign Secretary, was personally attracted to the idea, but told House that it was politically totally unacceptable. House decided to leave his concept in the hands of such thinkers and writers as Lord Loreburn, a former Lord Chancellor, Lord Mersey, and the editors of the *Daily Chronicle* and the *Economist*. He felt that if the idea was ventilated publicly, then there was a chance that a populace, sickened by the slaughter in France, might force the issue. It was a modest example of political fixing, and House organized a 'lobby' which though it was vocal, carried very little power. This was basically due to his abysmal lack of knowledge of what went on in England outside the drawing-rooms of Mayfair and the clubs of Pall Mall.

Page was against the idea. He was far too imbued with the British vision of crushing German militarism for all time to lend the cause even his tacit support. Peace, he believed, could only be made amid the ashes of Berlin, and even then America should have a firm say in ensuring that militarism never reared its head again. However, before the dialogue between Page and House developed or the lobby could start their campaign, Kapitän-Leutnant Schwieger sunk the concept without trace. The dawn of 6 May brought thick fog to the U-20, and the log records visibility at thirty yards. By 6.30 a.m. it had cleared somewhat though here and there were dense patches which the morning sun could not penetrate. At 7 a.m. the Harrison Line steamer *Candidate* came out of a fog bank and into the U-20's path. She immediately took evasive action and Schwieger got away two rounds with his deck gun before the fog cloaked both ships. Thirty minutes later the fog shifted and the U-20 found itself some fifty yards from the *Candidate*. After two grenades had been thrown, the *Candidate* hove to and the crew were allowed to abandon ship. There were no casualties, and the U-20's boarding party climbed aboard at 8.20 a.m. They stayed an hour and then drawing off a quarter of a mile put a torpedo into her, but the ship refused to sink. Schwieger closed up and a dozen rounds from his deck gun into the waterline sent the *Candidate* to the bottom at 11.25 a.m. The crew were picked up safely by a naval patrol boat which concentrated on its mission and did not attack the submarine. Schwieger allowed the patrol boat to depart unmolested.

An hour later the U-20 made an abortive attempt to attack a White Star steamer which escaped into the fog-banks and then at 1 p.m. the submarine encountered the *Candidate*'s sister ship, *Centurion*. Schwieger torpedoed her without warning, and the torpedo struck in the bows just by the bridge. The crew abandoned ship and again there was no loss of life. The torpedo did not sink the *Centurion*, and so once more the U-20 had to close up and this time fired another torpedo into her at pointblank range. Even then the *Centurion* took an hour and twenty minutes to go down.

The *Centurion* was the first ship for almost two weeks to have been sunk without warning, and there are several points here which are relevant to the *Lusitania* story. The first and possibly the most significant is that time and time again the first German torpedo did not sink its target. For that reason most submarine commanders preferred a surface attack and the sure use of their deck gun. To ensure a torpedo hit a submarine had to get well ahead and almost exactly abeam. Unless the angle of impact was almost ninety degrees it was rare for the torpedo to explode and even then, in many cases, the damage was insufficient to sink the ship. Schwieger noted in his log that his torpedoes were next to useless against any ship which had her bulkheads and watertight hatches properly secured. The fact that von Rosenberg in the U-30 would appear to have scrupulously observed the Cruiser Rules may possibly have lulled the decision-takers at the Admiralty into a sense of false security. Perhaps they thought that the Germans were behaving like gentlemen even though the public was inevitably told a different story. The crew of the *Candidate*, for example, were widely described as having had to take to the boats under a hail of shellfire,[1] and no mention was made of the fact that the U-20 had stood off to allow their rescue.

Von Rosenberg and Schwieger were not paragons of virtue, but nor were they pirates. They both had a profound distaste for their orders to sink without warning, and wherever they felt there was no danger at all to their submarines, the record shows that they invariably observed the Cruiser Rules. If they were convinced that their intended victim was unarmed, they had always challenged. Where there was the slightest doubt or danger, a torpedo attack would be launched without warning. The U-20's boarding party on the *Candidate* had discovered that she carried two sandbagged emplacements armed with machine guns, and was fitted with a six-pounder gun on the stern. As a result her sister ship, the *Centurion*, got short shrift. Both the U-20 and the U-30 carried the standard volumes of *Jane's Fighting Ships* and *The Naval Annual*, and the U-20 carried a civilian pilot as well, whose secondary duty was to assist in the identification of targets whose nationality was in doubt.

Schwieger was a more cautious seaman than von Rosenberg, and was not so inclined to give any potential target the benefit of the doubt. His personal record would indicate that he was both more ruthless and more easily frightened. On a previous voyage he had attacked a hospital ship without warning, and even though he missed, had justified his action in his report by claiming that it was sailing out from England, could not have been carrying wounded, and was therefore just another ship. It was flimsy logic at best. More recent was his memory of his last voyage when after making a surface challenge in the North Sea, he had had to crash dive to avoid a ramming attempt. He had escaped but had had to limp home with a badly damaged periscope and water leaking in through the joints whenever he submerged. Four of his fellow submarine commanders had been killed in the past nine weeks and on this trip he was determined not to take any unjustifiable risk whatsoever. He expected that his three actions between Kinsale and the entrance to St George's Channel would shortly bring a determined hunt for him. On the afternoon of 6 May, soon after he had sunk the *Centurion*, he established his position as twenty miles due south of the Coningbeg light, and after posting a look-out remained on the surface whilst he made a written appreciation of the situation. This survives in his war diary.

A further advance to Liverpool, the actual theatre of operations, given up for the following reasons:
(1) In view of the thick fog during the last two days, the calmness of the wind and the state of the barometer it is not to be expected that it will become clear in the next few days.
(2) In view of unclear weather it is not possible to see in time the keen enemy watch that is to be expected in St George's Channel and the Irish Sea – fishing steamers and destroyers – and accordingly a dangerous situation right along and travel under water.
(3) At night when not entirely clear the chance is ruled out of any watching on surface in front of Liverpool for outgoing transport, for the reason that escorting destroyers cannot be described in

proper time. Moreover it is to be assumed that transports if any leave Liverpool AT NIGHT and are escorted.

(4) On the trip all the way to St George's Channel the consumption of fuel oil has become already so great that a return from Liverpool southward around Ireland would no longer be possible. It is my intention to enter upon the return trip when two-fifths of the fuel oil is used up and it is my intention to avoid the trip through the North Channel, if at all possible, on account of the type of watch in operation that was met with by the U-20 up there on the last long-distance trip.

(5) There are still only 3 torpedoes available, of which it is my intention to conserve so far as possible two for the return trip.

It is therefore decided to remain to the south of the entrance to the Bristol Channel and attack steamers until two-fifths of the fuel oil is used up, especially since here a greater opportunity for attack is met with *less* counter-action than in the Irish Sea near Liverpool.[2]

By 6 p.m. Schwieger noted in his log that the fog had again closed down to thirty yards' visibility and that he could no longer see the Coningbeg lightship. He decided to 'submerge to twenty-four metres and overnight head for the open sea so as to be able to recharge my batteries far off from the lightship'.

The Admiralty was the first to be informed of the U-20's attacks, but they took their time in passing on the information and took no countermeasures. Lethargy seemed to have paralysed them. Hitherto escorts had been rushed from Milford Haven to Fastnet to protect cargoes of mules and the diversion of the *Transylvania* and *Ausonia* to Queenstown at the first hint of the presence of a U-boat indicates the customary prompt procedure that the War Staff adopted whenever a threat materialized in these waters. Incoming information was posted on the war map, and copies of it went to each Sea Lord and to the Directors of the Operations, Intelligence and Trade Divisions. Each of these three men could initiate a request for an escort and the Director of the Trade Division, whose concern the *Lusitania* was, could without seeking further authority order a diversion into Queenstown as he had done in the case of the *Ausonia* and the *Transylvania*. The detachment of counter-submarine forces from Milford Haven or the west coast ports would have been a matter for the Sea Lords, or at least two members of the Inner Staff or War Group.

News of the sinking of the *Candidate* reached the Admiralty at 11 a.m. on 6 May, but Admiral Coke at Queenstown was not informed until 10.59 a.m. the following day. But even without the knowledge of what had happened to the *Centurion* and the *Candidate*, the situation appeared so grave to Coke that he had to do something about it. He was forbidden to initiate any instruction to any ship not under his command without recourse to the Admiralty. He was further handicapped in that he was not allowed to send any specific information over his radio. His signals were always to be of 'a general and negative nature'. The precise brief given him in his Admiralty instructions was as follows: 'Do not order any ship into any definite area, but merely imply that certain areas are unsafe.'[3] The reason for this was the Admiralty were worried that the Germans would intercept and decode the messages, and then head for the areas indicated.

At 7 p.m. Coke studied the day's reports of submarine sightings, and with the memory of the *Earl of Lathom* fresh in his mind decided to warn the *Lusitania* to the best of his ability. His message reached Captain Turner at 7.50 p.m. just as he was about to go down to dinner and the passenger's concert. 'Submarines active off the south coast of Ireland.' Turner's hands were tied as well. He was not allowed to divert from his course without specific instructions from either the Admiralty or a British warship. At the moment his instructions were to approach Liverpool by coming south around Ireland. His one alternative was the diversion along the west and round the north coast, but this he could not adopt without orders. He anticipated meeting the *Juno* around dawn the following morning, and expected her to order him either northabout or into Queenstown if the threat persisted.

The signal was the first direct message the *Lusitania* had

received, though shortly after noon she had heard and acknow-ledged a general Admiralty instruction sent to all British mer-chant ships homeward bound. This had hardly concerned the *Lusitania* except that the last phrase had said 'Submarines off Fastnet'. Turner had accordingly reduced his speed slightly so that he rounded Fastnet during the dark and was steering a course whereby he would clear it by at least twenty-five miles. He did not dare go further out in case he missed his rendezvous with the *Juno*. He had taken other precautions. All the lifeboats were swung out on their davits, their canvas covers removed, their oars and provisions checked. Double look-outs had been posted, all watertight doors and bulkheads not essential to the working of the ship had been closed. The stewards had been ordered to blackout all the passengers' portholes and the passengers themselves had been asked not to show any unneces-sary lights. There was little else Turner could do, except to join the passengers at dinner.

Coke's warning to the *Lusitania* was copied to the Admiralty, and is marked as having been received there at 7.25 p.m. It merely served to underline the fact that the man on the spot was worried about the *Lusitania*. Although this worry was almost international, it did not appear to have percolated through to the Admiralty, whose collective telescope appeared permanently affixed to its blind eye. Captain Webb of the Trade Division did nothing. Captain Hall of Intelligence was dining at Greenwich, Admiral Oliver was in the United Ser-vices Club, Churchill was having an early supper in Paris before his drive to Calais, and the senior officer on the spot, Lord Fisher, worn out and distressed, had gone early to bed.

At the American Embassy, Walter Hines Page was writing to his son, and in his second letter of that week, he was pouring out his forebodings. On 2 May he had written: 'Peace? Lord knows when! I almost expect such a thing. . . . If a British liner full of American passengers be blown up, what will Uncle Sam do? That's what's going to happen.'[4] Now he was writing to tell his son of House's forthcoming return, and he revived his earlier premonitions: 'We all have a feeling here that more and more frightful things are about to happen.'[5]

In the smoking-room of the *Lusitania* Captain Turner stood up and faced his passengers. It was customary on these occasions for the captain to make a short speech, but this evening was different, for every passenger shared Page's foreboding, and some of them had asked Turner direct. They had watched the swinging out of the boats, the sudden blackout of their cabins. They had accepted his request not to light their after-dinner cigars outside on the deck, and they had all felt the *Lusitania* slow down. What, they asked the captain, is happening? Turner explained that there had been a submarine warning and that he had reduced speed so that they cleared the Fastnet during the hours of darkness or early dawn. He stressed that these were just routine precautions, and that in the morning they would find a cruiser alongside which would shepherd them into Liverpool on schedule. 'On entering the war zone tomorrow,' he told the passengers, 'we shall be securely in the care of the Royal Navy.'[6]

Turner was on the bridge at dawn the next morning, Friday, 7 May. The fog had come down overnight and visibility was again a mere thirty yards. Somewhere ahead of him Turner reckoned was the *Juno* and hopefully the Fastnet was behind him. However he could not place blind faith in his dead reckoning, and he slowed down to fifteen knots and commenced sounding his foghorn. The siren moaned through the fog, a plaintive call for the *Juno* to hear, but she was by now a hundred miles to the east and closing on Queenstown where she would dock around noon. A hundred and twenty miles ahead of the *Lusitania*, Schwieger stood in the conning tower of the U-20 whilst his batteries were charged and the fog swirled around him. He decided that if it had not cleared by the time the charging was finished, he would set course for the Fastnet and home around the west coast of Ireland.

Both Turner and Schwieger posted extra look-outs and went below to have their breakfasts.

Colonel House called on Sir Edward Grey shortly after breakfast. At noon that day House was to have an audience with King George V and Grey would accompany him. Grey had asked him to call early as he wished to take the opportunity for a 'short talk'. To House's surprise when he arrived at the Foreign Office, Grey's car was waiting, and Sir Edward was in the main hall. Taking House by the arm he said that it promised to be such a wonderful May morning, he had thought it better that they pass the time together by driving to Kew Gardens to see the almond blossom. They arrived there shortly after 10 a.m.

Sir Edward steered House across the dew, immaculate in their frock coats which were *de rigueur* for a royal audience. The sun had come out and Sir Edward, a famous ornithologist, motioned silently to House to stop and listen to a blackbird's song. As it finished he remarked, 'There's a sound you will not hear in Texas.' Thereafter his conversation was halting. Shyly he told House of his own garden in Northumberland, a garden which he had had to plan and cultivate from London. He regretted that never in the last fifteen years had he had the chance to visit it when the blossom was out. House recalled a faint sense of the ridiculous, as though he was a young girl walking with a tongue-tied beau, waiting for him to summon up the courage to propose. Gently he tried to steer the conversation back to matters of immediate importance. Grey suddenly stopped still and said apropos of nothing: 'What will America do if the Germans sink an ocean liner with American passengers on board?' House stopped walking and thought a moment, and searching into his mind he formulated his reply with the fluent chorus of the birdsong all around him. He chose his words with care. 'I believe that a flame of indignation would sweep the United States and that by itself would be sufficient to carry us into the war.'[7] His reply seemed to loosen Sir Edward's tongue for thereafter he talked fluently and frankly, regretting that House's plan for 'Freedom of the Seas' had come to nothing. He made it quite plain that it was the certain opposition from Kitchener and Churchill that made it such a political hot potato.

In Queenstown Admiral Coke studied his plot with growing concern. Since dawn four separate sightings of the U-20 had been reported, and at 9.20 a.m. he was informed of the sinking of the *Centurion* the previous day. At 10.59 a.m. came the news of the sinking of the *Candidate* and a few minutes later a signal from the Admiralty addressed to all British ships which echoed Coke's warning of the previous night. 'Submarines active in southern part of Irish Channel last heard of 20 miles South of Coningbeg Light vessel make certain "Lusitania" gets this.' That position was by now twenty-eight hours old and though Coke's later sightings had all gone to the Admiralty, inertia appeared to have gripped the war room. No directions, instructions, or updating of the position were given.

The 'all British ships' warning was passed to the *Lusitania* and acknowledged by her at 11.52 a.m.

At 11 a.m. Schwieger had finally decided to return home and submerged after sighting one of Coke's patrols just off the entrance to Queenstown Harbour. He decided to stay submerged until noon and then take a quick periscope look around. To his west the fog cleared and Captain Turner increased his speed from fifteen to eighteen knots. The signal saying that there was a submarine twenty miles south of Coningbeg presented him with a problem. This position was exactly in the middle of the entrance to St George's Channel, and his instructions were to take a course down the centre of it. It appeared to Turner that here was the most likely spot where the Germans would lie in wait for him. Anxiously he scanned the horizon for the *Juno* but there was no ship in sight. He concluded that he had missed her in the fog. The coast of Ireland was still an indistinct blur on the horizon and he ordered a modest change of course to draw a mile or so closer so that he could establish his precise position. If he was going to have to play ducks and and drakes with a U-boat amongst the shoals and rocks of Coningbeg, he needed to know exactly where he was, and after his Atlantic crossing on 'dead reckoning' he was not sure within twenty miles or so. There was also the danger that the fog would close in once more leaving him close to a dangerous coast to his port side and the mountains of Wales ahead. He did not wish to grope for the narrow entrance to St George's Channel in such conditions. Coke was busy checking his forces and their locations. He found he had a total of nine fishing boats of the auxiliary patrol, two motor boats and the yacht *Scadaun* dispersed over an area of almost 200 miles. The *Scadaun* was on detached duty escorting the auxiliary tug *Hellespont* from the area of Fastnet to Queenstown and the *Hellespont* had a radio. He decided to detach the *Scadaun* from the tug and order her to search the area between Fastnet and Queenstown for submarines.

Alfred Booth was in the Cunard office in Liverpool and read in his morning paper of the loss of the *Centurion* and the *Candidate*. He felt the same apprehension of danger as Captain Turner and immediately hurried to Admiral Stileman, the Senior Naval Officer Liverpool, and demanded that steps be taken to warn the *Lusitania*. Booth was always reticent as to what Stileman agreed to do, but he came away from that office convinced that the *Lusitania* was to be diverted into Queenstown. He telephoned his cousin George and told him so, and George Booth sent a telegram to Paul Crompton aboard the *Lusitania* to await him at the Cunard office at Queenstown.[8] The telegram told him to disembark there and come directly to London via Fishguard on the Irish packet. Alfred Booth, until the time he died, would only concede that Stileman had agreed to take certain steps, but that the tragedy occurred before they could be put into execution.

Around 11 a.m. Coke claimed that he spoke with both the Admiralty and Admiral Stileman in Liverpool. There is no record of what was said, but Coke has stated that he asked for permission to divert the *Lusitania* and could not get a firm decision. He was told to make sure that the *Lusitania* got the Admiralty message addressed to all British merchant ships which warned of a submarine having been seen twenty miles south of Coningbeg.

The tug *Hellespont* was a merchant fleet auxiliary as was the *Lusitania* and, like her, was referred to in signal parlance as an

MFA. Unfortunately the *Lusitania* had the call sign MFA. Coke wished to inform the tug that her escort *Scadaun* was to search for submarines whilst she was to come to Queenstown as quickly as possible. The escort had been ordered by the Admiralty and Coke could not have cancelled it without Admiralty clearance. Perhaps Coke asked the Admiralty for permission to divert the MFA into Queenstown. Any positive explanation is impossible and conjecture is the only answer as two signals are missing from the Admiralty signal register for 7 May – according to the head of the Admiralty Archives. The Admiralty however categorically denies and has done so before four courts of law – and over fifty-seven years – that any message coded or otherwise was sent to the *Lusitania* at 11.02 a.m. on the morning of 7 May. Fortunately a certified copy of the transmission log of the naval wireless station at Valentia has survived and this clearly shows that the *Lusitania* received a two-word message in naval code addressed to MFA at 11.02 G.M.T. which was promptly acknowledged by the *Lusitania* with the code word of the day 'Westrona'. The message was taken to Captain Turner who took some time to decode it, as it was the first he had ever received in that code. To the end of his life he was adamant that it instructed him to divert into Queenstown. In the event the *Lusitania* was probably diverted by accident. Possibly it was by design and was Coke's way of trying to ensure her safety; for his message to the tug *Hellespont* was certainly sent to the *Lusitania*. Unfortunately it was sent a few moments too late.

At noon Schwieger heard the throb of propellers above him, and a few moments later he came up to periscope depth and saw the *Juno* heading away from him into Queenstown. He also noticed that the sun was fully out, the fog had cleared, and with the exception of the *Juno* rapidly disappearing in the distance there was no other shipping around. After a twenty minute delay to give *Juno* time to get clear he surfaced and headed back towards Fastnet at full speed. Forty miles away was the *Lusitania* and Captain Turner had finished decoding Coke's

146

MFA signal a few moments before. At 12.15 G.M.T. he swung the *Lusitania* to port so violently that several passengers lost their balance and chaos was created in the galleys below. The *Lusitania* headed for the shore.

The King received Colonel House most graciously and they talked the small talk that monarchs reserve for visiting statesmen. House talked of Kew, the blackbirds and the kindness with which he had been received. The King stood looking out of the window, one hand toying with some papers on a desk. With his back to the Colonel he suddenly remarked, 'Colonel, what will America do if the Germans sink the *Lusitania*?'[9]

At 1.20 Schwieger saw a smudge of smoke on his starboard bow, and soon saw the four funnels of a steamer some fourteen miles ahead heading towards the coast. He promptly submerged and set a course that would take him ahead and abreast of his target should it turn to starboard and take a course parallel to the Irish coast and towards Queenstown. Such a course would give him a perfect flank shot. In the meantime he sang out to his pilot as the crew went to attack stations. 'Four funnels, schooner rig, upwards of 25,000 tons, speed about twenty-two knots.' The pilot replied, 'Either the *Lusitania* or the *Mauretania*, both armed cruisers used for trooping.' At that very moment the *Mauretania* was 150 miles away at Avonmouth loading troops for the Dardanelles. Schwieger believed he had found the target he had been sent to sink.

As the *Lusitania* closed to the coast, Turner could make out a lighthouse on the top of a high bluff standing out to sea. He reasoned correctly that it was probably the Old Head of Kinsale and promptly ordered a change of course to starboard which would take him into Queenstown. He was now seventeen miles off shore and twenty-five from safety. Ever a cautious man he ordered the officer of the watch to take a series of four point bearings on the lighthouse so as to help him establish his precise position before he navigated his way into Queenstown without either tugs or pilot, and through the only channel swept daily for mines. The course change led him directly into Schwieger's trap and the log of the U–20 relates what happened then with a professional simplicity.

2.35 p.m.*
The steamer turns starboard, takes a course to Queenstown and thus makes possible a drawing near for the firing. Up to 3 p.m. ran at high speed in order to get a position up-front.

3.10 p.m.
Pure bowshot at 700 metres range. (G torpedo 3m. depth adjustment), angle of intersection 90°, estimated speed 22 knots. Shot strikes starboard side right behind the bridge.[10]

Not only Kapitän-Leutnant Schwieger was shattered by its effect.

* Schwieger's clocks were of course set to German Time, one hour ahead of the Greenwich Time observed on the *Lusitania*. These have been corrected to GMT in the narrative but German Time has been retained in direct quotations.

12

Schwieger had little faith in his torpedoes and his log which describes the effect of one G type on the *Lusitania* reflects his awed surprise. He had estimated the speed of his target at twenty-two knots and correspondingly allowed that speed in calculating the deflection needed for a bow shot. His intention had been to fire as the bows touched the crossed wire in his sights which would give him a hit in the forward boiler room. The first indication of a hit was a waterspout rising just behind the bridge and slightly forward of the front funnel. His log account which he dictated to the pilot standing beside him as he watched through the periscope, continues:

An unusually heavy detonation takes place with a very strong explosion cloud (far beyond front funnel). The explosion of the torpedo must have been followed by a second one (boiler or coal or powder?). The superstructure above the point of impact and the bridge are torn asunder, fire breaks out, smoke envelopes the high bridge. The ship stops immediately and heels over to starboard quickly, immersing simultaneously at the bow. It appears as if the ship were going to capsize very shortly. Great confusion is rife on board; the boats are made ready and some of them lowered into the water. In connection therewith great panic must have reigned; some boats, full to capacity, are rushed from above, touch the water with either stem or stern first, and founder immediately . . .[1]

The U-20 cruised closer and made a circuit of the ship, Schwieger pivoting the periscope and noting that because of the list many of the port boats could not be lowered. He observed that his torpedo had struck slightly forward of where he had first thought, and accordingly revised his estimate of the ship's speed to not more than twenty knots. Then he handed the periscope to the pilot who taking a quick look said: 'By God, it's the *Lusitania*.' Eighteen minutes after the torpedo struck, the *Lusitania* had completely disappeared. Schwieger closed down the periscope and headed out to sea.

The torpedo struck the *Lusitania* slightly forward of the bridge on the junction of the longitudinal bulkhead and the transverse bulkhead which divided the reserve coalbunker and the lower orlop hold. The immediate effect was for the force of the explosion to blow both into the lower orlop hold and down the full length of the longitudinal bulkhead or bunker which by now, towards the end of the voyage, was almost empty. It did not penetrate into No. 1 boiler room or the stokehold that was immediately forward of the boilers. Nor did the boilers explode, and the evidence for this assumption is from the only two survivors from No. 1 room, a fireman and a trimmer who were both working there at the time. Their statements were sworn before a Board of Trade Inspector in Liverpool on 18 and 19 May 1915.[2] The fireman, Thomas Madden, stated that he was working in the forward section of the stokehold ahead of No. 1 boiler when the torpedo struck. He placed the explosion as coming from the forward end of the ship on the starboard side. No water came into his boiler room for two or three minutes, and he had time to run to the watertight exit door to find himself shut in. On his return he found water pouring through the loading aperture in the bunkers, and it was then about eighteen inches deep on the floor plates. The list and the current of water pouring in made him lose his footing but eventually he found his way to an escape ladder and climbed up to the boat deck through a ventilating shaft. Trimmer Frederick Davis's account exactly confirms Madden's story. He too escaped through the ventilator.

The water rushing down the starboard bunker compartment also burst into No. 2 boiler room through the open bunker hatches. Trimmer Ian McDermott was the only survivor from No. 2 and he also stated that the boilers did not explode in his room. He too escaped through the ventilator shaft as the list and the pressure of water had prevented the overriding mechanism for the watertight doors from being opened.

Almost immediately after the impact the *Lusitania*'s bow dipped into the water and No. 3 boiler room took only a small amount of water as it rose with the stern of the ship out of the water. No. 4 boiler room took no water from the impact nor did the engine rooms. Any water that subsequently entered them came from the eventual sinking of the ship. The crew of No. 3 boiler room all made their way up to the boatdeck and No. 4 was empty as it had been closed down.

The G torpedo had failed to blow in the inner bulkhead of No. 1 boiler room, but just further forward *something* blew out most of the bottom of the bows of the ship. It may have been the Bethlehem Company's three inch shells, the six million rounds of rifle ammunition, or the highly dubious contents of the bales of furs or the small 40 lb boxes of cheese. Divers who have been down to the wreck unanimously testify that the bow has been blasted by a massive internal explosion and large pieces of the bow plating, buckled from the inside, are to be found some distance from the hull.

Whatever the cause of the second explosion, it was not the boilers and it occurred farther forward, was larger than the first and did far more damage. Nor was it a second or third torpedo. Expert opinion – physical inspection and Schwieger's log and torpedo inventory – confirm that. It is probable that the still sealed records of Captains Hall and Gaunt at the Admiralty[3] provide the only definite clue to its cause. The Admiralty's consistent and adamant refusal – even though by the thirty-year rule these records could be officially disclosed – tends to confirm that the second explosion was caused by a contraband and explosive cargo which was forbidden by American law and which in any event should never have been placed on a passenger liner. The result of Schwieger's torpedo was the flooding of the starboard coal-bunkers and a 15 degree list. The result of the second explosion was the sinking of the *Lusitania*.

Leslie N. Morton was the starboard look-out in the bows

and Able Seaman Thomas Quinn the look-out in the crows nest. Both saw the track of the torpedo, and both shouted it to the bridge. Quinn in his Board of Trade deposition afterwards stated that 'it came abaft the foremast' which would correspond with Schwieger's revised estimate, and with the No. 5 lifeboat being destroyed by the consequent spout of water. Morton stationed sixty feet below Quinn told a conflicting story. He said that as soon as he had reported to the bridge he left his post and had rushed to the forecastle hatch leading down to the crew's quarters when the torpedo hit. The height of the *Lusitania*'s foredeck above the waterline and the position of the forecastle hatch in the centre of this deck make it a physical impossibility to see the waterline on either side of the foredeck and both flanks of the ship behind the bridge are obscured by the bridge itself. Leslie Morton later made several statements in evidence and under oath which include the observations that he saw not only the conning tower of the submarine, but *two* torpedoes and that 'as far as I could judge from forward'[4] 'they struck the side of the ship between Nos. 2 and 3 funnels and below No. 3 funnel respectively'. Both areas were invisible to him from the forecastle hatch. At this time Morton was only eighteen and it was his first voyage on the *Lusitania*. He was also in the hands of learned counsel who led him skilfully through this evidence.

Morton's qualification of 'as far as I could judge from forward' does not appear to have been taken at the value which doubtless Mr Morton, who died in 1972, meant it to be. The result of his evidence which was all the more convincing because he had personally saved many lives and was most properly regarded as one of the heroes of the occasion was to start the canard of two or more torpedoes which struck in the middle and towards the stern of the *Lusitania*. Such impact points would hardly account for the almost immediate immersion of the bows, and Morton's affidavit does contain the remark that when he ran to his boat station about a minute or so after the explosion the sea was already coming over the main bulkhead on the foredeck.

Almost every survivor had his own idea as to where the torpedo had struck, but three simple points confused the majority. The first was that most witnesses, including Morton, mistook the path of bubbles which marked the track of the torpedo, for the torpedo itself. Schwieger had set the running depth at 3 metres or slightly over 9 feet, and the bubbles were the compressed air from the driving motor rising to the surface. A bubble of compressed air in sea water, if there is no tide, takes from 6½ to 8 seconds to rise 9 feet, so that with the *Lusitania* travelling at 18 knots and the torpedo travelling at 45 knots, the torpedo would strike the side of the ship 9 seconds before the bubbles showed alongside, and when they did show they would surface well aft of the actual point of impact.

The second confusing factor depends on equally basic calculations and at the time of impact confused even Schwieger himself. The spout of water which he observed flying into the air had to travel up and then come down again. The *Lusitania*'s boats were 68 feet above the waterline and from AB Quinn's deposition it must have been the *descending* water and wreckage which landed on No. 5 boat, virtually wrecking it. The impact of the torpedo was some forty feet forward of the waterspout observed by Schwieger, and at least ninety feet ahead of No. 5 lifeboat.

The third and last confusing factor was the cloud of smoke, coaldust and apparently steam which numerous passengers and crew took for the explosion of the torpedo. It was not steam but white damp from the coaldust. The explosion of the torpedo in the extreme forward end of the starboard longitudinal bulkhead – used as a coal-bunker – blew a blast of its explosive gases down the entire length of the five-sixths empty and dusty compartment and the resulting cloud of dust, smoke and damp escaped through the ventilators which led from the top of the bunkers to outlets beside each funnel. These ventilators were there to prevent pockets of white damp building up. In retrospect, it is only too simple to realize that witnesses hearing a massive explosion and seeing a great belch of smoke and possibly inflammable white damp burst from the base of the funnel nearest them should immediately assume they were standing at the seat of the explosion.

This prolix discussion of the true point of impact is not intended to prove one witness wrong at the expense of another. A straightforward survey of the wreck has shown exactly where the torpedo struck. This discussion is required to explain the numerous truthfully offered but differing eye-witness accounts which were considered at the successive inquiries after the event. While it may seem sophisticated to a layman, there has never been any doubt in the minds of the naval or Cunard authorities as to where the torpedo struck. By its very act of exploding within the ship it recorded its exact location on the bulkhead door, fire and flooding indicators on the bridge and three of the five bridge staff survived, among them the master Captain Turner.

Turner was standing on the bridge when the look-outs hailed that there was a torpedo approaching from starboard. The message was acknowledged by Second Officer Heppert, who promptly told the Captain, but even as he did so, the torpedo struck as Turner ran to the starboard side. Within ten seconds, according to Turner's recollection, the ship took a 15 degree list so that it was almost impossible to stand on the deck. He shouted to the quartermaster to close all the water-tight doors that were not already closed and scanned the indicator which showed which bulkheads were secure and whether there was fire or flood in any compartment. At this moment, according to Turner, 'there came a second rumbling explosion and the indicators on the "telltale board" appeared to go berserk for most of the forward compartment'. Turner knew in his heart that in that moment he had lost his ship, and as the bow dipped into the water he gave the order to lower the boats and abandon ship. Then he instructed Second Officer Heppert to tell the yeoman carpenter to check the damage forward, and raced up the ladder to the navigation bridge above, from where he could see the boat decks down both sides of the ship. He immediately saw that the port boats had swung in against or over the rails, while the starboard boats had swung outwards. Smoke and dust was bursting from every ventilator and a gentle wind was blowing it towards him. Turning away from the smoke he felt wind on his face and realized that the *Lusitania* was still under way, throwing an appalling strain on the transverse bulkheads and making it impossible to put the boats into the water safely. He immediately ordered full speed astern.

In the engine room, George Little, the Senior Third Engineer, applied steam pressure to the astern turbines, but as he had been warned by Mr Laslett of the Board of Trade before they left Liverpool, there was a blowback and one of the two main steam pipes fractured, neatly blowing off the top of a condenser on the boat deck and nearly decapitating Third Officer Lewis who was standing nearby. In his excitement and in order to take the pressure off the astern turbines, Little placed the engine room controls back to 'full ahead'. However, as a result of the feed-back, the steam pressure had dropped from 190 to 50 lb, but this gave just enough headway to make it dangerous to launch the boats. Turner saw a great belch of steam burst out between the third and fourth funnels and realized what was happening. He immediately shouted to the deck officers not to let any boats be actually launched, called Staff Captain Anderson up to him and ordered him not to allow any boats to be put into the water until 'he thought the headway was sufficiently off the ship'. Anderson acknowledged the instruction and sent a message to the bridge suggesting that they flood the port side trim tanks in order to balance the list. Turner accepted that they would lose a little buoyancy, but agreed and immediately gave the instruction. It was useless because the crew to operate the flooding valves had already raced to the boats.

For a minute or two the list stabilized at 15 degrees but then the *Lusitania* began to heel still further to starboard, and Turner called down to Heppert to tell the quartermaster to shout out to him as each degree of list was registered on the list indicator. It was obvious to him that within minutes the *Lusitania* was going to capsize, unless she hit the bottom with her bows before she did so. Four minutes had now gone by and already the foredeck was completely under water. Through the forward hatches and over the bulkheads the sea was pouring into the ship. Turner tried to head her towards the Old Head of Kinsale tantalizingly close in the afternoon sunlight but the bow – now invisible below the surface – would not come round. Unknown to him, the rudders were already almost out of the water.

Down below on E deck the initial list had put the portholes under water, and as it slowly increased, those on D deck were submerged as well. Through each porthole the water poured at the rate of $3\frac{3}{4}$ tons a minute and survivors' statements show that at least seventy-four portholes on these decks were known to have been open. Ten minutes after the torpedo struck and six minutes after the D deck ports were submerged, Turner conceded that no matter what they did his ship was doomed and he signed to Anderson that despite the still appreciable headway on the ship, it was time to put the boats into the water. In that six-minute interval, at least 1500 tons of water had entered through the open ports besides that coming in over the bulkheads as the bows sunk lower and lower.

At 2.23 p.m. Mr Johnston, the quartermaster, called up to Turner that the list was now 25 degrees and Turner called down to him, 'Then save yourself.' Johnston picked up a lifebelt and stepped into the sea which was now lapping gently over the starboard side of the bridge. In his own words he 'let the tide take me where it wanted to'.

Turner was now alone, high up on the port side of the navigation bridge. He stood there gazing up at the boat decks which now reared high above him as the *Lusitania*'s stern rose higher out of the water. As the revolving propellers came clear the headway diminished and seconds after that the bow of the *Lusitania* struck the bottom, momentarily halting the inclination to capsize. Turner gripped the signal halyards and was surprised to be joined by the ship's doctor who laboriously climbed up to him. Whether to offer assistance or just because it was momentarily a place of safety, no one knows. The

Lusitania was now literally standing and pivoting on her bow which rested on the granite ocean floor, and ever so slowly she commenced to settle, at the same time turning over on to her starboard side. She had three minutes of life left. Her decks all the way up to the stern, which was almost a hundred yards away, and above the bridge, now towered over Turner and the doctor, thronged with people, some still frantically attempting to lower the remaining boats towards the stern.

As the stern slowly settled towards the sea, the bulkheads into the boiler rooms finally gave way and No. 3 boiler exploded blowing off No. 3 funnel. When the steam cleared, the *Lusitania* was gone. Only six of her forty-eight lifeboats were afloat amongst the wreckage, and there was not a rescue ship to be seen. The water was dead calm, the sun shone brightly and Junior Third Officer Albert Bestic was surprised to find the water so warm. He had been desperately trying to launch the port boats and after realizing it was a hopeless task, had gone into the great entrance hall where a number of first-class passengers were standing – seemingly unconcerned or unaware that they had literally only seconds in which to save themselves. There he had met Alfred Vanderbilt and the theatre producer Carl Frohman who were unconcernedly tying lifejackets to a series of Moses baskets in which many of the infants aboard had been sleeping in the ship's nursery after their lunch. Bestic attempted to alert them all to the danger but Vanderbilt merely shrugged.

As the waters rose higher, Frohman allegedly quoted, from *Peter Pan*, 'Why fear death? It is the most beautiful adventure in life.'

A rush of water then swept Bestic out through the doors, over the rail and into the sea. Now lying on his back amidst the wreckage and the cries of those around him he heard the wails of the babies in their wicker baskets as they floated around him. The hastily tied lifejackets did not survive the turbulence caused by the wreck settling far below them, one by one the cries ceased and Bestic found himself seemingly alone. He recalled that he had not the strength to take off his lifejacket and allow himself to drown. He could not forget the fiasco of the lifeboats and until he died in 1969, he found even the memory of those eighteen minutes almost impossible to live with.[5]

13

The *Lusitania* carried forty-eight lifeboats. Twenty-two of them were the conventional wooden type, clinker built and suspended from davits – eleven to either side. She also had twenty-six collapsibles which had a hollow wooden base and canvas sides which could be erected either on board or in the water. These were carried on the decks, and were secured there with wooden chocks to prevent them sliding about. They would float away of their own accord should there not be time to launch them. Eight of these collapsibles were stored on the after deck and the remaining eighteen were stowed directly beneath eighteen of the wooden lifeboats whose keels rested on a wooden frame which in turn secured the collapsible to the deck. When the wooden boats were swung out they hung just above and outside the collapsibles. In emergencies and before filling them with passengers the wooden boats were to be lowered to the level of the collapsibles which provided a platform from which to pass from the deck to the lifeboat.

Because of the *Lusitania*'s tendency to heel, experience had shown that when the conventional boats were swung out and lowered to the level of the collapsibles, they built up a dangerous oscillation, swinging in and damaging both themselves and the collapsibles alongside them. To prevent this a canvas-covered snubbing chain had been fitted which led from the edge of the deck to the inboard gunwale of the wooden boat. This damped down the outward swing, and acted as a buffer on the inboard side. This chain was fastened to the inboard gunwale by a link and pin. Each set of davits carried a hammer with which to knock out the pin, and also to free the chocks holding the collapsibles in position. Both types of boat had capacities ranging from fifty to seventy persons, and both types unladen weighed marginally under five tons.

The responsibility for all the boats on the port side was that of Staff Captain Anderson, while the starboard boats were under the First Officer. Both the port and starboard boatdecks were subdivided into two subsections, one of five sets of davits, the other of six. Each subsection was supervised by a junior officer. There were eleven pairs of davits to each side, but the shortage of able seamen meant that lowering crews were only available for ten pairs on each side of the ship, one AB to each davit; his function was to lower the falls, and once the conventional boat was in the water, to recover them and attach them to and then lower the collapsible. It was not planned to lower the collapsibles on the stern deck, but it was the function of the carpenter and his yeomen to free the chocks which secured them so that they would float free if the ship sank. The boats' crews were made up from senior members of the engineering and steward staffs, and each crew member was briefed as to how and when he should release the pin which secured the snubbing chain. Able seamen whilst they were allocated a boat station were not allocated places in the conventional boats which were lowered first. Their 'boat places' as opposed to 'boat stations' were in the second wave of boats to be lowered. The whole system depended on every man going to his correct station. There were only forty-one ABs to handle the forty davits which made up the stations, numbered from one to twenty; the odd numbers being on the starboard side, the even on the port.

Third Officer Albert Bestic was in charge of stations two to ten on the port side. It was his first trip aboard an ocean liner for he had only joined Cunard in New York. His first duty had been to conduct the port side boat drill and he noted in his pocketbook at the time that owing to the coaling barges alongside it had been impossible to lower any of them. The drill had consisted purely of mustering what men he had available and allocating them to their stations. He was not personally acquainted with any of the engineers and stewards who made up the crews, and knew them only from the master list which he had been handed by Staff Captain Anderson. Two days after the disaster he swore an affidavit before a Board of Trade Commissioner that no boats had been lowered in the practices, but this affidavit, though it was made by the officer who had conducted the drill, was never used at any inquiry to counteract other statements which claimed that not only had the boats then been lowered to the water but had been rowed around New York harbour.

After the torpedo struck, Bestic ran to his station at Captain Turner's command to make the boats ready. When he reached it, Staff Captain Anderson had already shouted the order to lower the lifeboats down to the level of the collapsibles, but many passengers had not waited for this and every boat on Bestic's station was already full. Many of the davitmen had not yet reached their station, and on number two Bestic noticed that he had only one man present and he was on the forward davit. Bestic went to the stern davit and hoisted himself up on it so that he could see what was going on and in order to try to bring order into the confusion which was only too evident. As he climbed the davit he realized that the great list would preclude the lifeboat being lowered clear of the ship's side and that the moment the tension was released on the snubbing chain, the lifeboat, already heavy with passengers, would swing inwards. He shouted for men to push the boat outwards so that it would clear the ship's side. Above the clamour, and as willing hands climbed on to the collapsible to carry out his order, he heard the clang as someone knocked out the pin of the snubbing chain and was able to draw himself backwards just in time. No. 2 boat crashed inwards, crushing the passengers on the collapsible, and then both boats slid forward towards the bows, carrying the remaining passengers before them until it pinned them against the bridge superstructure.

Determined to stop a recurrence, Bestic clambered up to No. 4 station, but he was too late and No. 4 boat crashed in, and then slid inexorably down on to the wreckage of No. 2.

Bestic recalled weeping with anger and frustration as he desperately fought his way to No. 6 where Anderson, realising what was happening, was trying to persuade the passengers aboard to disembark so that the boat could be manœuvred over the side. Many of the boats were filled with women and children, and numbers of the first-class male passengers, recognizing the danger, helped Anderson and Bestic to persuade them to disembark, but as quickly as people vacated their places, others climbed board. Anderson shouted two orders, both of which became confused. First, he ordered the women and children out of the way while the crew and male passengers tried to ease the heavy boats over the side. Second, to stop others climbing into the emptying boats, he shouted that the ship was not going to sink and sent Bestic back to the bridge to ask Turner to flood the port trimming tanks so as to reduce the list. By the time Bestic returned, Anderson's orders had become garbled into 'no women and children in the boats' and men to come to the port side to help counteract the list. As Bestic stood hanging on to the side of the bridge shouting above the din to Turner high above him, he watched excited passengers swarm into boats, 6, 8 and 10. One by one these suffered the fate of 2 and 4. Bestic's boat station looked as though a cyclone had hit with the splintered boats piled on top of each other and the passengers, and the whole awful heap sliding further forward as the bows lurched lower.

On No. 12 station, Anderson managed to re-establish some form of order. The pin had not been released, and he persuaded many of the passengers to leave the boat whilst this was done and with the help of volunteers manhandled it over the ship's side. Then he loaded it up again and commenced to lower away. The list was by now amost twenty degrees and the flank of the *Lusitania* resembled the north face of the Eiger. It was a slope of almost eighty degrees, studded every few inches with the snap-headed rivets which fastened the plating. Each rivet projected an inch above the plating, and already the rivets were catching under the lower edges of the planks of the clinker-built lifeboats. Anderson realized that they would rapidly tear the planks to pieces and shouted out to those aboard No. 12 to use their oars as a cushion between the rivets and the side of the lifeboat. The order was acknowledged and No. 12 grated slowly down the side of the ship. The list prevented the lowering crew from seeing the lifeboat's position.

When the boat came level with the promenade of the deck below, it started to come inboard and lodged on the balustrade. Passengers on this deck attempted to climb into it whilst those aboard pushed them off with their oars. Someone shouted to the lowering crew invisible above them 'lower away' but one or other of the men on the davits lost control and the stern of No. 12 dropped suddenly, throwing all aboard her into the water below. For a moment the boat hung by the bow fall, then that parted and No. 12 slid down the rivets and onto the passengers beneath.

Boat No. 14 was also eased over the side. As lowering commenced *Lusitania*'s bow struck the bottom. For a moment the ship flexed and the men at the davits simultaneously lost control. No. 14 fell straight down onto the wreckage of No. 12, but miraculously landed on an even keel. Some twenty survivors climbed aboard and the ship's barber managed to paddle No. 14 clear of the ship before the lifeboat slowly sank under them as water poured in through the strained and rivet-holed planks. It was now impossible to push the remaining boats over the side, but nevertheless everyone went on trying. As they did so the water crept up towards them, driving those aboard ever higher towards the stern. This crowd impeded those still trying to get the boats away. Somehow No. 16 was bodily hoisted over the side only to fall directly into the water where it broke up and sank. No. 20 splintered to pieces on the edge of the ship.

At No. 18 station occurred one of those incidents that haunt the lives of those responsible. The *Lusitania* was now standing on her bow with her stern well clear of the water. The starboard list had increased to twenty-five degrees, and the slope between stern and bow was approximately forty-five degrees. The port boat deck was thronged with a pushing, shoving crowd which threatened to engulf everything before it. Boat 18, packed with passengers, still hung high in its davits and a seaman stood on the gunwhale with an axe. It was his intention to cut the falls and release the pin as soon as the sea came level with the boat. A passenger – the instigator of the incident – either did not know of this plan or disapproved of it. The passenger was Mr Isaac Lehmann of New York City and the following day from his hospital bed in Queenstown he made a remorseful affidavit as to what occurred.

I ran down to the D deck to my state room ... to get a life preserver. ... Somebody certainly had been in in my room already and taken my life preserver. I don't know whatever possessed me, but I looked in my dress suit case and got hold of my revolver, as I figured this would come in handy in case of anybody not doing the proper thing. ... I rushed up to A deck ... and stood on one of the collapsible boats which lay on the deck covered with canvas. There were quite thirty or forty people on the boat already, and I asked why this boat was not launched and put down into the sea. I again asked why the boat was not put into the water, and said, 'Who has got charge of this boat?' One man who had an axe in his hand, answered that orders had been issued by the Captain not to launch any boats. My reply was, 'To hell with the Captain. Don't you see that the boat is sinking? And the first man that disobeys my orders to launch the boat I shoot to kill'. I drew my revolver and the order was then obeyed.[1]

The seaman knocked out the pin, and the boat loaded with people fell down onto the collapsible, and thence rolled down the steeply inclined deck, scything a path through the throng of passengers struggling up it. Lehmann records seeing at least thirty people crushed to death close to him and he himself suffered a severely injured leg. At that moment, the *Lusitania*, as though she could not tolerate any further indignity, sank quickly and with no more fuss than a great burst of steam and what Lehmann, who found himself in the water alongside, remembered it 'sounded like a terrible moan'.

The starboard boats were commanded by First Officer Arthur Jones, and Third Officer John Lewis had charge of stations 1 to 9. On this side the boats very naturally swung clear of the ship, but they swung so far out as to make it both difficult and dangerous to climb aboard. The snubbing chains held the boats some six feet from the edge of the deck. When they were released, the gap increased to just over ten feet. The deck listed towards the water making it difficult for the men on the davits to obtain sufficient purchase. Nevertheless almost all the boats were lowered to the water. No. 1 boat was the first down, but just two ABs were the only persons aboard it. Both had been allocated to port side stations, but in the confusion they went to the wrong boat. One of them, J. C. Morton – a brother of the lookout who had sighted the torpedo – told what happened:

... the passengers refused to get into the boat when we went to lower it into the water. We tried to get them in but they refused pointblank. .... I lowered the boat into the water with the idea of the passengers sliding down the falls but after I had done this the passengers refused to slide down. I then found that because of the way on the ship I could not disengage the falls from the boat so I tied a rope to the side of the ship, slid down it into the boat and was followed by AB Brown. Then we cut the falls hoping that the rope that I had tied on would hold us, but the speed of the vessel carried it away and we slid down the side of the ship and collided with boat No. 3 which had just been lowered. Boat No. 3 crushed No. 1 so Brown and I climbed into No. 3.[2]

The damage to Boat No. 1 could not have been very severe, because it was one of the six surviving boats out of the complement of 48 to arrive intact at Queenstown.

No. 3 boat had two persons in it when Morton and Brown climbed aboard. Both were members of the crew. As the *Lusitania*'s list increased and the bow sank the forward end of the starboard side came nearer to the water. It became an easy job for passengers to jump down into No. 3 and she was quickly filled to capacity. However, the headway on the ship pulled the snubbing chain taut, and the hammer had been left above on the davits. Inevitably the davits tilted the lifeboat over and then pressed it into the water. The sinking *Lusitania* took No. 3 boat to the bottom still held fast by the snubbing chain. AB Morton and his brother, who had left his station on boat No. 13 to join him, both jumped clear and swam to safety.

No. 5 boat had been wrecked by the descending mass of water and wreckage caused by the two explosions. No. 7 was lowered into the water and filled with passengers but once again the davits caught and crushed the boat before it could be pulled clear. There is no evidence as to whether the snubbing chain was released or not. No. 9 and No. 11 both reached the water safely and pulled clear of the ship. Both were lowered with only a few persons aboard, but afterwards picked up a great many from the water. No. 13 was lowered safely with sixty-five passengers and pulled away, as did No. 15 which First Officer Jones managed to lower, despite the sloping deck, with over eighty aboard. Rowing away from the ship he discovered No. 1 floating empty and transferred half of his load. Both boats pulled back to the ship under his command to collect passengers who had decided to swim for it. No. 17 was filled with passengers but the liners' rising stern and the sloping deck made the davit crew lose control and all aboard were tumbled out. No. 19 almost suffered a similar fate but the accident occurred when it was almost into the water and only a dozen or so were thrown into the sea.

Of the twenty-six collapsible boats several survived and a Mr Lauriat, a passenger from Boston, later published and sold an account of his own experience on one of them. It would appear that Lauriat, a Mr Gauntlett and a Mr Brookes were all survivors from No. 3 when the snubbing chain took her down. They all swam to a collapsible boat where they were joined by the Morton brothers. Lauriat's account is amply confirmed by a statement made the following morning by James Brookes of Bridport, Connecticut, and as Brookes's statement was made almost on the spot it would be fairer to reproduce parts of it.

At the time the torpedo struck, Mr Brookes was up at the telegraph office immediately behind the bridge. His first paragraphs describe his witnessing of the swinging out of the boats the night before. He then states that he noticed the snubbing chain, and he continues:

There was a dull explosion and a quantity of debris and water was flung into the air beside the bridge. The waterspout knocked me down beside the Marconi office. This explosion seemed to lift the ship hard over to port and was followed soon after by a second rumbling explosion entirely different to the first. . . . I remained amidship on the starboard side until the boat deck was awash and the remaining starboard boats (Nos. 3 and 7) were alongside the ship but still attached by the chain mentioned earlier. . . . I assisted a number of ladies into one of these (No. 3) and endeavoured to assist the sailor in releasing the chain. We were absolutely unable to do anything with our bare hands and there was no tool nor hammer with which to release the pin which was holding the chain. The ship at this time was continuously sinking on the starboard side and the sailor and myself still continued trying to release the boat from the chain until the davit reached the position of crushing the boat in the middle and seeing that there was no possible chance of getting clear, the sailor and myself stepped to the gunwale and dived overboard. We swam as fast as possible away from the wreck fearing the funnels might fall on us and got well clear until, as the ship rolled over on to her starboard, I noticed the wireless aerial descending through the air and was struck by it as it went down. The sea at this point was filled with wreckage of all kinds, dead bodies of all ages, many with life preservers on . . .

Mr Charles Lauriat with two sailors and myself swam to a collapsible boat which must have been washed from the deck and climbed aboard. The two sailors cut the cover off and then we began to pull people from the water until we had rescued 34. Then we attempted to raise the sides but found the supporting iron stays were broken and though there were row-locks there were no oars. . . . We rowed towards the shore with some oars and wreckage we picked from the water and almost two hours later were picked up by a sailing trawler which was the only sail in sight. We arrived at Queenstown at exactly 9.30. Upon landing we found the American Consul ready to do everything in his power and taking the names of American survivors as fast as they arrived.[3]

The American Consul in Queenstown was Wesley Frost. In addition to his normal consular duties he attempted to discover exactly what had happened aboard the *Lusitania*. He succeeded in obtaining affidavits from every American survivor, and these were forwarded by him to the State Department and to the Board of Trade in London. It says much for the attitude of both institutions that not one of this series of thirty-five affidavits was ever used in either the British or American inquiries. The State Department cleared their archive for public inspection in 1965, but of the copies sent to the Board of Trade, though at the time of the 1915 Inquiry they would have been invaluable in determining many of the mysteries surrounding the *Lusitania*, no trace remains except the acknowledgement to Mr Frost of their safe receipt. The Board of Trade took depositions on oath from every one of the 289 members of the crew who survived. Only thirteen of these are available at the Public Record Office and they all possess a curious lack of originality. Without exception, even those signed with a mark by an illiterate seaman, they place the torpedo's impact as well aft, amidships or both. Similarly each one commences with the sentences: 'At the time of sailing the ship was in good order and well found. The vessel was unarmed and possessed no weapons for offence or defence against an enemy and she has never carried such equipment. Boat drill was carried out before leaving New York.'[4] On this unanimous testimony the Board of Trade based their inquiry.

Admiral Coke was told shortly after 2.15 that an SOS had been received from the *Lusitania* saying 'Come at once – big list', and estimating her position as about ten miles south of the Old Head of Kinsale. He immediately ordered the *Juno*, which had arrived in harbour shortly after noon and still had steam up, to go at once to the scene. Shortly after *Juno* had left a message from the lighthouse keeper on the Old Head reported that the *Lusitania* had sunk. Coke sent out 'everything that would float' and asked the harbour masters at Kinsale and Oysterhaven to do the same. Then he reported the sinking and a summary of his actions to the Admiralty.

Admiral Oliver received the signal shortly before 3 p.m. and at once took it to Fisher, who seemed to take the news calmly. It was not until Oliver mentioned that the *Juno* was on her way and would doubtless wireless a full report that Fisher seemed to react. He ordered the *Juno* to be recalled at once. He had no wish for a recurrence of the 'livebait' tragedy. The *Juno* was in sight of the survivors in the water when she received the recall signal and turned back to Queenstown; as a result almost two hours elapsed before the first rescue ships started picking up survivors. A motley collection of fishing smacks and naval patrol craft was still searching the wreckage for survivors when darkness fell. All that remained in the water drifted westwards on the tide which set its burden gently ashore on the sands of Garretstown Strand and the mudflats of Courtmacsherry Bay. At dawn the next morning the beachcombers of these two villages picked a grisly harvest with over two hundred bodies in their tally. Further west at Schull, Bantry, and below the rocky headlands of the Kerry coast, searchers scoured the jetsam of successive tides, spurred on no doubt by the financial incentives officially announced by Cunard and anxious relatives. An ordinary body earned £1, an American £2, and a jackpot of £1000 was offered for the remains of Alfred Vanderbilt.

14

The telephone and telegraph cables between England and Ireland were controlled by the government, and Admiralty censors vetted everything that passed. The censorship was due more to the activities of the Sinn Feiners than those of the Germans, but on this occasion it granted the Admiralty a breathing space. The bare announcement that the *Lusitania* had sunk reached London newspaper offices, Cunard and the American Embassy shortly after 4 p.m. Despite the time differential the first message received in New York was not until 9 p.m. London time. The recipients believed that all the passengers had been saved, and the late evening editions of the London and New York newspapers confirmed this reassuring news. In New York the *Evening Telegram* reported that the liner had been beached and all aboard were safe.

At the American Embassy Ambassador Page decided to go ahead with his dinner party. It was not until shortly before his guests arrived that he received news of the terrible extent of the disaster. Page handed the first such bulletin to his wife. It told of almost a thousand casualties, including at least a hundred Americans. The dinner went on as planned, but it was a macabre social occasion. Throughout the meal the butler quietly handed Page fresh telegrams, each yellow envelope upon a silver salver. Page read the contents aloud. Conventions were forgotten and for perhaps the first time in the social history of the American diplomatic corps, the ladies stayed whilst the port decanters were passed around. Page remembered that the news seemed to have numbed everyone. There was little or no denunciation, there was no discussion of any of the consequences of the sinking, except that it was universally accepted that the United States would enter the war. The most vociferous proponent of this view was the guest of honour, Colonel House, who informed all present that the United States would enter the war within the month.

This feeling was shared by the American ambassadors in Berlin and Brussels, who immediately and without waiting for instructions from the State Department, began to make preparations for closing down their embassies. President Wilson was told just after the end of a cabinet meeting. He went off into the White House garden and cried silently for several minutes. Then, recovering himself, he established a precedent for presidents in times of world crisis – he went out and played a round of golf.

The Admiralty censors were galvanized into feverish activity, and newspaper correspondents' cables from Ireland to New York were scrutinized as much for information as for censorship. This resulted in long delays and the first really definite news did not reach British or American editorial offices until well after midnight. The *New York Times* gave the story a special edition and carried some hair-raising accounts. One passenger – an obscure Toronto newspaperman called Ernest Cowper – achieved international prominence with his eyewitness account of having seen the submarine on the surface a hundred yards away from the ship, hurling torpedoes into the side. He claimed that other passengers had told him that poison gas was used and praised the efficient and orderly manner in which the boats had been lowered. The recall of the *Juno* was denied. An Admiralty spokesman explained that she had been delayed by a U-boat which tried to attack her and prevent her humanitarian mission. Similar accounts appeared in almost every newspaper in the world. In Sweden and Germany the sinking was applauded, but the more sober journals in these countries expressed great sympathy for the passengers and stressed the contraband nature of the liner's cargo.

On Wall Street almost 600,000 stocks changed hands in a frantic hour of trading, and leading industrials slipped badly,

Bethlehem Steel for example dropping from 159 to 130. At the house of Morgan there was an edgy atmosphere, not improved as every minute the tickertape wiped millions off their portfolios. Harold Nicolson in his biography of Dwight Morrow gives a revealing cameo of the scene:

Jacob Schiff of Kuhn Loeb and Co. came round to 23 Wall street and entered the main partner's room. Mr J. P. Morgan himself was standing in the room. Mr Schiff approached him with some timidity murmuring regret at this unfortunate outrage. Mr Morgan was completely ungracious; he made some cutting rejoinder and turned on his heel. Crest-fallen and crushed, old Mr Schiff walked sadly from the building. An awkward silence followed. 'I suppose', said Mr Morgan to his partners, 'that I went a little far. I suppose I ought to apologise.' The silence remained both awkward and prolonged. Dwight Morrow drew a writing pad towards him and scribbled these words: 'Not for thy sake, but for thy name's sake, O House of Israel.' He tore off the sheet and passed it across to Mr Morgan. The latter read it, nodded in complete acquiescence, reached for his hat and hurried across to Kuhn Loeb and Co. to apologise.[1]

The tenor of the responsible American press suggested that the ultimate crisis in American-German relations had been reached. The White House had promised regular bulletins and the *New York Times* believed that Wilson would summon Congress for a special session. Joseph Tumulty, Wilson's secretary, discussed the morning papers with the President who confided that he had spent many sleepless hours thinking about the *Lusitania*. Possibly what distressed him most were the cogent observations of most of the shipping correspondents who hinted that the speed of the sinking might well have been due to an explosion of contraband cargo. Wilson telephoned Lansing and ordered him find out immediately from Customs Collector Malone if the *Lusitania* had carried any contraband. It was a Saturday and Malone was out, so Mr Wolsey of the Treasury was given the assignment of finding him. Lansing had a detailed report in writing from Malone by noon, which stated that 'practically all her cargo was contraband of some kind'[2] and listed great quantities of munitions. Nevertheless, Lansing and Wilson were the first to realize that if it became public that over 100 American lives had been lost because of the Administration's lax interpretation of neutrality, it would be most unlikely for them to survive the inevitable political holocaust.

Survival must have been uppermost in the minds of the Admiralty officials who worked throughout the night of Friday 7 May and the following weekend. Admiral Oliver called Captain Webb, Director of the Trade Division, to his room and the two men initiated a stream of signals and instructions, some of them indicating that there was something to conceal. Almost the first instruction sent to Coke asked him to 'ensure that bodies selected for the inquest had not been killed or mutilated by means which we do not wish made public'.* Coke's reply set them a problem. Kinsale was an ancient borough and proud of its rights. The Kinsale Coroner, Mr John Horgan, was not prepared to allow bodies washed ashore within his jurisdiction to be taken from it before he had performed his official duties. Horgan either intended to cause trouble or, as Coke suggested, wanted publicity. However, he was a vocal and active supporter of the Sinn Fein movement, and as such might very well bring in a verdict adverse to the English authorities.

Oliver did not have time for legal niceties. Some time very early on the Saturday he contacted Sir Frederick Smith, Solicitor-General. F. E. Smith, who had been at the American Embassy dinner the night before, was well aware of the enormity of the disaster and its political connotations. He

* This signal was the first to be despatched and reached Queenstown shortly after 3 p.m. The main effect was that the Royal Navy attempted to stop local fishermen landing survivors at Kinsale. Edward White, the owner of the drifter *Elizabeth*, picked up eighty survivors and towed them in their lifeboats twelve miles to the harbour at Kinsale. What happened then is described in a letter to Alfred Booth from Walter D. Fair, a marine engineer who was at the scene. 'They had arrived off the mouth of Kinsale harbour and would have landed the passengers in another twenty minutes when they were overtaken by the Navy tug *Stormcock* whose captain instead of allowing White to proceed at once to the nearest land insisted upon the transfer of the survivors to the *Stormcock*. . . . I understand that he threatened White that if he did not stop he would sink his boat.'

promptly secured agreement from the Board of Trade that they would hold an official inquiry, and Lord Mersey, the Commissioner for Wrecks, agreed to conduct it. This had the effect of silencing all newspaper speculation as to the cause of the sinking as the subject became *sub judice*. Many of the reporters' cables were mentioning the second explosion and quoting passengers' statements that there was ammunition aboard. Once the matter was *sub judice*, the press reports contented themselves with details of heroism and fulminations at the bestiality of the German U-boats. Smith arranged for all inquests to be conducted at Queenstown, and then contacted the Crown Solicitor for Cork and ordered him to stop Horgan's Kinsale inquest, which was scheduled for Monday 10 May at 10 a.m. Horgan however jumped the gun and commenced his inquest on Saturday afternoon, travelling himself to Queenstown in the morning and personally serving notice to attend on Captain Turner and as many survivors as he could find. Coke reported to London what was going on, but said there was no real need to worry. John Horgan has left an account of the proceedings: 'I convened at the quaint Old Market House of Kinsale ... by my side a jury of twelve shopkeepers and fishermen. Humble honest citizens all listening to the terrible story as survivor after survivor went into the witness box.'[3] He told how Captain Turner testified that there was one torpedo followed soon after by a massive internal explosion, but he got little more than this as Turner collapsed in tears. Horgan continued:

Half an hour after the Inquest concluded, my friend, Harry Wynne, the Crown Solicitor for Cork, arrived post haste with instructions from the Admiralty to stop the Inquest and prevent Captain Turner from giving evidence. That august body were, however, as belated on this occasion as they had been in protecting the *Lusitania* against attack.

Horgan did not publish his strictures. He wanted the headlines after all, and he made them with a verdict which formally indicted the Kaiser on a charge of 'Wilful and wholesale murder.'

If Horgan was an irritation, there was worse to follow. Coke reported to the Admiralty after a detailed discussion with Cunard's marine superintendent, Captain Dodd, that either a *salvo* of torpedoes must have been fired into the ship, or possibly part of the cargo had exploded. He added that Captain Turner had complained bitterly to him of the *Juno*'s absence. Most important, in the light of later events, he confirmed that the attack had taken place some fifteen miles south of the Old Head of Kinsale and that the ship eventually sank some three miles further inshore. The wreck had been buoyed and the co-ordinates placed it as 12·2 miles south and two points west of the Old Head.

Oliver, realizing that he would have no assistance from Fisher, who seemed unable to grasp what had happened, signalled to Churchill at Sir John French's headquarters on Sunday 9 May that 'naval and political considerations indicate an early public statement which doubtless you will wish to formulate'. He had no reply. Together with Captain Webb he prepared a report for the consideration of the Board of Admiralty on Churchill's return. Oliver carefully vetted the signals whilst Webb sifted through the mass of instructions issued to masters by the Senior Naval Officers at each port. Reading the memorandum they prepared that weekend, one is immediately struck by the omissions and the blatant anti-Turner attitude. Both Webb and Oliver had all the information they needed to realize that Turner had followed his instructions to the letter, and the records show that they did so realize. There was no doubt that the *Lusitania* had been torpedoed by a submarine, but the factors that had contributed to her speedy sinking, which might have been embodied in the memorandum, were studiously omitted. So also was the fact that no escort had been provided and that Turner had expected one.

One of the first things Oliver considered was the list of signals to and from the *Lusitania*. He noticed Coke's two-word coded instruction to 'MFA' and immediately signalled to him for an assurance that the operators at Valentia did not know the significance of the codes they were handling. On receiving this assurance, he omitted the instruction to divert to Queenstown from the list of signals being prepared for Churchill's return. The page containing this vital signal is also missing from the Admiralty signal register. At the same time Webb prepared a minute[4] which has survived, saying that Coke's diversionary signal had been sound in the circumstances and that it was better that he had taken the initiative rather than lose time by communicating with London.

Sir Courtenay Bennett was cabled and asked precisely what sailing instructions he had given, either verbally or in writing, to Captain Turner before he left New York. Sir Courtenay replied immediately that there had been none, as he had not been given any to give him. Webb then discovered that on 16 April an advisory memorandum had been prepared which recommended the naval practice of zigzagging as a method of reducing the danger of submarine attack. The *Lusitania* had sailed from England on 17 April, so Webb asked Captain Frederick, Assistant to Admiral Stileman, the S.N.O. Liverpool, to confirm that Turner had been given this before he sailed. Frederick replied that if anyone had done so, he certainly had not. In fact it is highly unlikely the memorandum had even reached Liverpool by then. Captain Frederick's formal letter of receipt is dated 2 May.[5] However, to lend his own memorandum weight, Webb assumed that Turner had received the recommendation and added strictly edited and convenient extracts from the dozens of frequently contradictory advices and instructions issued since hostilities began. The editing is suspect. For example, Webb ignored instructions which stated German submarines rarely operated within sight of land, but included one which said that 'the greatest danger was in the vicinity of ports and prominent headlands'. He used an instruction that warned ships not to use their peacetime trade routes and omitted to mention that the *Lusitania*'s peacetime route was to clear the Fastnet Rock by a mile or two and then steam parallel to and about two miles offshore. Webb knew that the closest *Lusitania* had come to land was fifteen miles, when she was struck, and that until she received a direct order to divert to

Queenstown she was some twenty-five miles out to sea. He omitted to mention that her speed and boiler power had been reduced. Lastly he laid emphasis on a standard message issued to all British ships homeward bound which instructed them to keep in mid-channel. This applied to the Irish Sea and St George's Channel. It did not apply to the Atlantic off the south-west coast of Ireland.

It is probable that Webb's actions were motivated by self-preservation, to protect himself as Director of the Trade Division and the Admiralty official directly responsible for the *Lusitania* and to conceal the decision of the Lords of the Admiralty who had hazarded the ship and her passengers in dangerous waters in the face of hitherto unparalleled submarine activity. His memorandum and its conclusions were to dictate the course of all inquiry into the affair, and those conclusions are as inaccurate as they are harsh. After a summary of the messages and the instructions, Webb stated:

It will thus be seen that in addition to printed orders in the Master's possession, he received definite warning that submarines were active off the Irish coast, and that he should avoid headlands and steer a mid-channel course.

In spite of these warnings the vessel appears to have been almost exactly on the usual trade route, and so far as is known at present was torpedoed 8 miles off Old Head of Kinsale. The vessel was apparently on this normal course, and was proceeding at a speed of 18 knots. The distance from the scene of disaster to Liverpool is approximately 240 miles and, proceeding at 18 knots, the 'Lusitania' would have arrived off the Bar shortly after 4 a.m. on the morning of the 8th. This would have been making his port at daybreak, which is in accordance with Admiralty instructions and appears to be the only instruction which the Master did carry out. On the morning of the 8th May the 'Lusitania' could have crossed the Bar at any time between 4 a.m. and 9.30 a.m. The Master, therefore, had five hours in hand, and could have covered an extra distance of 90 miles without losing the tide.

He might, therefore, have steered a course well out of sight of the Irish Coast, and more in mid-channel, and still have arrived at

Liverpool in time to get his tide, while not exceeding a speed of 18 knots. If he had taken the precaution of zigzagging, in accordance with the memo. of the 16th April, he could have worked out a zigzag at say, 22 knots, which would have given him a distance made good equivalent to a speed of 18 knots, assuming that this was what he wanted.

Further, when he was approaching the Irish Coast there was no need for him to come in to the land. It was within his power to raise steam for a higher speed, to have kept well out to sea, and to have made St George's Channel on a northerly course after dark.

The Master, therefore, had several alternatives as to the course and speed at which he should proceed through the dangerous area, in which, as he had been informed, submarines were active. Instead of this, he proceeded along the usual trade route at a speed approximately three-quarters of what he was able to get out of his vessel. He thus kept his valuable vessel for an unnecessary length of time in the area where she was most liable to attack, inviting disaster.[6]

In retrospect, it is difficult to decide whether Webb was a knave, a fool or both. The probability is that he was both. His omissions can only be categorized as dishonest. His statements that Turner could have zigzagged at twenty-two knots, was on the normal trade route and was in possession of written orders to zigzag fall into the same category as his omissions. So does the statement that Turner was torpedoed eight miles off shore instead of fifteen. Webb's tactical alternatives are those of a man who would appear likely to have done himself serious injury if allowed to play tactics in his bath, let alone the Western approaches. However, he was a career captain in the Royal Navy and his alternatives demand examination as presumably they were examined by the Board of Admiralty before they decided to offer Turner's head to the public.

Webb suggested that Turner should have timed his arrival at the bar at 9 a.m. Apart from the fact that this would have been gross disobedience of the written orders he had from the Admiralty and the wireless messages, it would have given him no time to spare should he have again met fog. If he had missed the tide he would have been caught in what the Admiralty had told him was the most dangerous place of all, and would have had to remain outside the bar until the following tide. Furthermore, Webb invited Turner to take the *Lusitania* through the narrow entrance to St George's Channel in the dark and without having fixed his position after an Atlantic passage, a procedure which, if discovered, would have probably cost him his master's certificate as such an action was totally against both Cunard's and the Board of Trade's regulations.

Captain Webb submitted his memorandum to Admiral Oliver who initialled it and laid it before Lord Fisher in the afternoon of Thursday 13 May. Shortly after it had been submitted, the Foreign Office sent round a copy of an urgent cypher signal from Sir Cecil Spring-Rice, the Ambassador in Washington, which stated that Sir Courtenay Bennett wished to draw attention to several reports he had sent on the subject of alleged German infiltration of Cunard. Sir Cecil had added a personal footnote to Sir Courtenay's request: 'Germans in New York seem to have known that "Lusitania" was in great danger and impression prevails that her course was known or misleading directions given by wireless in our code.'[7] Webb promptly made a selection of Sir Courtenay's reports, attached Sir Cecil's despatch to them and sent the bundle in to Fisher together with the following annotations.

1. The circumstances in connection with the loss of the 'Lusitania' are so extraordinary that it is impossible completely to disassociate the disaster from the facts reported by Sir C. Spring-Rice.[8]

It was a good if inelegant opening, but Webb did not continue with a summary of Sir Courtenay's allegations which said that possibly some of Cunard's New York staff might have German sympathies. Instead, he neatly interposed his own suggestion that Captain Turner was a spy, but the inference unless one read the complete file was that the idea came from Sir Cecil Spring-Rice.

2. In taking the course he did, the Master of the 'Lusitania' acted directly contrary to the written general instructions received from the Admiralty, and completely disregarded the telegraphic warnings

received from Queenstown during the hours immediately preceding the attack.

3. On the facts at present disclosed the Master appears to have displayed an almost inconceivable negligence, and one is forced to conclude that he is either utterly incompetent, or that he had been got at by the Germans. In considering this latter possibility it is not necessary to suppose that he had any conception of the loss of life which actually occurred and he may well have thought that being close to the shore there would be ample time to run his ship into a place of security before she foundered.

Webb went on to discuss the possibility that a spy in the Cunard New York office could have passed on the instructions to Turner, but omitted to tell his masters that there had been no instructions in the first place. His first three paragraphs were sufficient for Fisher, who seized his pen and began to annotate the memorandum in green ink, violently underlining the suggestion that Turner was in German pay and writing in the margin: 'Fully concur. As the Cunard Company would not have employed an *incompetent* man – the certainty is absolute that Captain Turner is not a fool but a knave!' Fisher liked the idea of running the *Lusitania* ashore, writing 'Quite true' in brackets. Probably he read the memorandum again because he made a further annotation in the margin: 'I hope Captain Turner will be arrested immediately after the Inquiry, *whatever* the verdict or finding may be.'

Obviously not satisfied with his efforts, Fisher then made a further and more positive note, ending with a suggestion which he addressed jointly to the Secretary of the Admiralty, Sir William Graham Greene, and to Churchill. 'I feel *absolutely* certain that Captain Turner of the Lusitania is a scoundrel and has been bribed. No seaman in his senses would have acted as he did. Ought not Lord Mersey to get a hint?' Fisher signed his name and passed Captain Webb's confection through to Churchill who was to read it the following day.

Fisher's eager acceptance of Webb's thesis must have stemmed very largely from a sense of personal desperation. He must have known, as every sailor knew, that inadequate protection had been the prime cause of the U-20's success. He realized that he had been wrong in regarding the Irish coast as a backwater and he had deeply resented the claims the Dardanelles operation was making on his escort cruisers and destroyers. He was old, he was tired and he had spent the previous two weeks fighting a bitter and losing battle with Churchill over yet further depletions of the home fleet to try and bolster the sagging offensive at Gallipoli. Hence his concern for the *Juno* and doubtless his worry that the Navy he loved would be blamed for the loss of the *Lusitania* as justly as the charges that had followed the 'livebait' squadron debacle had been unjust. To postulate further is uncharitable, but the straw offered by Webb was a plausible straw, made even more so by Webb's deliberate concealment of the facts.

Friday 14 May was a difficult day for Churchill who had returned from France the previous Monday. *The Times* had let loose a sensational report of the shell shortage on the Western Front, which had been deliberately leaked to them by Sir John French during the previous weekend. The author of the story was the military correspondent, Colonel Repington, and possibly it was no coincidence that he and Churchill had shared transport and hospitality in France the previous weekend. The object of the furore was to displace Kitchener, but in the political imbroglio which resulted after Fisher's resignation a coalition government was the only solution and the Conservatives' price for a coalition was that Churchill must go. At the War Council meeting that morning, all present saw that Fisher and Churchill were in grave dispute over the Dardanelles and that evening Churchill did his best to effect a reconciliation with Fisher. It was close to midnight when he had the chance to go through his papers. When he came to scrutinize Webb's memorandum either he blindly accepted Fisher's viewpoint, or else he recognized the threat the Navy's failure to protect the *Lusitania* would pose to his political career. More than anything else, the allegations that he had hazarded the 'livebait' squadron had wounded him deeply, and political animal that he was, he would have been foolish had he not scented political danger, no matter how Webb had blurred the true facts. Taking a fresh sheet of minute paper he wrote his comments in a firm hand. It is very evident that Churchill appreciated Webb's forensic talent for character assassination, for he decided that if Webb could wield the knife so well, he had better have a hand in both judgment and execution. 'Fully concur with D.T.D. [Director of the Trade Department]. I consider the Admiralty case against the Captain should be pressed before Lord Mersey by a skilful counsel, and that Captain Webb should attend as witness, if not employed as assessor: we shall pursue the Captain without check.'[9]

Though Churchill initialled his agreement with Webb and Fisher's views he did not initial Fisher's suggestion that Lord Mersey get 'a hint'. However, on the next day, the 15th, Lord Fisher resigned.[10] Lord Mersey received a note signed by Captain Webb which enclosed a number of relevant papers concerning the forthcoming inquiry into the loss of the *Lusitania*, including a copy of Webb's memorandum. This note stated: 'I am directed by the Board of Admiralty to inform you that it is considered politically expedient that Captain Turner the master of the *Lusitania* be most prominently blamed for the disaster.'[11]

15

Ambassador Page telegraphed Wilson at 5 p.m. on Saturday 8 May, summarizing British opinion:

Official comment is of course reticent. The freely expressed unofficial feeling is that the United States must declare war or forfeit European respect. So far as I know this opinion is universal. If the U.S. do come in, the moral and physical effect will be to bring peace quickly and to give the U.S. a great influence in ending the war and in so reorganising the world as to prevent its recurrence. . . .[1]

The President did not share Page's views which he minuted, were 'not his own but what he takes to be public opinion', and immediately burnt the telegram. Page was right. The British public did hope that timely intervention by the United States would stop the carnage on the western front, but those who dictated British policy did not want America walking tall in a reconstituted Europe. The Foreign Office instructed Spring-Rice in Washington that his immediate aim was to ensure that the United States remained both neutral and a fruitful source of credit and supply. Page, realizing this, regretfully telegraphed:

The aristocratic element of English life, which enjoys social and governmental privileges and is what we would call reactionary, consciously or unconsciously, hopes for American inactivity to justify their distrust of democratic institutions. Their feeling is that Great Britain will emerge from the war more powerful than ever, and they are content that the U.S. should be of as slight influence in the world as possible.[2]

It was Page's belief that by intervening the United States would earn the respect and the moral leadership of the world.

Lansing and House, who were putting pressure on the President, had a different motivation, and it was Page who unconsciously identified it weeks later when he described the convictions of some of the more intelligent English liberals. These tallied with the soundly researched conclusions of the politicians and those businessmen who knew the true state of England's indebtedness to America.

Men here know that Great Britain will come out of this war at the best with great financial and commercial embarrassment, and at the worst practically bankrupt ... and they know that the U.S. will have a prodigious advantage over any other country for a generation or two which (barring some great misfortune to us) will mean a prodigious advantage for all time. . . . Their predominant financial grip on the world, which is their main grip, will be gone.[3]

Lansing and House, with their ears firmly attuned to Wall Street, shared this viewpoint, and were also wise enough to realize that the United States could not now afford to let Britain lose the war. However, Lansing had his political ear closer to the ground than the others, and knew that armed intervention by the United States would never be carried through Congress. He counselled an immediate break in diplomatic relations with Germany but suggested that the U.S. be confined to the role of Allied supplier and creditor until the opportune political and financial moment, which he saw as some time shortly after the Presidential election of 1916. Until then, he reasoned, America must keep her quarrels with Germany defused until a suitably emotive moment.

Lansing had judged the temper of America accurately. While the East Coast press and Theodore Roosevelt thundered for war, the central and western states were distinctly cool. If America was to join the conflict it would have to be as the result of an emotive spark. The spark was to hand but the powder of America was damp and there was insufficient wind to sweep the flame of war across the continent. Wilson realized this, but misjudged the temper and the power of the East Coast press. On 10 May, looking 'serious and careworn', he made a speech to a mass audience of recently naturalized Americans in Philadelphia.

The example of America must be a special example. The example of America must be the example not merely of peace because it will not fight, but of peace because peace is the healing and elevating influence of the world and strife is not. There is such a thing as a man being too proud to fight.[4]

Biting criticism forced him to retract and declare that this was not a declaration of policy. In England both America and her President were regarded as craven cowards. As such they were savagely lampooned. When the word 'America' was mentioned in the theatres, the audiences booed and hissed. In Flanders an unexploded shell or dud was nicknamed 'a Wilson', whilst Colonel House confided to Page that he felt 'as if I had been given a kick at every lamp post coming down Constitution Hill'.[5] One result of this backlash was that when Wilson's Cabinet met on the morning of 11 May to discuss America's note of protest to Germany it was obvious to them all that for domestic policitical reasons, at least, it would have to be abrasive.

Secretary Bryan, Josephus Daniels, the Secretary of the Navy, and the Postmaster General, Mr Burleson, all believed that matters could be resolved without a break in diplomatic relations. L. M. Garrison, the Secretary for War, favoured a break and the commencement of active hostilities. Wilson, advised by Lansing who was not in the Cabinet, thought that a break could be effected without recourse to war as an inevitable result. After three hours of discussion no final agreement on policy had been reached, so Wilson, wishing to keep his options open, sent the draft of the 'note' down to Lansing and asked him to work on it. Lansing called in Garrison and also with Wilson's permission as 'time was short', Joseph P. Tumulty, the President's personal secretary and as hawkish as Garrison. Between them they produced a hardened version of the President's draft that would allay any public apprehension that the Administration was pro-German. When it was published, on

11 May the *Baltimore Sun* was to comment that it showed 'all the red blood in the message that a red-blooded nation can ask'.[6] Wilson preferred this version to Bryan's milder drafts. Most important, it referred to the *Lusitania* as an 'unarmed ship'.

Bryan had written to the President three days earlier, pointing out the continuing dangers of allowing American citizens to travel on munitions ships. It is probable, and in later life he claimed so, that he also mentioned his earlier warnings about the *Lusitania*'s status and cargo. Wilson, while he privately agreed with Bryan, in his reply expressed his worry over Lansing's point that if American citizens were to be warned, the Administration should have done so at the time it issued its notice to Germany holding that country to 'strict accountability'. To issue such a warning now would be a direct admission that the government had failed in its duty. Bryan suggested to the President that at the same time as he formally handed the note to Count Bernstorff, the German Ambassador, the American press should be confidentially briefed with a 'statement' as follows:

The words 'strict accountability' having been construed by some of the newspapers to mean an immediate settlement of the matter, I deem it fitting to say that that construction is not a necessary one. In individual matters friends sometimes find it wise to postpone the settlement of disputes until such differences can be considered calmly and on their merits. So it may be with nations. The United States and Germany, between whom there exists a longstanding friendship, may find it advisable to postpone until peace is restored, any disputes which do not yield to diplomatic treatment.[7]

Bryan wrote this draft fully aware that sooner or later there would be some revelations concerning the cargo of *Lusitania*. He was not pro-German. He was desperately concerned with justice and a genuine and committed pacifist. He had every reason to believe that the President shared his views and for that reason had dropped his own attempt to secure the Democratic nomination, in favour of Wilson.

He was partly right. The President appreciated Bryan's point, but did not like either his phraseology or his stealing the thunder. He sent back a note by return agreeing that the press should be given an off the record statement, but stipulating that this should come direct from the White House. He also enclosed a draft of his idea of the statement and asked Bryan to sign it if he agreed and return it to him. Bryan read the President's draft:

There is a good deal of confidence in administration circles that Germany will respond to this note in a spirit of accommodation. It is pointed out that, while Germany is not one of the many nations which have recently signed treaties of deliberation and inquiry with the United States upon all points of serious difficulty, as a means of supplementing ordinary diplomatic methods and preventing, so far as feasible, the possibility of conflict, she has assented to the principle of such a treaty; and it is believed that she will act in this instance in the spirit of that assent. A frank issue is now made, and it is expected that it will be met in good temper and with a desire to reach an agreement, despite the passions of the hour, passions in which the United States does not share, or else submit the whole matter to such processes of discussion as will result in a permanent settlement.[8]

Bryan realized that despite the campus syntax, Wilson was implying that he hoped that if Germany and America could not settle the *Lusitania* controversy by diplomatic negotiations, then the matter would be referred to the cooler atmosphere of a court of arbitration. Bryan accepted his President's draft, signed it and sent it back to the White House. Unfortunately, he took a copy, and even more unfortunate, late on the evening of the night before he dispatched the formal note to the German Government – he showed it to Lansing, who not realizing that it was the President's handiwork, expressed his personal disapproval and declined to endorse it; not that as legal counsellor to the State Department he had been asked to do so. His function was to advise on, not to create, his superiors' policy. Lansing saw the statement, which he believed to be Bryan's, as the stepping-stone to the position he coveted – Secretary of State.

The following morning Bryan was discussing routine matters on the telephone with Joseph Tumulty. He remarked that he was 'very much pleased' with the President's suggested 'draft' of the *Lusitania* statement. Tumulty asked Bryan what on earth he was talking about. Bryan, realizing that he had made an error, changed the subject and immediately afterwards sent an urgent note by hand to Wilson asking him to caution Tumulty 'to keep silent upon this important matter'.[9] Bryan was too late. Tumulty, suspecting that Bryan had pulled a fast one behind the Cabinet's back, had already contacted Lansing and asked him exactly what the draft contained. Lansing explained and added that he personally did not agree with it. Nor did Tumulty who on finding that Lansing shared his views, told him that Garrison and several other members of the Cabinet would support a protest. Tumulty asked if he could mention to the President Lansing's dislike of the statement and Lansing authorized him to tell Wilson that in the light of the new draft statement he felt his own position over the *Lusitania* was 'becoming difficult'. Tumulty then called each of the hawkish Cabinet members in turn after which he went in to the President and warned him that he suspected a Cabinet revolt was brewing. He did not tell him that this revolt was very largely due to his own activities. Wilson, faced with the choice of a major Cabinet split over an emotional public issue, decided to cancel the off-the-record statement.

The Tumulty plot of which there are numerous versions has been exhaustively examined by American historians. However, it may not have provided Wilson's only motive for withdrawing the statement. Circumstantially there was a stronger reason, which is better documented. That same day, 13 May, Lansing lunched with Captain Gaunt at the Shoreham Hotel, Washington. It was a regular engagement which both found useful. Gaunt's reports home reflected a detailed knowledge of what was happening in the higher echelons of the Administration, which would only have come from Lansing, and many of them mention him by name. Lansing had briefed Gaunt about a probable split in the Cabinet as early as 8 May and at the same time cautioned him that there would be 'considerable public excitement as the details of the *Lusitania* became known'.[10] In return Gaunt often proffered titbits of information which Lansing could use to his own advantage. Mostly these dealt with which manufacturer would get which Allied contract, but the previous February Gaunt had supplied information which had led to several German diplomats and four officials of the Hamburg-Amerika Line being implicated in a criminal matter. On 1 March 1915 the four H.A. officials had been indicted by a Grand Jury but the embassy officials had been ignored because of their status. The serious criminal charge had been 'issuing a false manifest in order to obtain a clearance certificate'. Lansing and Gaunt evidently shared a sense of humour worthy of Talleyrand.

To these Shoreham lunches Lansing usually brought a guest, and this day his guest was L. M. Garrison, suitably Secretary of State for War, and no friend of Bryan. Just as they started, Tumulty arrived to join them, remarking he had just had a very difficult half-hour with the President. Gaunt was full of fascinating stories. He told how British Intelligence had discovered that there were contingency plans within the German Embassy should America enter the war, which entailed sabotage and an armed insurrection in New York. He alluded to the British eavesdropping on the German diplomatic cables, and revealed that the Germans believed that the American Government would be exposed for its benign attitude towards Allied munitions shipments. He gave as his opinion – and left Garrison in no doubt – that any softening of the diplomatic note to Germany would be regarded by the Germans as an admission on the part of the Administration that they were just as much to blame for the unexpectedly great loss of life. Lastly he told how three Germans had been found aboard the ship just after she sailed. He did not mention the camera, but referred to it as a 'device'.[11]

After lunch Garrison went straight to the President. It would appear that he had an attentive audience, for Wilson took two immediate steps. Firstly, he summoned William J. Flynn, the Chief of the Secret Service, and ordered him to carry out an immediate inquiry into the activities of the German Ambassador and his staff. In doing so, he authorized Flynn to tap the telephones of the German Embassy and the private homes of the Ambassador and his attachés.[12] It was an unprecedented move for such a publicly committed pacifist and idealist to take. Secondly, and *after* he had seen Flynn, he sent a personal note to Bryan:

I have heard something . . . which convinces me that we should lose all chance of bringing Germany to reason if we in any way or degree indicated to them or our own public, that this note was merely the first word in a prolonged debate. I will tell you what I have in mind when I do not have to write it . . . please withdraw the message [Wilson's revised off-the record statement to the press] altogether. If we say anything of the kind, it must be a little later, after the note has had its first effect.[13]

Bryan was completely at a loss. He took Wilson's note into Lansing's room and plaintively remarked that he 'could not understand the President's change of mind'. Lansing did not enlighten him.

The American note of protest to Germany of 11 May 1915 was a historic and deliberately abrasive document. It omitted the customary diplomatic opening and closing civilities. It was uncompromising in its insistence that American citizens had the right to sail the high seas in any ship they wished, even if that ship was a belligerent and armed merchantman. It echoed the phrase 'strict accountability', stressed that the *Lusitania* was 'unarmed' and closed with the solemn warning that 'the United States would not omit' any word or any act necessary to performance of its sacred duty of maintaining the rights of the United States and its citizens and of safeguarding their free exercise and enjoyment. The phraseology alone must have dispelled any notions that the German government still held as to American neutrality. *The Times* hailed it as a literary masterpiece, the *English Review* saw Wilson's elegant phrases as 'struggling for the soul of the German nation', while the Berlin *Vossische Zeitung* remarked trenchantly that the responsibility for the death of so many American citizens, which is deeply regretted by everyone in Germany in a large measure, falls upon the American government. It could not admit that Americans were being used as shields for English contraband. In this regard America has permitted herself to be misused in a disgraceful manner by England. And now, instead of calling England to account, she sends a note to the German government.[14]

Lansing and Wilson were well aware of the weakness of the American thesis and only too conscious of the political implications should the truth about the *Lusitania*'s cargo emerge. On 10 May Lansing had prepared one of his personal memoranda, in which he correctly forecast the essence of the German reply. He believed that Germany would allege that the *Lusitania* was armed, was carrying munitions and possibly infringing the laws of the United States. He balanced these arguments with the suggestion that the pliable Dudley Malone could testify that she was unarmed and not carrying any cargo forbidden by law, but minuted that the point to stick to was an American citizen's right to travel on whichever ship he wished. His original handwritten note is illuminating as it includes the phrase 'based on the assumption that the alleged explosives did explode'. At this time no one had ever hinted that the *Lusitania* was carrying explosives and Lansing has crossed out the word 'alleged'. Lansing passed his memorandum to the Government Solicitor's department for their opinion on the international case law concerning the matter. Their reply must have disconcerted him. After reviewing the known facts they gave the following opinions:

1. Britain had obliterated the distinction between merchantmen and men of war.
2. Therefore Germany had every right to have sunk the *Lusitania*.
3. If Germany had not sunk the *Lusitania*, then a valuable cargo of munitions would have passed through to Germany's enemies.
4. There was no basis in International Law for the United

States claim that the life of an American citizen was sacro-
sanct even when aboard a belligerent ship of any category.
5. That England had recognized this fact during the Russo-
Japanese war and had published a warning to her citizens
against their taking passage in belligerent vessels.
6. That the owners and operators of the *Lusitania* appeared to
have committed a breach of Section 8 of the Passenger Act
of the Navigation Laws of the United States.[15]

Lansing retained these opinions in his personal archive and
there is no record that he either showed them to or discussed
them with the Secretary of State.

Bryan's position was becoming increasingly isolated. A
curious incident with Constantin Dumba, the Austrian Ambassador, accelerated his departure from office. On 17 May Dumba
paid a formal call on Bryan in the course of which he understood the Secretary of State to have remarked that the 'United
States was anxious for a peaceful solution to the problem, and
hoped that the German Government would reply to the
American note in a friendly spirit'. Dumba possibly misunder-
stood or perhaps Bryan had intimated his personal feelings too
strongly. Whatever did happen, Dumba promptly cabled
Vienna that 'The United States desires no war. Her notes,
however strongly worded meant no harm, but had to be written
in order to pacify public opinion of America. The Berlin
Government therefore need not feel itself injured but need
only make suitable concessions if it desires to put an end to the
dispute.'[16] The cable was routed to Vienna via Berlin and the
German Foreign Minister, Alfred Zimmermann, had a copy
of it before him while he was talking to J. W. Gerard, the
American Ambassador.

Gerard had irritated Zimmermann by ostentatiously and
personally booking sleeping-car accommodation for himself
and his staff in the expectancy of America entering the war.
Zimmermann remonstrated with the impulsive Gerard and
playfully quoted from Dumba's dispatch. Gerard promptly
cabled his version home and Bryan's political future looked

bleak. However, he had kept a record of what was actually said at the interview and had sent a transcript of it to the President the same day. Wilson had replied with a note saying 'I think your position in the conversation with the Austrian Ambassador was admirable'.[17] Whether or not Bryan did say something in confidence and Dumba broke that confidence will probably never be established. What Dumba's cable did reveal, however, was that there was a substantial difference between the State Department's public voice and the voice of public opinion. But contrary to some published accounts, it was not the Dumba incident that led to Bryan's resignation, though undoubtedly it was a contributory factor.

Germany's formal reply to the American note was delivered by Count Bernstorff on 28 May. It deeply regretted the loss of American lives, offered compensation, but refused to concede that the sinking was 'an illegal act'. It justified the U-20's attack with six countercharges, two of which had been anticipated by Lansing.

1. The *Lusitania* was an auxiliary of the British Navy.
2. It was armed.
3. The British Government had authorized the use of the U.S. flag as a 'ruse de guerre'.
4. British merchant vessels were instructed to ram or otherwise destroy German submarines in the event of a surface challenge.
5. The *Lusitania* carried munitions and contraband.
6. It had been used and was being used for the passage of Canadian troops.

To support these allegations, the Germans enclosed photographs of the orders issued to British merchantmen, together with a lucid commentary on the history and arming of the vessel. To give their note added effect they remarked that the British had been the first to declare a war zone.

On the same day Dumba called on Bryan and informed him that a series of allegations concerning the *Lusitania*'s cargo were

in the process of being verified and that if they were sub-
stantiated, copies of them would be forwarded to the State
Department. It is apparent that he gave more than a casual
insight into their nature, because Bryan, with just cause,
believed that in due course substantiation would be forthcoming. Whilst Dumba was with Bryan, Gustav Stahl, the former
acquaintance of young Neil J. Leach, was making an affidavit in downtown New York, in which he claimed that while
he was helping Leach and his baggage on to the ship, he had
seen concealed guns. A copy of this statement was formally
deposited with the State Department and unfortunately a third
copy was given to the *New York Times*.

The substance of the various allegations contained in the
German reply has already been examined. What is relevant
here is to place the consequent actions of Bryan and Lansing
in the correct time context. It is also impossible to ignore
the fact that Stahl's affidavit and the talk about others to
come coincided very neatly with the delivery of the German
note. Perhaps too neatly.

Bryan was deeply distressed by the German charges and by
Dumba's news, but Lansing was made of sterner fibre – perhaps
because he had more to lose. In a memorandum to the President
and to Bryan he noted that the German reply was sarcastic and
probably intended for home consumption. He regarded the
copies of the British orders to merchantmen as absurd forgeries.
On the other allegations he minuted:

· I cannot bring myself to admit that the facts are pertinent and
entitled to investigation. The only question which might be considered as possible of investigation would be whether or not the
Lusitania was an auxiliary of the British Navy, but that appears so
manifestly contradicted by the presence of passengers on board and
the vessel clearing on its regular trade route that it offers slender
excuse for enquiry.[18]

The President agreed with Lansing. Despite Bryan's
emotional appeals that at least the State Department make a
token inquiry into the allegations, he was overruled. The

President and Lansing drafted America's reply which, whilst it was written in considerably milder terms than its predecessor, contained the passage:

Of the facts alleged in your excellency's note, if true, the government of the United States would have been bound to have taken official cognizance. Performing its recognised duty as a neutral power and enforcing its national laws, it was its duty to see to it that the *Lusitania* was not armed for offensive action, that she was not serving as a transport, that she did not carry cargo prohibited by the statutes of the United States, and if in fact she was a naval vessel of Great Britain, she should not receive clearance as a merchantman. It performed this duty. It enforced its statutes with scrupulous vigilance through its regularly constituted officials and it is able therefore to assure the Imperial German Government that it has been misinformed.[19]

Bryan categorically refused to sign the note, arguing yet again that at least the facts should be checked before it was dispatched. He queried Lansing's use of the words 'not armed for offensive action' when in the first note he had said 'unarmed'. However, the President would not hear his protestations, and Bryan resigned on 8 June, hoping that by doing so he would give the public a glimpse of what was going on. The note was formally delivered the following day signed by Robert Lansing, Acting Secretary of State.

Gustav Stahl's affidavit received short shrift. Fortunately the Grand Jury which had indicted the officials of the Hamburg-Amerika Line was still empanelled. Stahl was asked to testify before it, and repeat the substance of his allegations. On 3 June 1915 immediately after leaving the witness box he was taken into custody by the Secret Service. After three days without charge or formal arrest he was indicted on a charge of perjury and ordered to pay a personal bond of 10,000 dollars pending his trial. Third party sureties were not accepted and without further ado he was confined in the Tombs prison where he waited three months without trial. Eventually he made a five-minute appearance, pleaded guilty and was sentenced to eighteen months' imprisonment and a fine of one dollar. No evidence was offered against him except that of Dudley Field Malone who made a written deposition stating that a personal search by him had failed to discover any guns aboard the *Lusitania*. Neither Cunard nor any responsible official was subpoenaed and Stahl was quietly deported to Switzerland once the fuss had died down. In 1924 the American Government agreed to pay him compensation of 20,000 dollars.

Lansing had one more hurdle to surmount. On 12 June the British Government, emboldened by Stahl's arrest, asked him for formally sworn evidence to the effect that none of the German allegations were true, as had been stated in the American note and which had formed the basis for Stahl's arrest and indictment. Lansing passed the problem to Wilson who wrote a carefully worded minute in reply. As he did so, he must have had Malone's report on the true nature of the cargo either before him or obsessively present in his thoughts.

I think perhaps that it would not be wise to send the collector's report regarding the *Lusitania* to Great Britain for the use of the Court of Enquiry, and that it would be better to ask the Treasury Department to supply the British Ambassador with sworn statements of the customs officials concerning the particular points mentioned by him. . . .

Lansing took the President's point. In the event Lord Mersey's inquiry had to rely not even on a sworn statement, as Malone refused to make one, but on a letter written by Malone to the Cunard manager in New York stating that 'All items shown on the manifest of the *Lusitania* were permitted to be shipped on passenger steamers under the laws of the United States'. Malone did not elaborate on this and made no mention that he was referring to the first one-page manifest, not the twenty-four page supplementary. This hurdle cleared and Stahl locked in the Tombs, the way out of the *Lusitania* impasse seemed open. The thornier questions could be left to Lord Mersey, and as Lansing constantly emphasises in his memoirs, he had immense respect for British justice.

16

At the Admiralty's request, the Board of Trade 'ordered a formal inquiry into the loss of the steamship *Lusitania*'. It was conducted before the Rt Hon. Lord Mersey, Wreck Commissioner for the United Kingdom, sitting at the Central Buildings, Westminster, on 15, 16, 17 and 18 June, 1 July and at the Westminster Palace Hotel on 17 July. His Lordship was assisted on naval matters by Admiral Sir Frederick Inglefield, K.C.B., and Lieutenant-Commander H. J. Hearn, R.N., and on matters affecting the merchant marine by Captains D. Davies and J. Spedding. These four sailors acted as Assessors. There were seven sittings, of which four were public, two *in camera* and one, at the hotel, of which the public was not notified until after it had taken place. The report of the court which was announced on 17 July 1915 stated that 'the loss of the ship and lives was due to damage caused to the said ship by torpedoes fired by a submarine of German nationality whereby the ship sank. In the opinion of the Court the act was done not merely with the intention of sinking the ship, but also with the intention of destroying the lives of the people on board.'

Lord Mersey prepared an annex which accompanied the report in which he explained or qualified his findings. In the following account of the 'Mersey Inquiry' the order in which the evidence was taken has been rearranged, but the evidence, though condensed, has not been edited.[1] The *in camera* sessions which were three days apart, have been taken as one hearing. There is little doubt, as will be seen from the transcripts quoted, that Lord Mersey was aware that discussion of certain questions was not in the public interest.

Lord Mersey was the first baron of his line and originally came from the Liverpool area. He had been an eminent and successful barrister specializing in maritime and Admiralty law and achieved international eminence with his conduct of the Board of Trade Inquiry into the loss of the *Titanic*. As a judge he was autocratic, impatient and given to bouts of testiness, much of it excusable as Admiralty cases tended to be full of witnesses who had little respect for the law or the lawyers who conducted it. In those days seamen distrusted lawyers. A merchant seaman in the witness box could never appreciate that he was there to help the court. He was nearly always convinced that he was there to defend himself. A relic no doubt of the grim days of Admiralty discipline, for this was an age when the cat o' nine tails was still a memory in the minds of the older men. Off the bench Mersey was a plump, mild, scholarly person, fond of good food and rare books. He furnished his house with an equally rare taste. Politically he was a Liberal, and his company and conversation were widely sought after, for he never lacked the courage to state his views, which were frequently radical and which had attracted the sympathetic ears of Colonel House. England, however, was at war, and Lord Mersey saw his first duty as to the national interest.

He did not approach the subject with an entirely fresh mind, for he had been most ably briefed by Captain Webb, and before the trial had received no fewer than seven detailed letters from Admiral Sir Frederick Inglefield who was the Admiralty's nominee as Chief Assessor. Churchill's suggestion that Captain Webb should take this function had not been put into effect. Instead, Sir Frederick, who had hauled down his flag as the Admiral Commanding the Auxiliary Coastal Patrol Forces, was sent to sit in judgment on the fate of the ship which his own patrols had failed to protect. Shortly after the case he retired from the service at his own request. From the start Sir Frederick either believed, or had been told to believe, that Captain Turner was guilty. He had studied Captain Webb's memorandum before the case started, and was aware of Churchill's and Fisher's comments. It is probable that in any ordinary court of law he would have been debarred from taking part. Churchill's and Fisher's strictures could have left little room for independent thought. The three other assessors came to the case with open minds. The two merchant captains were experienced men, while Hearn, though yet to command a ship of his own, was a submariner. Throughout the case they hardly uttered a word. At the end they unanimously found that Captain Turner had acted for the best throughout.

The questions the court was asked to answer were drafted by the Board of Trade. However, in the interests of security these questions had to be submitted to an 'Intelligence Advisory Committee' set up by the Admiralty before being placed before the court. This committee struck out nineteen of the forty questions which for one reason or another they considered came too near the bone. Some of the twenty-one surviving questions were carefully emasculated, most significantly in the case of the Board of Trade's original three-part question:

1. Were any instructions received by the Master of the 'Lusitania' from the owners or the Admiralty before or during the voyage from New York as to the navigation or management of the vessel on the voyage in question?
2. If so, what were those instructions?
3. Did the master carry out such instructions?[2]

The Admiralty deleted the second part of the question, to which only Inglefield and Mersey knew the answer. To be precise, they could only have known what Captain Webb had told them were the master's instructions. Therefore the Assessors had to decide if the master had obeyed orders, without being allowed to know what the orders were. Lord Mersey was further instructed that the Admiralty favoured a simple Yes or No answer to the two parts of the question that had been allowed to come before the court.

A subsequent question was also carefully tailored. The Board of Trade's draft read: 'What wireless messages if any were received by or transmitted from the 'Lusitania' on or during the voyage in question?' The Admiralty committee, realizing that this would expose Coke's critical signal, amended this to: 'Were any messages sent or received by the "Lusitania" with reference to enemy submarines during the voyage?'[3]

To assist the deliberations of the court, the Board of Trade nominated twenty-five witnesses and advertised in the *Shipping Gazette* that any passengers desirous of giving evidence should submit a proof of their evidence to the Board of Trade Solicitor. Five of the witnesses were selected from either Cunard or Board of Trade staff to give the elementary details of the ship's passenger-carrying capacity, proof of British registration and similar unimportant matters. The remaining twenty witnesses were drawn from the crew. It was a condition of the Merchant Shipping Act of 1894 that surviving crew members of a foundered vessel had to make a formal deposition as to what had occurred as soon as practicable after the event. By 28 May the 289 surviving crew members had done so, and on the basis of these depositions twenty witnesses were selected; 135 'proofs' were submitted by passengers who wished to testify and Wesley Frost, U.S. Consul at Queenstown, forwarded a further thirty-five affidavits which he had taken there from the American survivors immediately after the disaster. Frost's collection of statements were ignored and of the authors of the 135 'proofs' five were invited to appear before the court. During the hearing a further six members of the public volunteered evidence.

Not one of the passengers who referred to an explosion further forward than amidships appeared. Moreover, as has been stated, the crew depositions showed a remarkable unanimity, commencing, as they do, almost without exception: 'At the time of sailing, the ship was in good order and well found. She was unarmed, having no weapons for offence or defence against an enemy and she has never carried such equipment. Boat drill was carried out before the vessel left New York.' In the depositions of those selected to testify there was no mention of anything more than slight difficulty with the port-side boats. The passengers' 'proofs' tended to be repetitious, and it is illuminating to study the more cogent of those that were not used. For example, C. T. Hill, who had watched the arrest of the three Germans and was an experienced ocean traveller, had made a detailed and accurate summary of the whole voyage. Another typical and obviously sincere account was that of a young American passenger McMillan Adams, who raised a number of points which in normal circumstances would have been seized upon by any court of inquiry.

In the light of the evidence Lord Mersey was about to hear, it is relevant to study what was withheld from him. Adams spoke for a great many of the passengers.

I was in the lounge on A Deck . . . when suddenly the ship shook from stem to stern, and immediately started to list to starboard. . . . I rushed out into the companionway . . . While standing there, a second, and much greater explosion occurred. At first I thought the mast had fallen down. This was followed by the falling on the deck of the water spout that had been made by the impact of the torpedo with the ship. . . . My father came up and took me by the arm. . . . We went to the port side . . . and started to help in the launching of the life boats. Owing to the list of the ship, the lifeboats . . . had a tendency to swing inwards across the deck and before they could be launched, it was necessary to push them over the side of the ship. While working there, the staff Captain told us that the boat was not going to sink, and ordered the lifeboats not to be lowered. He also asked the gentlemen to help in clearing the passengers from the boat deck (A Deck). . . . it was impossible to lower the life boats safely at the speed at which the 'Lusitania' was still going. . . . I saw only two boats launched from this side. The first boat to be launched for the most part full of women fell sixty or seventy feet into the water, all the occupants being drowned. This was owing to the fact that the crew could not work the davits and falls properly, so let them slip out of their hands, and sent the lifeboats to destruction. . . . I said to my father 'We shall have to swim for it. We had better go below and get our lifebelts.'

When we got down to Deck D, our cabin deck, we found it was impossible to leave the stairs, as the water was pouring in at all the port holes. . . . Finally, we reached the boat deck again, this time on the starboard side, and after filling a lifeboat with women and children, we jumped into it. The lifeboat [No. 19] was successfully lowered until we were about twelve feet from the water, when the man at the bow davit lost his nerve, and let the rope go. Most of the occupants were thrown into the water, but we, being in the stern, managed to stay in. The lifeboat was full of water, but the sailors said it would float if only we could get it away from the LUSITANIA, which was now not far from sinking. My Father threw off his overcoat, and worked like a slave trying to help loose the falls from the boat. This, however, was impossible. B Deck was then level with the water, and I suggested to my Father we should climb up and get into another lifeboat. He, however, looked up, saw the LUSITANIA was very near its end, and was likely to come over on us, and pin us beneath. He shouted to me to jump, which I did. We were both swimming together in the water, a few yards from the ship, when something separated us. That was the last I saw of him. . . . After about an hour I was helped on to a collapsible boat which was upside down. It was at this time that we saw smoke coming towards us on the horizon out to sea, but as soon as the funnel was just in sight, it went away again from us. This must have been one of the boats that the German submarine stopped from coming to our rescue.

Later, another collapsible boat, full of water but right side up and with oars, came and picked us off our upturned boat. We rowed several miles in this sinking condition to [a] fishing boat . . .[4]

The case of the Board of Trade was assembled by the Solicitor-General, Sir Frederick Smith, who already knew quite a lot about the matter as, at Admiral Oliver's request, he had tried to halt the Kinsale inquest. He appeared with the Attorney-General, Sir Edward Carson, with Mr P. J. Branson and Mr I. M. Dunlop as their juniors as Counsel for the Board of Trade. Butler Aspinall, K.C., C. Laing, K.C., and A. H. Maxwell, appeared on behalf of the Cunard Company and Captain Turner, who were the only parties officially joined in the inquiry. The Canadian Government, numerous passengers and the trade unions representing differing categories of the crew also wished to appear, but though they were allowed to be represented, they were granted neither access to the witnesses nominated by the Board of Trade nor were they allowed to read the depositions and proofs of passengers and crew. They were not informed of the court's terms of reference or the questions which were to be answered.

The court assembled in the Central Hall, Westminster, at 10.30 a.m. on 15 June 1915. Lord Mersey with his Assessors sat on a raised dais at one end. In front of them and to their left were the witness box and the press benches. In the well of the court were a group of trestle tables around which sat the counsel for the Board of Trade, Cunard and Captain Turner. Behind them and to the rear of the court were benches and desks for the legal representatives of the passengers and crew, and at the back were some chairs for members of the public. Behind Lord Mersey was a row of chairs upon which distinguished visitors were invited to observe the proceedings. Invitations had been sent to every Embassy, but in most cases only the ladies attended. The United States Embassy sent Mr McBride, a distinguished naval architect. Even at this stage the American marine authorities had an inkling of what the evidence might show. Consul Wesley Frost had anticipated a part of it when he had reported to Lansing:

I am surprised that Germany has not protested that the loss of life was in large part due to negligence and inefficiency and that she has not asserted that on a German ship under similar circumstances far more passengers would have been saved. I discussed with Captain Dodd the marine superintendent of the Cunard Company this apparent over-confidence on the part of the ship's officers and he simply stated that the sinking of the 'Lusitania' in so short a space of time had 'totally upset all the company's scientific calculations'.[5]

The Attorney-General opened the proceedings and the first dissension came when the legal representatives of the Canadian Government, the passengers and the crew applied to be heard.

CARSON: My Lord, we have served the formal notices required upon the Captain of the ship and also upon the owners, and I understand that my friends Mr Aspinall and Mr Laing and others appear on [their] behalf. . . . I do not know that there are any other appearances in the case.

MACMASTER: I appear on behalf of the Canadian Government.

CARSON: Of course, the only formal parties are the parties upon whom the notice has been served.

MERSEY: Those, I understand, are the Owners and the Captain? .

CARSON: The Owners and the Captain.

MERSEY: And no one else?

CARSON: And no one else. . . .

He continued speaking and gave an outline of the torpedoing of the *Lusitania* which was listened to without interruption for almost an hour. As he closed a group of barristers at the back of the court rose to their feet one by one.

MR COTTER: I should like to make an application at this point to appear as representing 150 men of the 'Lusitania'.

CLEM EDWARDS, M.P.: I wish to appear on behalf of the National Sailors' and Firemen's Union, of whom about 150 men were lost.

The General Secretary of the Marine Engineers' Association and barristers representing the executors of Mr Vanderbilt and over 200 passengers, made similar applications. Lord Mersey listened to each and finally ruled that if they desired to put any questions they might put them through him, continuing:

. . . but I am not going to make anybody party to this Inquiry except those people who have been mentioned by Sir Edward Carson, namely, the owners and the Captain. Of course, it is understood that if at any time during the Inquiry I desire to clear the Court and to take any part of the Inquiry in private, the gentlemen who have spoken to me must retire. . . .

The design and construction of the *Lusitania* had been mentioned by Sir Edward Carson in his opening address. He had stressed that allegations had been made by the German Government 'that certain alterations and outfitting had been carried out' and he had refuted them in the most emphatic terms. 'There was', he declared, 'no such outfitting of the vessel as is alleged and fancied or invented by the German Government; and your Lordship will have the fullest evidence of that.' The best evidence would have been that of *Lusitania*'s designer, Mr Peskett, but unfortunately he had been taken seriously ill on the day of the disaster and was still incapable of assisting the court.* In his place Cunard had sent the assistant superintendent engineer, Alexander Galbraith. His examination was conducted by F. E. Smith, who led him quickly through the prosaic details of the *Lusitania*'s tonnage, speed and passenger capacity. Then Galbraith was asked the question Mr McBride, the American observer, and some of the excluded barristers wanted to hear: 'What was the structure of the vessel?' Galbraith began a brief description. He had been talking for not quite thirty seconds and had just mentioned 'bulkhead' when Lord Mersey interrupted him.

MERSEY: What point, Mr Solicitor, does all this go to?

SMITH: I thought the Court would desire to know what the construction of the vessel was at some time or other in the Inquiry.

MERSEY: But all these details produce no impression on my mind. We have other and much more important matters to enquire into.

SMITH: My Lord, that may be so, but at the same time surely it would be necessary, even if there were more important matters, that the Court should be informed of these things?

MERSEY: Is there to be any suggestion that this ship was not seaworthy?

SMITH: Until we know what suggestions are made in the course of the Inquiry, it is a little difficult to tell.

MERSEY: Have you any reason to believe that there will be any such suggestions?

SMITH: No, my Lord, I have no reason to believe anything. As to what will be suggested, I do not know.

* It was reported to the Finance Committee on 23 June 1915 that Mr Peskett had undergone an operation for appendicitis on the previous Friday.

MERSEY: If I might suggest it, I think you had better defer all these details until you do hear something in the nature of a suggestion.

SMITH: If your Lordship pleases. Then that disposes of the whole of the evidence of this witness . . .

No further evidence as to the design, structure, modification or conversion of the *Lusitania* was offered to the court. It was a strange decision by Mersey, who could well have heard it *in camera*. At the *Titanic* inquiry, which had brought him to international eminence, his strictures on marine safety and design had resulted in numerous committees and many improvements. The findings of the Admiralty committee as to the instability of vessels with longitudinal bulkheads had greatly influenced naval policy once the practical lesson had been learnt by the loss of the 'livebait' squadron. It is unlikely that Mersey acted through pique though he was well known for his overbearing manner on the bench, in dramatic contrast to the easygoing family man he was at home.

Among the barristers at the back of the court was Clem Edwards, M.P., who had appeared before Mersey at the *Titanic* inquiry on behalf of many members of the crew. It had been Edwards who had directed Mersey's attention to numerous shortcomings of the *Titanic*, and he resolved to attempt to reopen the design and bulkhead issue should an opportunity arise. This came the next day when the Third Engineer, George Little, was giving evidence. He had been examined by F. E. Smith's junior, Mr Dunlop, and Mersey had already suppressed his attempt to explain why there had been a drop in steam pressure by asking 'what does that matter?' Edwards was given permission to put some questions. He commenced by asking Little the layout of the bulkheads and watertight doors and had begun to get a detailed and practical reply when Mersey interrupted. Edwards at least gave as good as he received.

MERSEY: Supposing you get it all [this information], tell me, what does it matter?

EDWARDS? It matters nothing as to those who have gone

down in this ship, my Lord, but it matters materially as to steps that ought to be taken in the future.

MERSEY: Do you propose to enter into an inquiry as to whether this ship was built on the most scientific principles. I know something about these Inquiries and I am wondering when we shall come to the end of this Inquiry?

EDWARDS: We all know that your Lordship's knowledge of these Inquiries is unique, and I do not for a single moment propose to raise the elementary questions of construction, which, by your Lordship's direction, were referred to a certain expert committee after the 'Titanic' Inquiry—

Edwards paused so that Mersey could see the trap into which he had led him, then he sprung it: '—who have reported.'

MERSEY: What became of it?

EDWARDS: What has become of *them* [referring to the Committee's recommendations] is that they are being put on the shelf while all our attention is drawn to the war; but the suggestions and recommendations there recorded, if I may say so, constitute very refreshing fruit from the seeds which some of us were able so sow . . . I do think, if I may say so with profound respect, that it is germane to this Inquiry . . .

MERSEY: This gentleman is a third engineer. Do you think his answers are of any value on these abstruse points?

EDWARDS: . . . I should say they might be of very material value on the practical side; but if your Lordship thinks I ought not to pursue it, I will leave it.

MERSEY: No, I do not think anything at all, but I do not want to sit here to go through what I am afraid will turn out to be a perfectly useless Inquiry. You have tried it before, you know.

EDWARDS: With great respect –

MERSEY: I have said what I have to say, and I am going to leave it to your wisdom.

Clem Edwards took the hint and dropped his line of questioning. The matter was not referred to again, though later in the hearing he made a formal grievance to the court complaining that although he represented the relatives of over a hundred of the casualties and the greater part of the members of the crew who had survived, he had not been allowed access to either the witnesses or their proofs. He complained that Lord Mersey's handling of the inquiry was quite without precedent and that he had continually frustrated every attempt that he or any other counsel had made to ascertain whether it had been the torpedoing that caused the ship to sink or some other cause. He had not, he claimed, been allowed even to query the extent of the damage. Finally he accused the Board of Trade of trying to conceal material and relevant facts in their framing of Lord Mersey's terms of reference and their selection of evidence. It was a forlorn attempt, for no newspaper was allowed by the government censor to publish it.

The cargo of the *Lusitania* had not been the subject of public discussion though the German allegations had been publicly refuted. Discussion had been inhibited by an extension of the Defence of the Realm Act on 17 May 1915 which made it an offence to refer in any way to the cargo of any British or Allied merchantman. The Mersey inquiry promised to be the first full examination of the allegations or at least that was what the Attorney-General led the public to believe when he referred to them in his opening speech. He told the court that the *Lusitania* had left New York with

a general cargo, bound for Liverpool. Certain statements have been made which have become public, and certain allegations have been made as between the German Government and America. Notes have passed between them, and it is not inconvenient that I should tell your Lordship the statement which the United States have made as regards the requirements of their laws before the steamship 'Lusitania' sailed for Liverpool. . . .

Sir Edward then read the text of the American diplomatic note to Germany which had rebutted the German allegations in the strongest terms. He continued, 'May I say here . . . that that being a statement of the enforcement of the Regulations . . . at . . . New York, our evidence here fully confirms the statement that was made . . . your Lordship will have the fullest evidence of that from the witnesses we will call in confirmation of what was said by the United States Government.'

In neither the open nor the *in camera* hearings were there any witnesses or any evidence taken on oath as to the nature or content of the cargo. In Captain Turner's examination the cargo was referred to once in passing by Carson in his opening questions.

Were you the Master of the 'Lusitania'? I was.
On the voyage from New York to Liverpool? I was.
You started your voyage on the 1st May? Yes.
I will not go into the particulars of the crew and cargo, because we know what it was. What certificate do you hold? Extra Master.

Apart from this one remark, the only other reference came when Alfred Booth identified a copy of the manifest as being a true copy of the original. It was not. It was a combination of the original and the supplementary manifests and several of the more sensitive items had been less than adequately described. Shell cases became shell castings; aircraft magnetos and engine components became machine components, and much of the ammunition became 'metallic packages'. There was no examination of the manifest nor was Booth cross-examined on it. After Booth had left the witness box, and after a discussion of the precise boundaries of the German war zone, Lord Mersey expressly asked the Attorney-General: 'Is there anything you want to call my attention to, Sir Edward, in the manifest?'

CARSON: There are, as your Lordship will see if you look down the manifest, certain cases of ammunition and some empty shells, but no question has been asked hitherto as to them on that matter.
MERSEY: Not shells to be utilized?
CARSON: No, nor ammunition to be utilized. The ammunition was in cases as you will see; that is the only thing which can

have any materiality, but no suggestion has been made or asked as to this having had anything to do with the calamity.

The following morning, immediately Lord Mersey had taken his seat and before any witnesses were called, Sir Edward Carson produced the 'ample evidence' he had promised in support of the statements in the American note to Germany. It was not sworn to, though there is no doubt that its author was Dudley Field Malone, and it fell a long way short of the sworn declaration and production of witnesses that had been promised by the Attorney-General. Sir Edward addressed the court:

My Lord, with reference to the ship's manifest which I put in yesterday and with reference to what took place on the ship starting at New York, there is a letter I should like to read from the Collector of the Treasury Department of the United States Customs for the Port of New York. It is dated 2nd June of the present year and is directed to Mr Charles Sumner of the Cunard Steamship Company: 'Dear sir, – I have your letter of June 1st stating that you have received a cable from your Liverpool office, as follows: "Send declaration of proper customs officials showing no description of cargo was loaded in violation of American shipping law, particularly as regards passenger steamers". In reply to this inquiry I have to state all the articles specified in the manifest of the "Lusitania" are permitted to be shipped on passenger vessels under the laws of the United States.'

The cargo was not referred to again until after Lord Mersey had heard the final speeches of counsel and adjourned to consider his report. This was on 27 June when Ernest Moggridge, an official of the Marine Department of the Board of Trade, called on Lord Mersey at his home at 22 Grosvenor Place. His problem was a peculiar one. Apparently amongst the 'proofs' submitted by the passengers was one which contained serious allegations about the cargo of the vessel. It alleged that ammunition did explode and refuted the suggestion that more than one torpedo had struck the ship. The passenger in question turned out on inquiry to be a university professor and former army officer. The Board of Trade had not called him as a witness, but now two complications had arisen.

The passenger, Professor Joseph Marichal, was a French citizen married to an English wife. Marichal had complained not only to the Board of Trade but also to the Quai d'Orsay. Sir Francis Bertie, the British Ambassador in Paris, had recommended a procrastinating answer in order to stop Marichal publicizing his views, and this had been given. However, Marichal now intended to publish them. He had written to Cunard threatening legal action unless he was compensated for his losses. Moggridge wondered if Lord Mersey would see fit to reopen the inquiry and examine Marichal who, perhaps fortunately, was not legally represented. Lord Mersey agreed to do so and a room was booked for 1 July at the Westminster Palace Hotel. The Board of Trade agreed to furnish a witness who could give evidence as to the structure of the *Lusitania* and could testify that a torpedo hitting amidships would not ignite the cargo. The new sitting was not publicized, but a representative was invited from *The Times*.

Marichal's allegations had been received by the Foreign Office on 5 June and in the interval quite a lot had been learnt about him. He was a native of the department of Haute-Saône and had taken a degree in European languages at the Sorbonne. In 1902 on leaving university he had been drafted as a second lieutenant into the French army and stationed at Lille. At that time he was engaged to an English girl and he ran into trouble firstly for forging himself a weekend leave-pass and secondly for getting married without his colonel's permission. He was eventually summoned to appear before a military tribunal and invited to resign his commission. It was not a court martial in the English sense but it was a damaging blot on his record. Once out of the army, he had emigrated to Canada with his family and for the previous three years had been Professor of Romance Languages at Queen's University, Ontario. He had resigned his position the previous April and intending to settle in England had booked passages on the *Lusitania* for himself, his pregnant wife and three children. He had lost everything he possessed in the disaster, his wife had had a miscarriage, his children were separated from him and living on the charity of Birmingham City Council. His letter to Cunard was close to being an ultimatum though he stressed that he had no wish to make the matter public and that he would settle for compensation of £1000 which would enable him to bring his family together again, pay his medical bills and find a home. He added that if he could claim against the German government he would do so.

Marichal's allegations basically centred on the cargo. He said that the torpedo had struck the forward hold and that the second explosion had been followed by the rattling of exploding cartridges – a sound with which he was familiar from his army experience.

Lord Mersey re-opened the extempore proceedings in the Westminster Palace Hotel on 1 July and Marichal was called. Speaking in a heavy accent he alleged that the Admiralty were to blame for not providing escorts and that the reason why the liner had sunk so quickly was because the cargo had exploded. Mr Aspinall for Cunard ignored the allegation and concentrated on his character. He asked if he had written to the Cunard Company asking for an 'immediate allowance on account of the claim or else I shall have the unpleasant duty to claim publicly and in doing so to produce evidence which will certainly not be to the credit of your company or the Admiralty'. Marichal agreed that he had done so but stressed that this had been written *after* he had submitted a 'proof' to the Board of Trade and that he had expected the Board of Trade would have taken his evidence *in camera*. Lord Mersey then asked him if what he meant was that even if he had received some compensation on account from Cunard, he would still have spoken to the court as he had spoken today. Marichal replied yes, and reiterated that he wrote to Cunard *after* making his allegations to the Board of Trade solicitor. Mersey then said, 'I am sorry to have to say it but I do say it – that I do not believe you.' Marichal withdrew protesting that it was a disgraceful way to treat a witness.

Mr Laslett, the Board of Trade surveyor, was then called and after being told that the first torpedo had apparently hit the *Lusitania* no further forward than amidships gave as his opinion that no part of the cargo could have been within fifty yards of the point of impact.

The following morning *The Times* treated Marichal's allegations in scathing terms, and Marichal himself wrote to Lord Mersey enclosing copies of his letters to Cunard and the Quai d'Orsai together with his Board of Trade 'proof' which showed that he had been speaking the truth. He also threw down a challenge which his Lordship took seriously.

As you stated during the first 'Lusitania' inquiry that you were 'not going to believe' a statement made by several witnesses I ought to have been prepared for your despicable remarks concerning me. . . .

My impression is that you were exclusively bent on causing some sensation which would divert attention from very serious allegations against the Cunard Company. Had it not been so it was clearly your duty if convinced that I was untruthful whilst under oath to have had me prosecuted for perjury and not to insult me. . . . [6]

He asked Lord Mersey to rehabilitate his character when he delivered his judgment, otherwise he would be forced to continue with his action against Cunard and would call the letter his Lordship was reading into evidence. Lord Mersey kept the original but had copies of it and the enclosures sent round to the Foreign Office.

On 8 June the British Embassy in Paris claimed that 'it had received a communication from the French Ministry of Foreign Affairs as to the character and veracity of Mr Marichal'. They handed a statement to Exchange Telegraph news agency who transmitted it to almost every English newspaper. It began by referring to Joseph Marichal of Birmingham as Jules Marechal of Soho and gave a misleading and disparaging account of his military career. It went on to state that he had been convicted in Belgium in 1912 and 1914 for forgery and that he had been court-martialled and dismissed from the French army in 1913 for dishonourable conduct. It was a gross distortion of the facts as supplied by the French authorities and apart from maximizing his offences it had updated them by over ten years. Professor Marichal never received any compensation and was killed in action in 1917 while serving as a private soldier in the East Yorkshire Regiment. His family tried for many years to rehabilitate his character. His grandson who is still alive thinks further efforts would be 'a waste of time'.

17

The Marichal incident obviously disturbed Lord Mersey. It had occurred after he had closed the inquiry and the final stages had brought home to him that the *Lusitania* case was not so clearcut as his earlier briefings and Captain Webb's memoranda had made it out to be. He had considered only the bare minimum of evidence to satisfy his terms of reference from the Board of Trade. Some of the points obviously worried him when he considered his report; for example whether the *Lusitania* was armed or not, the evidence against rested on one question to Captain Turner, 'Was she armed or unarmed?' 'Unarmed.' Alfred Booth, the Board of Trade Inspectors, and the Design Engineer all escaped such inquiry. The much published claim that many portholes were open received equally short shrift. First Officer Jones testified that he was in the dining saloon when the torpedo struck. If any had been open, he claimed, they would have been closed as he had ordered it. The transcript shows how futile a remark this was. Mr Cotter, representing the stewards' union, had asked him:

COTTER: But it would be dangerous for the ship's safety if the ports were open, if she took a list to the starboard side, would it not?

JONES: Naturally.

COTTER: Did you go up the main companion way [from the saloon]?

JONES: Yes.

COTTER: Did you see any of the passengers going up that way?

JONES: Well, when we were struck there were about 100 people lunching in the saloon, and the moment she was struck of course we all got up and they preceded me out through both doors. I was about the last man to come out of the saloon. It was as I was passing through the door that I issued this order 'Close the ports' . . .

It would be academic to speculate who was there to carry out his order, and presumably the twenty-nine passengers' 'proofs' which stated the saloon ports were open were omitted by the Board of Trade for this reason. No other evidence was presented on the question of the portholes.

The Attorney-General had dictated the torpedoes' point of impact in his opening address when he stated that 'she was struck between the third and fourth funnels. There is evidence that there was a second and perhaps a third torpedo fired. . . .' The body of evidence to confirm this statement is a trifle confused. Seven witnesses referred to the impact point.

Between them they declared:

Near No. 5 boat [No. 2 funnel].
Forward of No. 2 funnel.
Forward of No. 1 boiler room [ahead of No. 1 funnel].
No. 1 funnel.
between Nos. 2 and 3 funnels, and the second one just under No. 3 funnel, as far as I could judge from forward.
I saw the wake between No. 2 and No. 3 funnels.
A big volume of smoke and steam came up between the third and fourth funnels.

Seventy-two depositions or 'proofs' which stated that the torpedo struck beside the bridge or close to it were not called in evidence.

Three crew members who did not see the impact testified that as the ship was sinking they saw the tracks of more torpedoes. Each man saw a different track coming from a different direction. This evidence was sufficient for Lord Mersey to find that 'the Lusitania was struck on the starboard side somewhere between the third and fourth funnels. . . . A second torpedo was fired immediately afterwards, which also struck the ship on the starboard side'.[1] Lord Mersey added that there was evidence that a further torpedo was fired which went to show that 'perhaps more than one submarine was taking part in the attack'. His findings did not mention or account for the fact that the *Lusitania* sank by the bow.

The debacle of the port side boats had scarcely received a mention. Leslie Morton, aged eighteen, who appeared to have found the time to observe and subsequently gave evidence on almost every point at issue, testified that when he went to the port boats there were no passengers there, that the boats were all empty and that no one was lowering them as it was obviously impossible to do so. Two passengers claimed that they saw a port boat spilled into the water owing to the davits breaking or the falls jamming, while a third stated that she got into a port boat but left it when asked to do so by Staff Captain Anderson. Possibly there was a distinct shortage of persons left alive from the port side to testify as to what had happened. Third Officer Bestic was called but his answers were carefully muted. He mentioned that he had tried to push out one boat which had swung inboard. He did not mention any accident to any boat, nor was he asked. The final question in his examination on this subject which lasted just over a minute, was 'Did any boats . . . for which you were responsible get away?' 'Not to my knowledge.' First Officer Jones unconsciously summed up the attitude of the inquiry to the port boats when he was asked in cross-examination by Cotter:

COTTER: Had you been over to the port side at all?
JONES: Yes.
COTTER: What did you see then with regard to the boats?
JONES: I do not remember a thing about the port side, so you might as well leave that out.

Curiously the only open criticism of the handling of the boats came on the first day during Captain Turner's brief appearance in public when he answered almost every question in monosyllables. Obviously he was feeling the pressure upon him but just once his natural outspokenness got the better of him. Cotter asked him: 'Was the crew of the "Lusitania" proficient in handling boats, in your estimation?' Turner replied with some emphasis: 'No, they were not.'

Cunard's counsel, Butler Aspinall, rose to his feet and with the silent acquiescence of the court carried out what must rank as a classical exercise in the art of re-examination.

ASPINALL: You told the gentleman who sits behind me that in your view the crew of the 'Lusitania' were not proficient in handling boats'.

Turner made no reply.

ASPINALL: I want you to explain that a little. Is it your view that the modern ships, with their greasers and their stewards and their firemen, sometimes do not carry the old-fashioned sailor that you knew of in the days of your youth?

TURNER: That is the idea.

ASPINALL: That is what you have in your mind?

TURNER: That is it.

ASPINALL: You are an old-fashioned sailor man?

TURNER: That is right.

ASPINALL: And you preferred the man of your youth?

TURNER: Yes, and I prefer him yet.

Wisely seeing the captain was beginning to seethe again, Aspinall changed the subject. No further evidence was called as to the efficiency or proficiency of the boat crews. But there is little question that many of the passengers present or of those who had made formal 'proofs' had their doubts. Both the Attorney-General and Solicitor-General wisely decided to limit the number of passengers to be called. F. E. Smith hinted this as broadly as possible to Lord Mersey, with the bland insolence for which he is chiefly remembered and which infuriated many of the judges before whom he appeared.

My Lord, with regard to the other passengers, the Board of Trade has a large number of statements made by passengers both of the first, second and third classes. I have read I think all those statements ... and I am bound to tell your Lordship that they involve, in my judgment, a very great deal of repetition and they do not develop specific complaints as far as my recollection of them goes. . . . I find myself in some little doubt as to how far I can usefully *assist the Court*.

His emphasis on the last three words was sufficient for the shorthand writer heavily to underline them, but Lord Mersey was slow to take the point and began to speak at a tangent. Smith interposed that 'the most convenient course would be if your Lordship would give me an opportunity before tomorrow morning of discussing the whole of the remaining balance of this evidence with the Attorney-General'. Mersey was still slow on the uptake. 'Does that mean that you want us to rise now?' 'It is 10 minutes to 4 my Lord.' 'Then it does mean that you want to rise.' The Solicitor-General descended into sarcasm: 'No, my Lord. There is nothing that I should like better than to go on taking evidence if it will amuse your Lordship to hear passengers called.' Lord Mersey eventually got the message. 'Then we will rise now.'

Captain Turner gave very little evidence in open court. Apart from his brief outburst about the boat crews on the first day he had spoken almost entirely in monosyllables and counsel had not probed into anything more interesting than his age, the type of certificate he held and whether or not the U-20 had given a warning before she fired her torpedo. He was present however throughout the opening hearings, sitting behind Aspinall in lonely isolation. Alfred Booth confided to his cousin that 'Poor Turner clings to Aspinall for support . . . he appears demused by the affair'.[2]

Turner was more than bemused. He was miserably unhappy. A whispering campaign had started in Liverpool and London that he was the cause of the disaster. Some militant female had handed him a white feather as he entered Central Hall on the first day of the hearing, and his wife gave him no support. In fact he never spoke to her again after the hearing. Whatever the original reasons for the breach, the disaster made it permanent.

The loneliness he must have felt, together with his domestic problems and the after-effects of losing his ship and spending four and a half hours in the water when just past his sixtieth birthday, made him a disconsolate figure and probably clouded his judgment when he stepped into the box for his *in camera* testimony. Facing him were two of the most brilliant lawyers in England and a judge who by his acerbity had already demonstrated that he was not prepared to give any witness an easy passage. In Turner's case Lord Mersey had also been instructed to prejudge the issue. Turner was to owe his survival from this ordeal to his counsel Butler Aspinall and to Lord Mersey's belated but profound respect for English law which surfaced dramatically towards the close of the hearing.

Before the inquiry had commenced Turner had been interviewed by solicitors for the Board of Trade and by 'someone at the Admiralty'. Captain Webb's allegations had been explained to him and he had been told that he had never been instructed to divert to Queenstown. He was handed a list of what purported to be all messages that had been sent to him. The vital signal was not there. His papers and the logs had gone down with the ship and he was later to tell Miss Every, 'It was all so confusing – like a bad dream.' He was not legally represented at any of the preliminary proceedings, and when he had realized that Coke's signal was not available to his defence, he had decided to say that the reason for coming in closer to the shore was to establish his correct position so that he could slide through the opening into St George's Channel without danger. He added that in order to do this he would have come into the mouth of the channel close to the land and not in mid channel as he had been ordered. Aspinall had formulated the defence that this was a proper course to take in view of the signal sent to Turner stating that the last known position of the U-boat was twenty miles south of the Coningbeg lightship that marked the entrance. Twenty miles south was exactly mid channel. It was a flimsy defence, but without the existence of Coke's signal it was the only one possible.

Turner had argued that the wireless operators would confirm the receipt of a signal, even if they did not know the code. There had been two wireless men aboard and both survived. David McCormick who had received the messages was ignored and his colleague, Robert Leith, was called. Leith had been on duty from 2 a.m. until 8 a.m. and was due to relieve McCormick again at 2 p.m. When the torpedo struck he was having a meal after spending the morning in his bunk. He was slightly late in relieving the watch but this was because at noon that day the Irish-English time differential of twenty-five minutes had been adjusted on the ship's clocks and the two operators had agreed to split the difference between them. The calling of Leith instead of McCormick was grossly unfair to Turner as Leith had no knowledge of what messages had come into the wireless room during McCormick's watch. The wireless log had gone down with the ship. Leith was examined by Sir Edward Carson who 'led' his witness into confirming the facts that the Admiralty wanted in evidence. There had been three coded messages to Turner, one from Coke at 11.02 a.m. and two from the Admiralty timed at 11.52 a.m. and 1 p.m. Sir Edward wanted only two.

CARSON: On Friday morning the 7th did you receive two Government messages?

LEITH: Yes.

CARSON: Which were from a wireless coast station?

LEITH: Yes.

CARSON: The first was at about 11.30?

LEITH: Approximately.

CARSON: And the other one shortly after 1 o'clock?

LEITH: Yes.

CARSON (*to the court*): There is no dispute if your Lordship remembers the evidence, I only want just to confirm it.

Sir Edward's phrase, 'if your Lordship remembers the evidence', can only refer to Captain Webb's memorandum or some other private briefing before the case as this was the first time the signals had been introduced into evidence. Leith was not asked any further questions on them by anyone present.

Turner was then cross-examined on his actions. Carson first of all took him through the various advisory memoranda alleged to have been given to him by the Admiralty. Earlier Alfred Booth had testified that all Admiralty advices went direct from the Senior Naval Officer Liverpool to the Captain. The S.N.O. had refused to confirm this but was not called to refute it in court. Turner told the court that the only advices or instructions that he had had in England came to him from Cunard. Aspinall did not cross-examine on this issue, but if Turner did not receive any vital advice or instruction, it is relevant that it would have been the Cunard Company's omission, not his own. However, Turner was asked in the case of every instruction except the zigzag advice issued on 16 April if he had received it on a certain date. On all of these he confirmed that he had and that he had been given them by Cunard. Sir Edward came to the zigzag instruction but did not specify its date or ask him if he had received it. Instead he asked, 'Did you read that?' Turner replied, 'I did'.

If the accusation is made that this account seems directed at exonerating Turner, it must be conceded that there is a most unlikely chance that he could have done so. Turner himself was convinced that he had read some such instruction and there was one issued on 10 February 1915 which urged masters on sighting a U-boat to take evasive action and ram if possible, 'if a submarine was sighted'. The evasive actions suggested were sharp alterations of course. His admission that he had read the zigzag instruction brought the Attorney-General's attempt at a knockout. 'Do you not see now that you really disobeyed a very important instruction?'

Turner made no reply. Later Butler Aspinall intervened.

ASPINALL: . . . You received that instruction?
TURNER: Yes.
ASPINALL: And you know of it?
TURNER: Yes, I know of it.
ASPINALL: . . . Now, what did you understand that to mean?

TURNER: I understood it to mean that if I saw a submarine, to get clear out of its way.

ASPINALL: If you saw a submarine?

TURNER: If one was in sight.

ASPINALL: If one was in sight, you understood then that you were to zigzag?

TURNER: Yes.

ASPINALL: You may be wrong?

TURNER: I may be wrong. . . . I certainly understood it that way.

ASPINALL: What has caused you to alter your view?

TURNER: Because it has been read over to me again; it seems different language.

Aspinall was to return to the question of the zigzagging later on in his closing speech, and he tried to introduce the earlier advice for evading submarines into evidence. But Sir Frederick Inglefield intervened and his use of words certainly let slip the true role of the *Lusitania* when he held that the 10 February advice was irrelevant as 'that order applies more specially to the early operations of these *cruisers*'. Lord Mersey must have taken the point because on his judgment notes in his transcript he has ringed the word 'cruisers' and marked it with both an exclamation and a question mark.

Turner was asked why he had not travelled faster by putting all available men on to the boilers and refiring No. 4 room so that he would have arrived at the Mersey bar some hours before the tide would permit him to cross it. He replied that it would have been dangerous because he knew submarines were operating in those waters. Lord Mersey, possibly scenting some truth in Captain Webb's allegations, interrupted: 'I am not satisfied about this. When . . . from whom did you get the information?' Turner replied it was general knowledge and though he could not remember how he heard it, he certainly did know about submarines having been active.

Mersey sarcastically asked him, 'It is not 12 months ago [that you heard it], I suppose?' Turner, not recognizing the innuendo of prewar knowledge of German operations, replied mildly, 'No, it was not that long.' Mersey spoke to the court in general: 'You see these answers are worth nothing when you test them. They are not worth much, any way.'

Mersey's sarcasm did once at least arouse Turner. Sir Edward Carson had challenged the master on his course and asked why he had come so close to the Irish coast. Turner replied, 'To get a fix'.

Mersey interrupted, 'Do you mean to say you had no idea where you were?' 'Yes, I had an approximate idea, but I wanted to be sure.' 'Why?'

Turner replied with what must have been the dignity of a sorely tried man, 'Well, my Lord, I do not navigate a ship on guess-work.'

Again it was left to Butler Aspinall quietly to point out that the mid-channel instructions referred specifically to the English Channel and St George's Channel, and the entrance to the latter was almost a hundred miles away from Kinsale. Turner's riposte must have brought home to Lord Mersey that he was after all conducting a court of law. Turner withdrew during the recess and Mersey invited Aspinall to comment on the captain's evidence so far.

Aspinall prefaced his comments by saying, 'What I want to emphasize . . . is this, that the Captain was, undoubtedly, a bad witness although he may be a very excellent navigator.' 'No,' said Mersey, 'he was not a bad witness.'

ASPINALL: Well, he was confused, my Lord.

MERSEY: In my opinion at present, he may have been a bad Master during that voyage, but I think he was telling the truth.

ASPINALL: Yes.

MERSEY: And I think he is a truthful witness. I think he means to tell the truth. . . . In that sense he did not make a bad witness.

ASPINALL: . . . I was going to submit that he was an honest man.

MERSEY: I think he is, and I do not think Sir Edward Carson or

Sir Frederick Smith have suggested anything to the contrary. . . . The impression the man has made upon me is ——

Here Mersey hesitated, and started again: 'I came here prepared to consider his evidence very carefully, but the impression he has made upon me is that he was quite straight and honest.'

Aspinall summed up for Turner as best he could. He concentrated on the precautions he had taken, and marked out his route on the chart. He emphasized that the captain had carried out all instructions. He conceded that he had not zigzagged and attempted to bring in the previous advice on what to do when a submarine was sighted, but Inglefield finessed this so firmly that Aspinall remarked: 'Yes, I think one may neglect that.' He did however pour scorn on the suggestion that Turner should have stood out to sea without a landfall and entered the channel by night. Without calling evidence he managed to gain Mersey's acceptance that safety came before Admiralty 'advices' to mariners. Lastly he produced for the court a devastating list of the ships which had been attacked or sunk within the previous six weeks along the route Captain Turner had to take, and this point erased Lord Mersey's reservations that Turner had improper knowledge of German activities.

F. E. Smith rose to make the closing address for the Board of Trade. Sensing Mersey's changed attitude he began by saying that of course it was not his function to conduct a prosecution but that he felt his case would produce 'some considerations which might or might not lead to an opposite conclusion to that on behalf of which Mr Aspinall has contended'. The Solicitor-General concentrated on the series of signals sent to the *Lusitania* and here Captain Webb's staff work let him down. The dialogue between Smith and Mersey must be reproduced verbatim, from which it becomes apparent that Webb, not content with exonerating the Admiralty, had prepared a further case against the captain and Cunard but had decided for some reason or other not to present it. Unfortunately, he had handed Lord Mersey one memorandum, which has survived in the Mersey Papers, and given a different one to the Solicitor-General. Unknowingly, F. E. Smith began to read from *his* version.

SMITH: On the 7th of May, a period when of course [the *Lusitania*'s] attention had been in the most pointed way directed to the fact that the general submarine menace had materialized at the particular point [south of Ireland] – on the 7th of May they received a message, 'Submarine area should be avoided by keeping well off the land . . .'.

MERSEY: Which telegram are you referring to?

SMITH: The one of the 7th of May, my Lord.

MERSEY: To whom?

SMITH: To all British merchant vessels.

MERSEY: Where is it referred to in the evidence?

SMITH: I will give your Lordship the reference.

MERSEY: Are you reading from the Admiralty Memorandum?

SMITH: Yes, my Lord.

MERSEY: Would you tell me where it is?

SMITH: If your Lordship will look 'it has been ascertained that the following wireless message passed' (it is towards the end of the page) 'on the 6th of May, the 7th of May and the 8th May.'

MERSEY: Are you reading from the Memorandum headed 'Lusitania'?

SMITH: Yes, headed 'Lusitania', my Lord.

Mersey handed his copy of Webb's Memorandum down and said: 'Where is it?' F. E. Smith compared his version with Lord Mersey's. 'It is very curious, my Lord. I cannot explain it at all. Your Lordship's copy is not the same as mine, oddly enough. I have a different document to the one your Lordship has.'

MERSEY: What is the document that you have got?

SMITH: Mine, my Lord, is an Admiralty Memorandum prepared by the officials of the Board of Admiralty and headed 'Lusitania'.

MERSEY: Could you find me any reference to it in the evidence, Mr Aspinall?

ASPINALL: No, my Lord . . . It is new.

SMITH: I have been working on it throughout the case.

Lord Mersey reached across and took a bundle of Admiral Inglefield's papers. These included the master copy of the log of the Valentia wireless station. He compared both versions of the Webb memorandum with the Valentia log and then summoned Sir Ellis Cunliffe, the solicitor to the Board of Trade, up to the bench. He handed him all three documents and asked which was correct. Sir Ellis replied that Inglefield's, the master copy, was correct. Lord Mersey coldly asked, 'What is the meaning of it, Sir Ellis, do you know?' Sir Ellis lamely replied that the only explanation that he could think of was that the Webb memorandum was phrased as it was 'in the event of it being thought that this might have been heard in open Court'.

Smith lapsed into his familiar acidity. 'I must confess I do not want it. I think it would be very unfair for me when it has not been put to the Master and had not been produced in evidence to found any further comment upon it.' Smith's point was that he had asked Turner if this was the list of signals he had received to which the captain had meekly replied yes. From Inglefield's master copy of the log it was plain there had been a message which had not been entered in evidence. This was Coke's coded signal at 11.02 a.m. It was immediately obvious to Mersey that he was being misled. Furthermore the master copy did not contain the signal about 'keeping well off the land' which had been entered in evidence and which a confused Turner had admitted he had received. Mersey kept any opinions he may have formed to himself, but he also kept Sir Frederick Inglefield's master copy and other papers. In his personal judgment notes he states that he found it difficult to understand why Inglefield had not called his attention to it before, as it must have been apparent to him from the beginning.

This episode seemed to take most of the steam out of

F. E. Smith's closing address. When he had finished Mersey spoke to the assembled counsel. He was now troubled in his mind by the Board of Trade's phrasing of the questions which comprised his terms of reference.

MERSEY: Now I should like to ask a question. I shall have to deal with this point, and having regard to the form of the questions – I suppose the form has been carefully considered – it is possible for us to give a very short answer. 'Were any instructions received by the Master of the "Lusitania" from the owners or the Admiralty before or during the voyage from New York as to the navigation or management of the vessel on the voyage in question?' You will observe, Mr Solicitor, that that does not ask, 'and what instructions'. Therefore that question can be answered by Yes or No. Then, 'Did the Master carry out such instructions?' Well, that question can be answered Yes or No, and I should like to know whether you think it wise that we should attempt to answer in detail. I will tell you what is running in my head. If we blame the Master, there is an appeal from our decision, and that appeal cannot be properly heard – at least, I think not – if we give a judgment which gives no reasons; I am talking about this particular voyage, of course; and I am not sure that it is desirable to give reasons, I mean in the public interest. I can conceive that the appeal might be heard in camera, and that the reasons that we give might never be heard of by the public, but the larger the audience to which these observations are made, the greater the risk, and I should like to know from you whether, as representing the Board of Trade, who propound these questions and put these questions before us, what kind of answers you really wish us to convey. I fancy – I do not know, because I saw a previous draft of the questions, and then I saw this draft of the questions, and this draft of the questions departed from the previous draft in this way, that the previous draft asked what were the instructions, and this draft does not, and as this was the final draft, I came to the conclusion that those advising the Board of Trade had purposely abstained from asking what the instructions were.

SMITH: That was so, my Lord.

MERSEY: Very well. Then, of course, if I understand that that is so, I should probably not attempt to refer to the instructions and should confine myself to a simple answer, yes or no.

SMITH: Yes.

MERSEY: Then comes the next question which I think is answered by the way you have answered the first question because if we are to go into details in answering the question, 'Did the Master carry out such instructions?' it would almost be impossible to avoid saying what the instructions were.

SMITH: Is your Lordship quite right in saying (I have not considered the point before) that an appeal would be in any way hampered by the fact that these questions had not been answered with greater fulness than your Lordship contemplates?

MERSEY: All I can say is that if the matter comes on appeal before a tribunal, according to my notion, it is very desirable that the tribunal should know what the reasons were which guided the tribunal below.

SMITH: Of course, I agree respectfully with your Lordship, but I think there would be no difficulty. At least, I should assume that there would be inherent powers in the Court of hearing it *in camera* there.

MERSEY: I assume so. I never heard of such a thing as taking an Inquiry of this kind *in camera* until this case.

SMITH: . . . It is possible that the difficulty which your Lordship indicates, that the Court will not have any fully detailed reasons for these answers, might be met by asking you in more detail what your reasons were, if that point arose.

MERSEY: It might be, and I could tell them by word of mouth.

SMITH: Yes.

MERSEY: Very well. Then I think that would be the most convenient course. Now I shall not close this Inquiry in case we should want any further evidence or in case we should want any further assistance from Counsel. I simply now adjourn it *sine die*.

When the court had been cleared, Lord Mersey invited his assessors to submit to him in writing their views as to whether or not the Master of the *Lusitania* was in any way to blame for the disaster. He asked them to do so independently and to hand them to him in a sealed envelope. Among the four only Inglefield felt Turner was to blame. He gave as his opinion that Turner should have headed out to sea and zigzagged about until nightfall, and suggested that the court 'returned a censure such as indicated by Captain Webb'.

Mersey disagreed, so Inglefield went behind his back to Sir William Graham Greene, the Secretary to the Admiralty. Sir William obviously did some pretty rapid canvassing for on 1 July 1915 he wrote formally to Lord Mersey, informing him that though Captain Webb's original memorandum had been written for his guidance, it did not necessarily reflect the current opinion of the Board of Admiralty. He continued:

By the First Lord's wish I have conferred with Sir Arthur Nicolson at the Foreign Office and he has now written to me to state that in the opinion of the Foreign Office, which includes that of Lord Crewe, there would be no objection to the publication of a censure upon the Master of the vessel on the lines of the last paragraph but one of Captain Webb's memorandum, viz., that the Master received suitable written instructions which he omitted to follow and that he was also fully informed of the presence of hostile submarines in the vicinity of the place in which he was torpedoed.

Mr Balfour agrees with Lord Crewe in this matter and desires me to inform you accordingly. If you should still have any doubts on the subject, Mr Balfour would be glad to see you at some convenient time.[3]

Graham Greene now had a new Board of Admiralty. On 15 May Fisher had formally resigned and retreated to sulk in Scotland. He had been emotionally and physically exhausted and disagreed profoundly with Churchill. He also feared being made the joint scapegoat for the Dardanelles imbroglio from which England was trying to extract herself. The shell crisis had led to the formation of a coalition government and the Conservatives' price of cooperation was that Churchill be dismissed and sent into the political wilderness. A. J. Balfour had become First Lord of the Admiralty. Heads were beginning to roll at the Admiralty and it is unlikely that Mr Balfour would have been fully briefed by Captain Webb.

Mersey made his report on 17 July. With new leaders at the Admiralty, he decided to follow his conscience as far as Turner was concerned. But as a whole his verdict assisted the Government. He castigated Marichal, found that all the portholes had been closed and that there had been no explosion of anything except at least two torpedoes. In the case of Turner he produced a masterly compromise.

Captain Turner was fully advised as to the means which in the view of the Admiralty were best calculated to avert the perils he was likely to encounter, and in considering the question whether he is to blame for the catastrophe in which his voyage ended I have to bear this circumstance in mind. It is certain that in some respects Captain Turner did not follow the advice given to him. It may be (though I seriously doubt it) that had he done so his ship would have reached Liverpool in safety. But the question remains, was his conduct the conduct of a negligent or of an incompetent man. On this question I have sought the guidance of my assessors, who have rendered me invaluable assistance, and the conclusion at which I have arrived is that blame ought not to be imputed to the Captain. The advice given to him, although meant for his most serious and careful consideration, was not intended to deprive him of the right to exercise his skilled judgment in the difficult questions that might arise from time to time in the navigation of his ship. His omission to follow the advice in all respects cannot fairly be attributed either to negligence or incompetence.

He exercised his judgment for the best. It was the judgment of a skilled and experienced man, and although others might have acted differently and perhaps more successfully he ought not, in my opinion, to be blamed.

The whole blame for the cruel destruction of life in this

catastrophe must rest solely with those who plotted and with those who committed the crime.

Lord Mersey was equally positive on another matter. Two days after delivering his judgment he formally wrote to Prime Minister Asquith, waiving his fee for the case and adding that 'I must request that henceforth I be excused from administering His Majesty's Justice.'[4] He was more forthright to his children. 'The *Lusitania* case,' he told them, 'was a damned dirty business.'

18

The State Department greeted Lord Mersey's verdict with undisguised relief. Each post had brought further allegations and accusations from militant pro-German Americans that the *Lusitania* had been an armed auxiliary carrying munitions. Secretary Lansing in every case except one merely acknowledged them but took no further action. Gustav Stahl's foolish affidavit had appeared in the *New York Times* and the Administration's countermeasures had been as swift as they were unconstitutional. In his affidavit Stahl had justified his presence aboard the *Lusitania* by saying that he had helped his friend Leach to carry his trunk aboard. Special Agent Bielaski had found the trunk in Stahl's lodgings – this was the only flaw in Stahl's story. The Chief Steward of the *Lusitania* confirmed that Leach had claimed to have lost his boarding pass and had been granted another, so Stahl could easily have gained access. His description of the mounting blocks of the gun, its canvas cover and its hiding place match the now known facts precisely. The truth is probably that when the photographic party failed to return, Stahl was a hasty substitute. But he was not of sufficient mental calibre to sustain his role and three months in the Tombs would not have stiffened his resolve.

Most of the other letters Lansing received were either well-meaning or the work of German propaganda organizations. However one was from a lady whose family to this day forbid her name to be mentioned, possibly because one of them in due course became a President of the United States. Her original letter is amongst Lansing's private papers which are open to scholars but not necessarily available for publication.[1] The gist of her letter and its provenance deserve attention. She claimed that she had recently been in London and had gone to tea with Clementine Churchill. Lord Fisher had looked in. While he was there he had a cup of tea and the lady asked him to help her get a priority passage back to New York. Fisher told her to be sure that she travelled either on the *Lusitania* or the *Olympic* as both carried a concealed armament. He offered to and did arrange her passage, which because of her date of travel was on the *Olympic*. She saw no guns, so explained to her steward what Lord Fisher had told her. The steward, realizing her connections, showed her how the decks could be lifted to reveal the gun rings and confided that it would take about twenty minutes to 'wheel the guns into position'. The letter asked that President Wilson be informed of these facts so that 'it would guide him in any decisions he might take'. Lastly it was stressed that it was not for publication.

The Mersey verdict was announced on 17 July, but the British Cabinet had been informed on 10 July. Sir Cecil Spring-Rice in Washington was told on the 11th, and he informed Lansing in a handwritten 'demi-official' note the same day. Lansing then turned over to the Treasury and the Attorney-General an explosive pile of papers which had been sent to him by the Austrian Ambassador Constantin Dumba three weeks previously, but on which his department had taken no action. The Treasury replied that they also proposed to take no action themselves and would leave the matter to the Attorney-General's Department. Some action was taken, but despite my determined inquiry no formal record is yet available to the public. Some of Lansing's other papers leave sufficient clues precisely to identify the allegations and to postulate what happened. These papers of Lansing's were 'declassified' by the American Government in April 1962. They have never been published.

On 22 June 1915 Constantin Dumba wrote to Lansing a personal and confidential letter from his country house in Lennox, Massachussets.

My Dear Mr Lansing,

I beg to send to you directly an official note accompanied by an

English translation referring to information about the sending of explosives on the Lusitania. I take at the same time the liberty to enclose the English translation of the correspondence between my Embassy, the Austro-Hungarian Consul in Cleveland, and Mr Ritter a chemist, whose affidavit seems to be important enough to justify a thorough investigation by the federal Authorities.

I wish to explain my point of view in this affair in order to avoid all misunderstandings and should lay particular stress upon absolutely excluding the press and the reporters from all proceedings and even keeping them in entire ignorance of my step. We don't assume any responsibility for the person, or the veracity and trust-worthiness of Mr Ritter, who is a highly nervous man, although a clever chemist and full of resources. We don't incriminate anybody, neither the British Military Attaché nor the Cunard Line. We simply put at the disposal of the State Department information which seems interesting and the nature of which can easily be controlled. The Embassy will be certainly attacked and slandered by some of the Pro-Ally papers if anything should leak out and be published about my Note. I therefore have the honour to ask you kindly to consider and treat my step and correspondence as strictly confidential and to insure me against unpleasant press-attacks.

With many thanks and kindest regards, believe me, my dear Mr Lansing, Yours very sincerely,

C. DUMBA[2]

The enclosed correspondence concerned Ritter von Rettegh's actions after his conversations with Captain Gaunt about the susceptibility of pyroxylin to sea water and his reading in the American press the eyewitness accounts of the *Lusitania*'s second explosion. He had mentioned this to the Austrian Consul in Cleveland who conducted through an eminent firm of local attorneys, Messrs Reed, Eichelberger and Nord, an extraordinarily deep investigation. Members of the Dupont shipping and packing gangs were interviewed and copies taken of the shipping documents and carriage notes of the barge companies in New York, also of the records of the New York, Philadelphia and Norfolk Railway and the Pennsylvania Railway. It transpired that several hundred tons of pyroxylin had been sent to the *Lusitania* as well as to certain other steamers loading for England. The one error in the allegations was that the consignment notes named Robert Fitzgerald as paymaster to the *Lusitania* when in fact Fitzgerald was the name of the traffic manager of G. K. Sheldon and Company, the Admiralty agent on the Cunard Dock. The pyroxylin was packed and sewn most unusually in burlap matting and was shipped in packages weighing between thirty-five and forty pounds. (The relationship to the unexplained 3813 40 lb packages of cheese is obvious.) Finally Dumba's enclosures included details of shipments about to be made with the names of the steamers on which the pyroxylin was to sail. There was also a short postscript saying that Ritter von Rettegh, in the opinion of one of the Embassy staff was 'not quite normal'. The State Department ordered Malone to send them the manifests of the steamers mentioned by Ritter and his informants, which confirmed that part of the allegations. Special Agent Barberini was ordered to check the carriage records of the railway companies and he also confirmed that such consignments had been made. These preliminary inquiries were organized by the 'office of the Second Assistant Secretary of State' and the results were sent to the Assistant Secretary, Mr Adee with the following notes: 'Mr Adee. This seems to be important. Has the Secy. [Lansing] seen it? Shouldn't it also be sent (*confidentially*) to the Atty. Genl.?' Adee agreed and he passed the material to Lansing writing on the docket, 'Dear Lansing, I have always had my doubts about the $150,000 shipment of "furs" by the Lusitania.'

The Secretary of State did nothing for two weeks and then sent copies of the complete file to the Attorney-General. From that point there is a gap in the archives. Guesses at the action taken can be hazarded from fragments of information. On 18 July the Cleveland Austrian Consulate was burgled by unknown persons and Ritter's papers were stolen. On 24 July Ritter was arrested for cheque offences and though he pleaded that he had never signed the cheques in question nor even seen them he was held in custody. On 2 August he appeared in court charged with 'utterances prejudicial to the peace of the

Nation under Section 5 of the Federal Criminal Code'. The trial was *in camera*. He was convicted and sentenced to one to three years. He claimed that he had been framed but there is no evidence available on which to examine his defence. The State Department records contain tantalizing glimpses that this was no simple case of petty fraud. There are a small group of coded telegrams in the National Archives identifying two witnesses in the Ritter case as a member of the Treasury Department secret service and a special agent of the Department of Justice.[3] Lastly, there is a coded telegram from the Attorney-General instructing the Cleveland Attorney-General on no account to release any information concerning Ritter to the press and not to proceed until a full report and instructions came from Washington. Perhaps Lansing was honouring Ambassador Dumba's request for privacy.

The Ritter affair was a narrow squeak for the Administration. The exact location of the truth still lies buried somewhere in the archives of the Department of Justice, and it is significant that the relevant file is still classified secret.

Researching into and writing of these events long after leaves one with a taste of despairing cynicism, but among the tangled threads of the U.S. reaction to the disaster there is one magnificent piece of classic American opportunism which deserves a place if only to lighten the narrative.

A newsreel team had filmed the *Lusitania*'s departure, and the film belonged to Morris Spiers, the owner of the Spiers Theatre Realty Co. of Philadelphia. On 14 June 1915 he approached Mr Powell, the British Consul in that city, and not only told him he had the negative of the film, but hinted that a man with a foreign accent had tried to buy it from him, because 'the picture gives a very clear view of the decks'.[4] Powell reported immediately to the Embassy in Washington who in turn sent an urgent cypher signal to London. The price of the film was 150 dollars for a print or 15,000 dollars for the negative. The Admiralty signalled back authorizing the Consul to purchase the film and negative forthwith.[5] Fortunately, Captain Gaunt had the sense to view it first and was able to assure London that

'There were no guns'.[6] Spiers missed his chance of 15,000 dollars and the lack of guns only goes to show that the Admiralty did not want the negative for its sentimental value.

The political dialogue over the *Lusitania* continued throughout the autumn and into the winter. The German Foreign Office remained remarkably stubborn and it was only the conciliatory manner of their Ambassador in Washington, Count Bernstoff, that prevented a break in diplomatic relations. Lansing himself favoured a break and possibly so did Wilson. Unfortunately, in August and September the British 'mystery' ship *Barralong* committed two separate atrocities that severely shook Wilson's and Lansing's pro-Ally stance.[7]

On 19 August the U-27 stopped the British cargo steamer *Nicosian* and gave the crew, which included eight U.S. citizens, time to escape before attempting to sink her with gunfire. Meanwhile another vessel came alongside flying the American flag and with a board fixed to her sides with the Stars and Stripes painted on it. It was the *Barralong*. She opened fire on the U-27 which speedily sank. The survivors climbed aboard the damaged *Nicosian*, or stayed treading water with their hands up. After picking up the *Nicosian*'s crew the crew of the *Barralong* shot every survivor from the U-27. The captain of the U-boat leapt overboard from the deck of the *Nicosian* when he saw what was happening and was shot by rifle fire. It was only the protests of the *Nicosian*'s American crew members to the State Department that made the affair public. The *Barralong* repeated this performance on 24 September upon the U-41 after she had stopped the steamer *Urbino*. The first lieutenant of the *Urbino*, Lt Crompton, reported the captain of the *Barralong* to the Admiralty and his report came immediately after a stiff note from Lansing about the U-27 incident. The Admiralty categorically denied both charges and awarded the *Barralong*'s captain (later drowned off Scapa Flow) an immediate D.S.C. Lansing voiced the Administration's doubts in a cypher signal to Ambassador Page on 18 October 1915 when he asked him to ' . . . obtain full and complete information . . . to determine whether – if these reports are true – it is not incumbent upon this government to change its lenient attitude toward the arming of merchant vessels'.[8]

In this mood he began to draft an almost complete reversal of his policy, whilst at the same time he maintained constant pressure on Germany to settle the *Lusitania* question. He accepted the German argument that in view of the invention of the submarine it was impractical for a merchantman to carry any form of armament if the Cruiser Rules were to be observed. He tested this thesis out on Wilson who approved it. Here then was the nub of a settlement to the *Lusitania* dispute. Germany would admit liability and America would press the Allies into disarming all merchantships and revising their orders so that they would automatically submit to a submarine's challenge.

Two factors stood in the way of this formula. The first was the temper of Congress. The British blockade was causing delays to mails, cables and cargoes. Valuable commercial information was being extracted by the censors and passed on to British firms. Cargoes were often impounded for weeks at a time and frequently confiscated. In the latter case Britain eventually paid full compensation, but in the meantime American businessmen were losing both money and markets. The resentment found its outlet in Congress and Lansing realized that once he achieved a settlement over the *Lusitania*, Congress would demand that he take an equally firm line with the British authorities.

President Wilson was standing for re-election in 1916. His attitude over the *Lusitania* had already alienated the German vote. He could not afford to make any more political enemies. Lansing informed the President that though he was now in a position to conclude a settlement with Germany, such an action would lead to 'grave political disadvantages as the anger of Congress is going to centre on England'.[9] The Germans had in fact submitted a note which would effectively close the matter.

The second reason why America did not want a settlement just yet was that Colonel House and Wilson had evolved a plan whereby America was to enter the war on the Allied side.

The plan depended on Britain's and France's agreement, and America needed to have some *casus belli* to justify intervention. House urged Lansing to delay the *Lusitania* case whilst he held secret negotiations with French Premier Briand and Sir Edward Grey. Unfortunately and without House's knowledge, Lansing had circulated the Allied ambassadors with an unofficial memorandum outlining his new policy for the disarming of all merchant ships. This had gone out on 18 January 1916. House learnt this in London on 24 January and cabled the President in no uncertain terms that such an action would irretrievably wreck their plan. Lansing had to turn a diplomatic somersault.

To help him do so, Wilson explained the House plan to him. America was going to propose a conference to end the war. The Allies would accept, and if Germany did not, then America would join the Allies. If Germany did accept, America would dictate terms agreeable to the Allies. If Germany did not accept these terms, America would declare war. Neither Wilson nor House had any mandate from the people or Congress for such an action. In the absence of this mandate the United States had to keep up the show of a dispute over the *Lusitania* so as to keep her options open. Not only was the peace of Europe at stake, so was Wilson's re-election. For both great causes, Lansing had to wreck the *Lusitania* settlement.

Lansing devised a Machiavellian solution.[10] From Berlin Ambassador Gerard advised him that the Germans suspected that there was a secret agreement between America and the Allies. If this was true it would give added impetus in Germany to the public and naval demands for a resumption of unrestricted submarine warfare. On 26 January Lansing invited Baron Zweideneck, the Austrian chargé d'affaires, to call on him. He showed him in confidence the circular about the disarming of merchantmen and intimated that the Baron was free to tip off his government. Zweideneck confided in return that there was increasing pressure to resume unrestricted submarine warfare unless the Allies disarmed their merchant ships, and suggested that perhaps between them they could both disarm Allied ships and avoid the horrors of attack without warning. Lansing fanned the Baron's enthusiasm by offering to let him use American diplomatic channels to get his message home, as London was delaying the cables. Zweideneck wrote his despatch which he handed to Lansing together with an English translation. Lansing read it and accepted it. It included the sentence: 'Mr Lansing would welcome an announcement from the Central Powers that they would henceforth treat merchantmen armed with one gun or more as auxiliary cruisers.'[11] The response was prompt. Germany and Austria announced that as from 8 February 1916 they would do just that.

The public uproar with which this announcement was received throughout the United States completely puzzled the Central Powers. Lansing had tricked the Baron and fostered the second period of unrestricted submarine warfare. He had kept America's options open and given her the grounds for repudiating the agreed settlement over the *Lusitania*. On 16 February Wilson wrote to him confirming that this was the course to be followed. 'I have no hesitation in saying that but for the recent announcement by the Central Powers as to the treatment they propose subjecting armed merchantmen and those which they presume to be armed, it would clearly be our duty to accept the [German] note as satisfactory.'[12]

Lansing admitted the trick long after the war, but at the time he made extraordinary efforts to make it seem like another 'Dumba incident', but this time with Baron Zweideneck in the role of Bryan. The same day as Lansing read the Baron's cable he wrote a minute for his archive saying, 'Call attention of Austrian chargé *if opportunity offers** to his use of the word welcome. I did not use this word but said, "If the German and the Austrian Governments intended to issue such a proclamation, then the sooner they do it the better."'[13] Lansing could have stopped the cable, advised the Baron promptly, or telegraphed a negating or corrective instruction to the American Ambassadors in Berlin and Vienna. Instead he waited until the Central Powers, having taken the rope he had

* Author's italics.

given them, publicly hanged themselves. He then formally repudiated the secretly agreed *Lusitania* settlement, thereby showing all America that Wilson's administration was firm and unyielding after all, and that President Wilson was the man who deserved their vote in the forthcoming election.

Bolstered by confidence Colonel House initialled the secret agreement with Sir Edward Grey on 22 February. Sir Edward had previously made a memorandum for the benefit of his Cabinet colleagues and the phraseology is interesting.

Colonel House told me that President Wilson was ready on hearing from France and England that the moment was opportune, to propose that a conference should be summoned to put an end to the war. Should the Allies accept this proposal and should Germany refuse it, the United States would *probably* enter the war against Germany. Colonel House expressed the opinion that if such a conference met it would secure peace on terms not unfavourable to the Allies, and if it failed to secure peace the United States would* leave the conference as a belligerent on the side of the Allies. . . .

What House and Wilson did not realize was that neither Britain nor France had any intention of allowing America to take a peace initiative. If eventually intervention was needed, they felt that America should enter the war on the same terms as the Allies and not under any moral obligation. The House–Grey Agreement was useful only to the extent that if its contents were leaked, America's integrity as an honest broker would be hopelessly compromised. It was a splendid insurance that the United States would continue to supply the tools and the credit whilst the Allies would finish the job.

* When President Wilson saw the draft he inserted the word 'probably' in this space.

19

The diplomatic impasse engineered by Lansing hindered the numerous claims for compensation filed by the survivors and dependants of those who had lost their lives. The State Department took the view that any attempt to prejudge the matter in the civil courts would prejudice America's negotiating position. For this reason they refused to release any information whatsoever to the numerous firms of attorneys engaged. Several of the claimants had given detailed statements to Consul Frost in Queenstown, but had not retained copies for their own use. Their applications for a sight of their own statements met with a remarkable degree of evasion. On 9 September 1915 Messrs Hunt, Hill and Betts, the New York attorneys for Mrs Gertrude Adams – whose husband had been drowned and whose son's affidavit has already been quoted – applied for a copy of the son's statement. The State Department referred them to the Treasury, which in turn referred them to the Attorney-General. From here they were advised to contact Consul Frost direct and when they did so he advised them that they should put their request to the State Department, who predictably sent them a duplicate of their previous reply referring the inquiry to the Treasury. Hunt, Hill and Betts never obtained Adams' affidavit and eventually asked him to make another. By this time he was serving with the American army and the military authorities refused to allow him to testify without State Department clearance which was not forthcoming until March 1918. Nevertheless ninety-four claimants represented by thirteen law firms continued to press their claims which totalled slightly over five million dollars.

Each alleged negligence by Cunard, citing the design, stability, open portholes, davits and navigation. Five specifically alleged that the *Lusitania* was carrying contraband and munitions of war, Canadian and other military personnel and that she was an auxiliary of the Royal Navy. Dudley Field Malone was joined as a co-defender with the company on these claims on the grounds that he should not have issued a clearance certificate. Should any one of the allegations be proved, Malone would automatically be indicted for involuntary manslaughter. The potential legal embarrassments were as dangerous as the political.

Cunard, faced with the multiplicity of claims, took the same defensive action as had the White Star Line after the loss of the *Titanic*. They presented a petition before the New York courts to 'limit their liability'. If this plea was accepted by the court it would have the effect of all the several actions against them being heard at the same time. An American judge, once he had agreed to allow Cunard to present such a plea, would hear all the evidence of all the claimants and his decision would be binding upon everyone. Should he find for Cunard, their liability would be limited to the value of the wreck strippings and salvage recovered, together with the monies received for passenger fares and cargo freight, less the costs of forwarding the shipwrecked passengers from Kinsale to Liverpool. Should negligence be proved against the company, damages would be limited to whatever amount had been paid into court at the time the 'plea in limitation' had been presented. Only if the claimants could prove that Cunard had broken the law or were 'privy to the disaster' could the damages be higher than the sum paid into court.

Cunard's solicitors, Hill, Dickinson and Co. of Liverpool, instructed Lord, Day and Lord of New York to enter 'a plea in limitation' on their behalf and pay 100,000 dollars into court. On 23 June 1916, in order to sustain this action Hill, Dickinson wrote to the Admiralty requesting permission 'to exonerate their clients'.[1] They asked that *all* the evidence presented before Lord Mersey be made available to them together with *all* the instructions and written messages which the Admiralty had withheld. No reply was received to this request, which was repeated at monthly intervals until December of that year. On 4 January 1917 Hill, Dickinson had to write regretfully to Lord, Day and Lord that:

We have been quite unable to obtain any answer from the Admiralty regarding our application as to what particulars may be furnished to you for the purposes of the proceedings in your country, and we are afraid that in the absence of instructions we cannot supply you with information. It will, of course, be readily appreciated that at the present time there is perhaps not much opportunity for officials of the Admiralty to deal with enquiries of this nature . . . but we had fully expected to be in a position to send you some definite answer long before this.[2]

Hill, Dickinson shared their American legal advisers' opinion that the Admiralty's tardiness would gravely prejudice their case.

America's entry into the war on 6 April 1917 promoted a slightly more cooperative attitude, for the Admiralty agreed that all the evidence laid before Lord Mersey in *open court* could be used in the American hearings. Sir William Graham Greene strengthened this evidence by writing a letter which implied that any other instructions or advices to the master which may have been given were not relevant to the navigation of the vessel and were only withheld so as not to assist the Germans. His letter, which was eventually accepted as evidence by the New York district court, contained the falsehood that the evidence heard in open court before Lord Mersey 'does include *all** the wireless messages which were sent by or on behalf of the Admiralty to and received by the Master of the "Lusitania" on her last voyage from New York'.[3]

In retrospect, Cunard's case had little on which it could be based but Lucius Beers, the senior partner of Lord, Day and Lord strove to construct a formidable legal edifice. The state of war also proved a godsend. Beers prevailed on all the lawyers

* Author's italics.

acting for the claimants to accept that because of the war it would be in order to take much of the evidence in London before a commissioner for oaths. At the same time he managed to obtain agreement that all the 'published' evidence established before Lord Mersey should be accepted *in toto*. This meant that Lord Mersey's findings became facts. It was not generally known that the 'published' evidence contained very little more than the introductory speeches of Sir Edward Carson and Sir F. E. Smith and their examinations of carefully selected members of the crew and passengers. Lucius Beers himself was aware that when the crunch came before the judge in New York, he would need some more witnesses, and anxiously cabled Hill, Dickinson saying it was essential that Captain Turner and as many others as possible should come to New York. Hill, Dickinson very wisely thought otherwise, and took a formal opinion from the redoubtable Butler Aspinall, who stated:

Captain Turner will be the principal witness. Whilst referring to him we might parenthetically deal with the point which was put to us in consultation viz:—whether in the American proceedings he should be examined in England or America. We emphatically advise the former. Captain Turner is a difficult witness and wants extremely careful and delicate handling. His idiosyncrasies are known here to those who have the handling of him; they are not known to the defendant's advisers in America, and without intending any disrespect to the extremely able counsel conducting the proceedings in America, we consider that Captain Turner's evidence is likely to be more satisfactory, as an article grown in England, than as the product of American forensic talent. . . . In fact speaking generally we think that as few witnesses as possible should be examined in America . . . we do not advise calling any passengers; none of them is of any real value, and passengers are usually dangerous witnesses.[4]

Meanwhile Lucius Beers wrote to Secretary Lansing, asking if there were still 'objections to the commencement of the *Lusitania* proceedings' and remarking that if the case was heard after the cessation of hostilities, the result might 'put those parties who have been instructing me at a disadvantage'.[5] On 24 May 1917 Lansing replied with a copy to the Department of

Justice, that the State Department had no objection, but that all parties must first submit their evidence to the Department of Justice in case there should prove a need to take part or all of the proceedings *in camera*.

In London, British claimants had also filed actions against Cunard and Hill, Dickinson advised Alfred Booth, Cunard's Chairman, that in Counsel's opinion it would be far better to have the American case decided first as it would be heard by a judge sitting alone and not by a jury. The letter continued.

Subject to your approval, we therefore propose to do everything we can to delay the trial of the English actions. . . . If you approve of Counsel's advice being followed, we propose to apply to the Court for an order for the evidence of the clerks who issued the tickets to be taken on commission in America. If this order were made, it would have the effect of the English actions not being heard for several months.

Booth approved and that is what was done.

The evidence for the American proceedings was heard in London by a commissioner sitting in the Law Society's building in Chancery Lane. No public were admitted but otherwise the cast was almost identical to that of the Board of Trade's production. A junior executive of Cunard, Charles Cotterel, watched the proceedings. His diary has survived.

Monday 11 June 1917
Left Liverpool by the 9.40 train with Mr Peskett and Captain Turner. Met Mr Pershouse* of Hill, Dickinson at the Howard Hotel at 3 p.m. Went to Paper Buildings for consultation with Counsel.
Counsel went over various points in the probable evidence and questions of procedure. Mr Aspinall decided on second thoughts not to go through the evidence with Captain Turner as it might flurry

---

* Managing Clerk of Hill, Dickinson but also a qualified barrister.

him. It was mentioned that the commissioner appointed was a Mr R. V. Wynne. On the name being mentioned both counsel said they knew him and their opinion seemed to be that he was an 'old woman'. . . . We then returned to the Howard Hotel where Mr Pershouse of Hill, Dickinson went over many of the salient points with Mr Peskett and Captain Turner which took until 7.15 p.m.

Tuesday 12 June

Met Hill, Dickinson and Co. and the various witnesses at the Hotel at 10.15 and proceeded to the Incorporated Law Society's Hall in Chancery Lane. The Commissioner took his seat at 11 a.m. and took the oath himself and then arranged procedure with both sides, namely Messrs Butler, Aspinall and Raeburn for the Cunard Company, Mr Scanlan for the Americans. The shorthand writer was called and the first witness called was Mr Peskett.

Mr Raeburn examined Mr Peskett on the construction of the ship, bulkheads, watertight doors, boats, davits and passenger and crew capacity. Mr Scanlan closely cross-examined him on various points the principal being mechanical davits versus the old style. . . . He also examined very closely on the question of the stability of the ship with compartments flooded. Mr Peskett said that the Company calculated that the ship would float upright with any two adjacent compartments flooded. Mr Scanlan tried to make him admit that this supposition was wrong in view of what happened.[6]

However, it appeared that Peskett had no precise knowledge of what had happened, and had not had either the opportunity or the inclination to find out. Although he had designed the *Lusitania*, he even refused to indicate the location of its boiler rooms. The shorthand transcript shows how he blocked Mr Scanlan's inquiries.

SCANLAN: Have you heard where she was struck by the torpedo or torpedoes?

PESKETT: Unofficially I have, Numbers three and four boiler rooms were opened to the sea by the first torpedo.

SCANLAN: Can you indicate on this plan of the ship those compartments which you understand to have been opened by the torpedo or torpedoes?

PESKETT: No; I cannot, I had nothing to do with this. I was

ill at the time. I was away six months . . . so I cannot speak on the subject.

SCANLAN: Have you read the petition which the Cunard Steamship Company has presented to the Court in America?

PESKETT: No, I have not.

SCANLAN: With regard to the getting out of the boats, have you been informed of the vessel taking a heavy list?

PESKETT: As I have said before I am not at all acquainted with the details of the loss of the ship.

SCANLAN: And it has not, I gather, been your business at all to make yourself acquainted with the circumstances which prevailed when the boats were being launched?

PESKETT: I have not done so.[7]

Scanlan managed to obtain an admission that, since the loss, geared davits had become compulsory on all passenger ships, but Peskett justified his use of what he described as 'old-fashioned davits' as they were more reliable. His scientific calculations had indeed 'been upset' as Cunard's marine superintendent had confided to Consul Frost, but Peskett had obviously put his head in the sand and had no wish to enlighten himself. His evidence can only be described as unhelpful.

Sir Alfred Booth (he had been made a baronet the previous January for his services to British shipping) also gave evidence. He too professed ignorance of what had happened. He claimed that he had not even read the transcript of the Mersey Inquiry and had no idea what wireless messages or other instructions had been given to the captain. Scanlan drew his attention to the fact that when Cunard had presented their plea to the American courts, Sir Alfred had sworn an affidavit that the instructions and signals as disclosed before Lord Mersey were the only ones that had passed. He asked Sir Alfred how, if he was unaware of them, could he have made such a statement? Sir Alfred explained that he was assured by those in authority that this was so. 'Who by?' asked Scanlan. 'The Admiralty,' Booth replied and explained that he had had a series of interviews but could not recall with whom he had spoken. Scanlan expressed surprise that the chairman of Cunard could not give more specific answers to what were very simple questions. Sir Alfred lost his temper. 'I have received all kinds of notes and requests from the Admiralty and I can no more tell you what they are than fly. So it is no use asking me . . . you might as well drop it, because I cannot answer you truthfully because I do not know.'

Under pressure from Scanlan, Booth admitted that there were other instructions but that he himself was unaware of their content. Commissioner Wynne taking the evidence intervened and asked him, 'Do I understand that these questions which are causing such difficulty refer to a state secret?'

'You are correct,' replied Sir Alfred.

Captain Turner, despite his prior coaching, also conceded that there had been a further instruction and gave a clue as to what it had contained.

SCANLAN: May I take it that you have at present in your mind all the instructions that the Admiralty issued?

TURNER: Yes, pretty well.

SCANLAN: Those which are disclosed by your company and those which are not disclosed . . .

TURNER: It would be a task to tell you what instructions I have had from the Admiralty and everyone else – I could paper the walls with them.

SCANLAN: I am talking about the instructions in this [he showed Turner the published transcript of Lord Mersey's Inquiry] with these three you could not do much papering.

TURNER: No, that is right.

SCANLAN: I understand some other instructions were received from the Admiralty than these mentioned here?

TURNER: You are quite right.

SCANLAN: I call for those instructions.

TURNER: I am afraid that you will have to call.

SCANLAN: Do you refuse?

TURNER: Yes. I refuse absolutely. All I can do is to respectfully refer you to the Admiralty.

SCANLAN: Had you received before the ship sailed from New

York on the 1 May 1915 any Admiralty instructions in addition to those which you have disclosed in answer to Mr Butler Aspinall?

TURNER: I cannot remember anything about them at all.

SCANLAN: Were the other instructions, that is the instructions which are not disclosed, advices from the Admiralty with reference to the navigation of the *Lusitania*?

TURNER: Yes, they tell which course to take.

Unbelievably, Scanlan, having established the existence and significance of the concealed message, did not follow up his advantage. Nor did he compare Turner's admission that the withheld instructions dealt with the navigation of the *Lusitania* with Sir William Graham Greene's letter which was read to the court after Turner had stepped down. Its text deserves a second examination.

... I am to state however that the memorandum ... does in fact include all the instructions advice and notices given to the 'Lusitania' which are relevant to the issues raised as to the navigation of the vessel and further that it does include all the wireless messages which were sent by or on behalf of the Admiralty to and received by the Master of the 'Lusitania'.[8]

Apart from establishing that the Admiralty was withholding material evidence, the evidence taken in London for the American trial proved to be of little use to the claimants. Turner, Peskett and Sir Alfred all escaped the rigours of cross-examination by American attorneys who probably would not have been so accommodating as Mr Scanlan. Transcripts of the London hearings were forwarded to all the parties involved and Cunard applied for a date to be set for the trial. Judge Julius B. Mayer scheduled 24 October 1917.

The claimants cross-petitioned to have the trial delayed until after the war, on the grounds that it would then be in order to force the Admiralty to produce the withheld evidence. Mayer – after consulting with the Chief Justice – turned them down. Angered by his refusal John M. Nolan of Messrs Nolan, Friedland and Digbey, attorneys for one of the claimants, asked

Senator La Follette, an ardent pacifist and a powerful publisher to lobby the Department of Justice. La Follette exceeded his brief. At that time his twin platforms were pacifism and women's suffrage. On behalf of Nolan, he approached William Jennings Bryan for his background knowledge and then Dudley Field Malone who had publicly supported women's suffrage. His approach to Malone did not go unnoticed by Special Agent Bruce Bielaski who reported the matter to the President. Wilson asked Secretary of the Treasury McAdoo to detail a private secretary to prepare a confidential report on Malone's conduct and attendance to his duties. The private secretary, W. B. Clagett, wrote personally to Wilson on 7 September that Malone was neglecting his duties and enclosed his attendance record which showed he was hardly ever in the office.[9] The same day Wilson asked for and obtained Malone's letter of resignation, which drew attention to the work he had done over the *Lusitania* and announced that he intended to devote his life to the cause of women's suffrage as he was not content with the Administration's attitude to it.

A fortnight later on 20 September, Senator La Follette made a speech at St Paul, Missouri, which he devoted to the *Lusitania* and Lansing's doctrine that the presence of American citizens aboard a belligerent vessel should give immunity. He claimed publicly: 'Four days before the *Lusitania* sailed, President Wilson was warned in person by Secretary of State Bryan that the *Lusitania* had 6,000,000 rounds of ammunition on board, besides explosives; and that the passengers who proposed to sail on that vessel were sailing in violation of statute of this country.' He went on to explain the spirit of the Passenger Act of 1882 and continued: 'Secretary Bryan appealed to President Wilson to stop passengers from sailing on the *Lusitania*. I am giving you some history that probably has not been given you here before.'[10]

The speech, which was widely reported, drew an angry response from the Senate which formed a committee to demand La Follette's expulsion. If the motion had been debated, a great many issues which remained unresolved for many years would have been exposed. To prepare his defence before the Senate, La Follette demanded the full manifest of the *Lusitania* together with copies of Malone's report and all other relevant information which the Treasury might hold. The Treasury referred him to Lansing who replied that these documents had been transferred to the archives as they were secret documents. Malone then wrote to Lansing and the Chairman of the Senate Committee offering to testify in La Follette's defence. Lansing had to act quickly. The Senate dropped their expulsion demand, Malone kept his silence and Judge Mayer adjourned the Cunard Company's petition until the following law term. La Follette had achieved a six-month delay for John Nolan. Unfortunately for the claimants, peace was still a year away.

Judge Mayer convened the hearing on 7 April 1918. It was a sterile and barely reported affair, despite the multiplicity of lawyers and the emotional issues involved. America had been at war for a year and tempers and attitudes had changed when the casualty lists began to come in. Before any evidence was taken, all allegations referring to contraband munitions, troops or guns were dropped. Judge Mayer expressed his pleasure by remarking, 'Good, now that story is forever disposed of.'[11]

New evidence relating to the stability of the ship was given, but on the orders of the Secretary of the Navy[12] it was given *in camera* and no reference to the sitting was allowed in the Court Notices, the *Law Journal* or the daily calendar of cases. Basically it confirmed the inherent instability of the vessel, and revealed that every American passenger ship with side bunkers was being or had been converted to a transverse system of bulkheads to avoid a repetition of the disaster.

On 23 August 1918 Judge Mayer found for Cunard on the grounds that the action of the U-20 was an illegal act according to the American interpretation of international law. From this premise he descended to the American case law that, where the direct cause of an accident was by an illegal act, there could be no negligence unless the owners and master of the vessel were privy to the U-20's action. As no evidence had been offered to him alleging such privity, Cunard was entitled to the judgment. Judicially Mayer's decision was as sound as it was convenient. He disposed of the *in camera* evidence by noting that as an illegal act had caused the disaster, he did not propose to examine the 'several interesting arguments'[13] that had been presented to him.

There were no appeals against the decision. The claimants met their own costs and the net value of the wreck strippings totalling £147 16s 8d was shared amongst them. Lord, Day and Lord's fees totalled 77,695 dollars 19 cents. In the light of the American decision Cunard settled all other claims out of court by paying the claimants' legal costs.

There was one small piece of evidence which had not been tendered before Judge Mayer for the simple reason that President Wilson still had it in his office. This was the *Lusitania*'s original manifest together with the twenty-four page supplementary one which Dudley Field Malone had handed to him. The President sealed the papers in an envelope, marked it 'Only to be opened by the President of the United States',[14] and consigned it to the Treasury archives, where it remained as secure from prying eyes as the *Lusitania* herself, three hundred and twenty feet down and twelve miles south of the Old Head of Kinsale.

Captain Turner returned to the sea, being torpedoed again when in command of the *Link* thirty miles west of Cyprus in 1917. He survived and after the war Cunard promoted him Commodore of the Line. In 1921 Churchill published *The World Crisis*, which contained an account of the *Lusitania* disaster, which can only be described as a more elegantly written version of Captain Webb's memorandum. *The World Crisis* is now recognized as a four-volume exercise in self-justification, most aptly described by Lytton Strachey when he remarked to Maynard Keynes, 'Winston has written a four-volume book about himself and called it The World Crisis.'[15] The account, given wide currency at the time, inaccurately exposed Turner as having been responsible for the disaster. He retired unable to face the public and hostile criticism of the Liverpool shipping world. He built himself a cottage at

Yelverton in Devonshire and took up beekeeping, but again he was located by the press, so he went to Australia for eighteen months to search for the sons whom he had not seen since the opening of the Mersey inquiry. The search was unsuccessful. Eventually, unable to resist the lure of Liverpool, he retired there to spend the last few years of his life with Miss Every looking after him. He became a great favourite with the local children, teaching them sea shanties and accompanying them on a fiddle. He died of cancer of the intestines in 1933 being bedridden for the last five years of his life and remarking to visitors with bitter humour: 'I am all right fore and aft but my longitudinal bulkhead's given way.'[16]

Admiral Sir Charles Coke was ordered to haul down his flag at Queenstown on 27 May 1915 and transferred to the reserve. Six months later he was re-employed as a temporary captain in charge of troop shipments from Halifax, Nova Scotia – a rank and mission which a former Keeper of the Rolls Room at the Admiralty archives remarks 'might possibly be taken as a mark of their Lordships' displeasure'.[17] Admiral Hood was promoted on 13 May 1915 to the command of the third Battle Cruiser Squadron and was killed in action at Jutland.

Captains Hall and Gaunt each rose to be Rear-Admirals and were knighted. Kapitän-Leutnant Schwieger was drowned in the U-88 on 17 September 1917 whilst Admiral Sir Frederick Inglefield died in his bed, as did Sir Alfred Booth and Lord Mersey who had accepted a Viscountcy in November 1915.

William Jennings Bryan stayed in the political wilderness, briefly appearing in the public eye at the notorious Monkey Trial in March 1925 when he defended the local belief that evolution was an improper subject and should not be taught in school. Robert Lansing was dismissed by President Wilson after the Versailles Peace Conference. He published his war memoirs in 1926 and then retired to fish bass at Henderson Harbour and play mentor to his favourite nephew, John Foster Dulles. Alfred Fraser remained a picturesque operator on the fringe of the sheepskin market and is remembered to this day with many a rueful shudder amongst the fur dealing community. Dr Ritter von Rettegh vanished into an anonymous limbo after his release from the Cleveland Penitentiary, while von Papen after becoming Chancellor of Germany closed his career as German Ambassador to Turkey in the last war from which position he mounted some remarkably sophisticated intelligence operations. Churchill went to France in command of the 6th Battalion Royal Scots Fusiliers and it was not until 1939 that he returned as First Lord of the Admiralty. The famous signal was flashed out to the Fleet 'Winston is back'. More discreet was his first memorandum to the Trade Department on 7 September 1939: 'Report the names of British passenger ships which, if sunk, would cause national despondency.'[18] The Trade Division replied naming the *Queen Mary* and the newly launched *Mauretania*, which had been built to replace the *Lusitania*'s sister ship of the same name. Both were promptly despatched to New York until they were required for trooping duties.

By January 1940 Britain and America stood in a relationship almost identical to that of May 1915. On 21 January President Franklin Roosevelt asked Edwin M. Watson, one of his secretaries, to bring him President Wilson's packet from the Treasury archives. The then Collector of Customs, Harry M. Durning, searched it out and handed it over. Watson sent it through to the President with the following note.

THE WHITE HOUSE
WASHINGTON
1-26-40
MEMORANDUM FOR THE PRESIDENT:
This is from Mr Durning, and is the original manifest of the S.S. Lusitania. He wanted me to open it but I was afraid to do it until you had seen it. I have thanked Mr Durning.

E.M.W.[19]

Epilogue

During the decade that has passed since this account was first published, many of the unanswered queries that I raised have been answered, at least as satisfactorily as existing records and memories allow. It is now generally accepted that the Admiralty and the politicians, each in their own fashion, deliberately hazarded the ship. The Admiralty's action was merely a cynical manipulation of the regulations that governed the type of cargo that may or may not be loaded on to a passenger ship. I am satisfied that, at the time, the politicians involved did not know the precise nature of individual cargoes. They knew that they were contraband, but there is no evidence that either the politicians or even the senior naval staff *in London* were aware of the deadly nature of that loaded aboard the *Lusitania* on her final and fatal voyage.

The *in London* qualification is important. The key British Naval Intelligence staff in New York cannot be exonerated so easily. They knew what they were loading on to the ship. They knew its inherently dangerous characteristics. They were aware of the warnings from the German Embassy and other pro-German factions. They were equally aware of the hazards that had faced the ship on her previous voyage and, being privy to the naval dispositions of the time, they knew the threats that faced her on the current passage. Their failure to ensure that Captain Turner was not informed and their omission to request for a special escort around the Irish Coast, as they had done on numerous occasions before, can only be described as negligence of the grossest kind. That is a charitable stricture. If the files of British Naval

Intelligence are ever revealed they may well deserve a harsher judgement.

A considerable canon of evidence has emerged to sustain the charge that the politicians, led by Winston Churchill and Lloyd George, had a policy of deliberately embroiling the United States. Much of this evidence emerged during the controversy which followed the publication of the first edition. The B.B.C., together with the late Mr Nicholas Tomalin, adopted this thesis, which was opposed with characteristic vigour by Churchill's grandson, Winston Churchill Jr, M.P. In a spirited exchange of letters to *The Times* Tomalin quoted a 1914 letter from Churchill to Walter Runciman at the Board of Trade. 'We need,' it read in part, 'to embroil neutral ships with the German submarines, and the ships we most need to so embroil are the Americans . . .'

Tomalin's letter was followed by one from Martin Gilbert, the distinguished historian, who has the position of official biographer to Churchill. He began by stating 'The policy of seeking to embroil America with Germany was not unique to Churchill . . . (Prime Minister) Asquith wrote to Venetia Stanley on this subject. "Winston, McKenna, Lloyd George etc. are full of blood and thunder, but they haven't half thought out the thing and its consequences . . ."'

Mr Gilbert then treated *The Times* readers to a quick taste of what would be contained in his forthcoming official study, *Winston S. Churchill, 1914–1916* (Cassell, 1973). He wrote,

Readers of my new volume will find many more examples of Churchill's ruthlessness in the prosecution of the war. He was one of the first Ministerial advocates of the bombing of military targets inside towns. He contemplated the violation of Dutch and Danish neutrality in an attempt to launch an invasion of Germany. He was prepared to allow neutral Spain to annex Britain's ally Portugal, hoping, thereby, to secure the use of Portuguese colonial ports for Britain. He was a persistent advocate of the use of poison gas against the Turks at Gallipoli; a policy rejected by the Commander of the troops on the peninsular . . . Further historical research in Britain's archives will reveal much more about 'embroiling the

U.S. with Germany' . . . A comprehensive book on this subject would certainly be worthwhile.

The allegation that the authorities on both sides of the Atlantic had mounted a cover-up operation was denied by few. The two principal challengers to this thesis were the late Stephen Roskill, the distinguished official historian of the Royal Navy, and a former deputy director of Naval Intelligence between 1944 and 1948, Commander Patrick Beesly, R.N. (Retd). Roskill contented himself by displaying the traditional hostility that academics reserve for trespassing journalists. He did not answer any of the queries posed in the book and went to the grave convinced, like Churchill and others of his time, that whatever had been done was right and that in any higher judgement he and his contemporaries would be exonerated – if only because God was not only an Englishman but had probably served his time in the Royal Navy.

Commander Beesly adopted a more open approach. Using his undoubted entré into the arcane world of naval intelligence he made his own searching inquiries. In 1982 he had the honesty and the courtesy to confirm publicly that not only was the *Lusitania* carrying explosive contraband but that, in his professional opinion, she had been shamelessly hazarded and that both these facts had been deliberately concealed from the public by the British and American authorities.

The issues that remain unanswered are more material ones, that over the last sixty-seven years have primarily interested potential salvors, and those shippers who lost valuable goods in the disaster and who hoped and still hope that they might be recovered.

For example, Sir Hugh Lane, the eminent art-dealer and Director of the Irish National Gallery, had been a passenger. He had briefly visited New York to be a witness in a legal action and was on his way home. He had a premonition that he might be drowned and shortly before he sailed he made a codicil to his will donating many of his finest paintings, then on loan to the National and Tate galleries in London, to

Ireland. Perhaps of more immediate interest was that Lord Duveen, a fellow art-dealer based in New York, had entrusted him with a crate containing twenty-seven masterpieces for inspection by the Irish Gallery trustees. It was a condition of Duveen's that the Irish Gallery insure the pictures. Sir Hugh paid the premium in New York – out of his own funds – but on behalf of the Irish Gallery. They were insured for $4 million. Sir Hugh went down with the ship. His body was never recovered, but his will and codicil were found in his office desk.

The English courts refused to acknowledge the codicil on the grounds that it had not been witnessed and Sir Hugh's London collection was denied to Ireland. This has been an emotional issue ever since and many Irish feel that at least they are entitled to the Lane pictures aboard the *Lusitania*, which were intended for them, and for which Sir Hugh had paid the insurance.

The confusion and the deliberate disinformation generated by the several cargo manifests fuelled the belief that there was a considerable quantity of bullion aboard. Rumours ranged from the theory that hundreds of crates marked 'corn beef' contained gold bars to alleged stories of millions of pounds worth of industrial diamonds secreted in the mailroom under plain cover.

In fact there is no evidence whatsoever that any bullion was aboard. None is listed in any manifest, Admiralty or Cunard document or any insurance claim. It is instructive to remember that at that period of the war Britain was a customer of the United States and any bullion crossing the Atlantic did so from east to west.

The mailroom did contain numerous sacks of registered mail and in total some two million letters and packages were loaded. Presumably many of these contained valuables or possible negotiable documents, cheques, money orders or bills of exchange.

The manifest also contains a mention of a 'package of gemstones', around which an intriguing and minor mystery remains, and to which I will return.

Apart from the cargo, the package of gemstones in the mail-room and other probably modest valuables amongst the registered mail, the *Lusitania* contains nothing to merit an expensive salvage operation, with one significant exception, and that is the purser's safe. The safe was situated in the purser's office which was on the promenade deck forward of the upstairs exit from the domed dining saloon with its white and gold marbled pillars which supported the painted dome. The safe was in an inner room and weighed 16 tons. Inside it was divided into several smaller compartments, many of which had separate locking systems and a range of 288 small safe-deposit boxes to which both the purser and the passenger who rented them held a key. The contents of the safe will not be known until it is recovered and opened, probably during the 1983–4 diving season. There are, however, grounds for some educated guesses.

It was a Cunard convention that passengers did not pay cash for goods and services. Everything from a deckchair ticket to a bottle of claret at dinner was signed for on a 'chit'. These were collated in the purser's office and passengers were asked to settle their accounts before they disembarked. It followed that few people carried cash upon their person, and in the days before travellers' cheques and credit cards travellers relied on a plentiful supply of gold sovereigns – the international currency of the time – and their letters of credit from their own American to European bankers. Their cash, whether it was currency notes or gold, was deposited for safety's sake with the purser. More valuable items such as jewellery, letters of credit, bearer bonds, etc., were usually stored in one of the small safe-deposit boxes which could be rented for the duration of the voyage.

Life aboard the *Lusitania* was not cheap. Cunard advised passengers that a gentleman's requirements for the few days at sea would probably cost him between £40 and £50. A typical example of such a passenger was Sir Harold Boulton, an English baronet who had settled in Canada and who was returning to England to enlist. In 1936 he wrote an account of the sinking which was published in the London *Evening Standard*.

The foghorn awakened me at 8.30 a.m. It continued to blow until about 11, when the fog lifted and the sun came out on a fairly calm sea. We were nearing the 'danger zone'. Several people, who had been too nervous to go to bed in their cabins the night before, were now picking up the rugs and pillows with which they made their temporary beds, and were going upstairs to tidy up. Many had slept in their clothes in the drawing-room, writing-room or lounge – any place they could find . . . Just before luncheon I went below and got from the purser the money I had given him for safe keeping the first day out. I had about 200 dollars which he changed for me into £42 . . .

Sir Harold's recollection was that he did so because he wanted his money with him in case anything happened and that he also wanted to settle the various small accounts that he had incurred aboard, tip his cabin- and dining-room steward etc. so that he could avoid the rush of the following morning's early disembarkation.

It is likely that quite a few passengers took similar precautions, for many of the survivors and the corpses washed ashore were carrying considerable amounts of money. In some cases packets of share certificates and even jewellery cases were found secured to their bodies. Others were already packing. The crew members' statements at the Mersey Inquiry reveal that baggage parties had been bringing up passengers' luggage from the baggage rooms since before dawn and there are several stories of passengers tripping over trunks and suitcases stacked outside cabin doors when they rushed below to collect their lifejackets from their cabins.

Nevertheless the purser's safe probably contains a great many valuables. Survivors' insurance claims for all the effects they lost during the disaster totalled £480,000 and, as rather less than 40 per cent of the passengers actually survived the total loss, the total could well be in excess of £1 million, though naturally this would have included clothes, luggage and items in their cabins. Despite this simple arithmetic there have been numerous reports that the safe contained millions in bullion, currency and jewellery, but no insurance claim of any kind has ever been made for this alleged treasure and no insurance company has ever admitted to underwriting such risks. The companies have had ample opportunity.

In January 1923 Germany agreed to pay full compensation in respect of loss of life, personal injury and loss of property and the United States government ordered the establishment of a Federal Commission to receive, collate and examine all the claims made. The eventual claims made totalled £5,124,000 of which £2.4 million was disallowed. The balance of £2.7 million was largely taken up by meeting substantial claims from life insurance companies. Vanderbilt and Frohman each had policies for $1 million. Incidentally, Lord Duveen's claim for his pictures was refused, the Commissioners saying that the claim should be made by either Sir Hugh Lane's estate or his insurers. It was never made. Amongst the items on which insurance was paid were $100,000 for a pearl necklace which had been in the purser's safe, and $6000 for the packet of gemstones which had been in the registered mailroom and which was mentioned earlier in this narrative. This packet has generated its own little mystery which can be told but not completely explained. The mail, specie and luggage rooms were in the aft section of the ship and slightly above the waterline. The complex stretched the full width of the hull and was bisected by a passage which ran from side to side. Access fore and aft was limited. Forward were the coal bunkers on either side, aft was the steerage flat. There was an exit or loading hatch at each end of the passage so that mail and other items could be loaded or unloaded from either side depending on how the vessel was docked. These were heavy steel doors which could only be opened from the inside and the complete area was 'secure' in that it was manned at all times.

The issue of *Sphere* magazine published in London on 15 May 1915 described what it called an 'interesting phenomenon seen just at the moment of sinking'. A survivor told their reporting team that he was standing on the stern about a minute before the ship sank and looking out over the port side of the ship which, due to the list to starboard, was considerably higher and had seemed safer. As the ship began her final steep, bow-first plunge to the bottom he noticed a hatch or door burst open down on the port side and a mass of smoke and debris stream out.

One possible explanation is that a build-up of pressure inside the hull forced its way up the now almost empty coal bunkers which terminated at the forward end of the mailroom, then burst through the bulkhead and blew off the port side mail-loading door. Another is that the trapped mail crew were trying to escape. There may well be other explanations but what is certain is that some of the registered mail *including the packet of gems* came out of that door either then or very soon afterwards. A clue to this emerged in Hansard, the daily written record of the Houses of Parliament during question time in the House of Commons on Thursday 12 December 1919. The question was asked by Mr McVeagh M.P. and addressed to the then Postmaster-General, Mr Pike Pease.

According to Mr McVeagh one of his constituents, a fisherman called John Hayes who lived in the village of Courtmacsherry, had recovered a parcel of diamonds from the sea. The package had been an item of registered mail which according to the information on the attached insurance label was valued at £23,000. After an understandable but un-explained lapse of time, Mr Hayes' solicitor had returned the parcel to the headquarters of the General Post Office in London with a request for either a reward or 'salvage'.

In reply, the Postmaster-General confirmed that not one parcel but 'parcels' had been returned to the G.P.O., but claimed that their contents had not been anything like either the value claimed, or what was stated on the label. 'Neither,' he commented somewhat drily 'did the Post Office agree with the claim for salvage which in law had to be at some risk or peril to the salvors.' He added that the Post Office solicitors had queried these points in writing to Mr Hayes and his advisers some ten months ago and had as yet received no reply.

It would appear to be an area into which neither party wished to delve too deeply or to answer any potentially embarrassing questions. Sixty years later only two things are certain. Firstly, a registered package or packages, one of which contained diamonds and which had been in the mailroom of the *Lusitania* had turned up in Courtmacsherry a few days after the sinking. Secondly, it is, and has been, an open secret for many years that after the events of 7 May 1915, several of the sea-going communities on the coasts of Cork and Kerry enjoyed a higher standard of living than they had hitherto.

The Early Salvors

The first public speculation as to what could be salvaged from the wreck appeared in the *New York World* on 27 October 1916. It carried a modest if speculative item saying that preliminary moves were under way to form a post-war syndicate that would attempt to recover the purser's safe. Using the now almost traditional clichés, it claimed that it contained 'a king's ransom in gold and jewels'.

This was followed almost immediately by a cheeky but understandable offer from the German communities of New York and Argentina, who announced that they were prepared to underwrite the full costs of a salvage operation, either to be carried out during the summer of 1917 by the neutral Dutch or by an international team 'once the current hostilities have been resolved'. The German offer had a qualification: should the expedition find that the *Lusitania* was either armed, carrying contraband or both, then it expected Cunard and the British government to pick up the bill. Understandably the offer was ignored.

The presence of the *Lusitania* and almost three hundred other wartime wrecks off the Irish coast led to the possibility of the liner's salvage being chosen as the keynote speech and debate at the 1918 annual conference of the Engineering and

Scientific Association of Ireland. Specialist speakers from the Admiralty and the Liverpool and War Risks Insurance Company attended and were allowed to speak. The Association found that 'owing to the great depth at which she lies, the water pressure will have crushed her. In all probability,' they concluded, 'the *Lusitania* has ceased to be a ship.' There were many who disagreed with this conclusion and who had the initiative and imagination to put their ideas into practice. However, before their attempts are examined, the position of the Liverpool and War Risks Company merits examination.

In October 1914, when Alfred Booth was shanghaied by Sir William Graham Greene, the Secretary to the Admiralty, to adapt the *Lusitania* to her officially designated wartime role, he was informed that the British government would arrange the insurance cover that was needed. The vehicle the Boards of Trade and Admiralty devised was in effect a State-owned insurance company, which was called the Liverpool and War Risks. This company not only issued cover for the shipment of materials needed for the war effort, it also indemnified the shipowners whose ships had been requisitioned or chartered by the government.

At the end of the war, the insurance company paid out to those who had used its services and found itself, as a natural result, the owners of numerous shipping casualties around the world. To be precise, it owned the hull and machinery of all the sunken ships, plus the salvage rights to those cargoes that had been 'war' or what were euphemistically called 'strategic' materials. Any potential salvor had a legal duty to seek the company's permission to operate on whichever ship it wished, and this permission was sparingly given. When it was granted, it was usually only to those firms who were on an approved list of what were and are called Admiralty Salvage Agents.

Today, the holdings and obligations of the Liverpool and War Risks Company are administered by the Salvage Association, an officially independent institution sponsored by Lloyds of London, but answerable to the government of the day. In the case of the *Lusitania*, the L. & W. R. owned all rights to the hull and machinery. They also owned and still own all those items of cargo which were covered by the Admiralty's blanket policy. However, there is a key point to be made in that the L. & W. R.'s ownership is based on only what is shown in the 'sailing manifest'.

Should an independent salvor attempt work on the *Lusitania*, which lies outside territorial waters, the Liverpool insurers would have very little redress. They would have to bring a case before the International Salvage Court which sits in The Hague, and by now readers may well understand that this or any other public forum was the last place that the government would wish to be questioned about the *Lusitania*. It was as neat a cleft stick as has ever been devised, and over the last sixty years there have been a stream of entrepreneurs who, firstly, spotted the unique legal position of the *Lusitania* and who, secondly, were seduced by the rumour and speculation regarding her cargo.

The position of individual property aboard the liner was more specific. The contents of the safe, of passengers' baggage or mail, or even Sir Hugh Lane's pictures, would be purely a matter of negotiation to be decided by the International Court in the event of a dispute. As a rule of thumb the salvor would be entitled to deduct his costs and split the residual value or profit – if any – between the original owners or their insurers.

The salvage arithmetic was attractive. An attempt could be mounted for, say, the safe or the pictures, and should anything else come up such as the hundreds of bars of copper or brass, or even the (by now to those who were in the know) shrapnel shells or Captain Gaunt's tubs of butter, there was very little the Admiralty could do about it. An added attraction was the incredible amount of superb quality brass or bronze fittings with which the ship was equipped. For example, the four propellers each weighed almost 20 tons, and were of the most expensive bronze alloy ever made.

The first operator in the field played it by the book. This was an Italian called Count Zainardi Landi who, with the backing of a Greek entrepreneur called Vincent Grech of

Constantinople, had begun salvage operations in the Dardanelles in 1919. Between them they had raised the German battleship *Goeben* and sold her for scrap. 'Raised' is perhaps a generous term as the ship was only three feet below high-water and the operation consisted of patching her holes and pumping her out. With their profits, the Count and his partner purchased an ex-Admiralty sloop called the *Buttercup*, and obtained a three-year contract from the Liverpool and War Risks Company to raise the *Lusitania* by floating her to the surface.

Landi claimed that he had a team of nine divers, whom he believed could patch the torpedo hole, and assuming the watertight compartments were intact, pump her full of air. The scheme was sufficiently impractical to appeal to the press and perhaps for that reason the Admiralty readily gave their permission for the operation. The contract had three interesting clauses.

Landi was to deliver the ship to an English breaker's yard and hand over all documents to the authorities. He would be entitled to the £3 million of bullion which he claimed was in the purser's safe, and 40 per cent of the residual value of the hull, machinery and cargo, the value to be unilaterally decided by the L. & W.R. The *Buttercup*, renamed the *Semper Paratus*, left Dover on 4 July 1923 and was next heard of 29 days later in the Levant. Apparently Landi had been unable to find the *Lusitania* and even if he had tried he does not seem to have been in the area very long. In the words of his rivals and with hindsight it is likely that Landi got himself a cheap ship and was extremely useful to the Admiralty. He had an exclusive three-year contract to work the *Lusitania* and whilst he had it no one else could make an attempt. If they did it would not be for either the L. & W.R. or the Admiralty to sue, for Landi's company, which was conveniently British registered, could simply take out a civil injunction. The issue that would be at stake would not be the *Lusitania*'s cargo but Landi and his company's *rights* to it.

The chief rival to the Landi campaign was an equally

enterprising American called Captain Benjamin Leavitt, who had successfully completed an extremely profitable operation raising several hundred tons of copper from the British schooner *Cape Horn* which lay in 318 feet of water off the coast of Chile. He sold his cargo on the New York market and promptly floated a public company called The Lusitania Salvage Company.

Leavitt's prospectus was to raise $500,000 in $1 shares. He estimated his costs at just under $300,000 and said that his plans were only to raise the valuables, in particular the purser's safe which he claimed weighed 30 tons and contained – he had obviously read the *New York World* – 'a king's ransom'. His share-offer was overscribed. Benjamin Leavitt and his crew sailed from New York on the steamer *Blakely* on which he made a down payment for a three-month charter.

Leavitt and the *Blakely* spent their three months searching for the wreck without success. Their credit expired in Ireland and Leavitt and his ship put into Swansea where the *Blakely* was promptly arrested for debt, as Leavitt had omitted to keep up the payments. Little more was heard of this first American salvor except that he signed on aboard a Welsh collier to work his passage home to face his shareholders. He bitterly claimed that all his efforts had been frustrated and darkly hinted that the *Lusitania* did not lie where Lord Mersey's inquiry and the Admiralty charts said that she did.

During the 1920s not a year went by without one or another foreign ship vainly scouring the area a few miles off the Old Head of Kinsale. There were Greeks, Dutch, Germans and Italians, their visits now only chronicled by the records of the Kinsale harbour-master and the bored lighthouse-keepers up on the Old Head itself. None of them is worth recalling with the possible exception of an eccentric who proposed a plan to pump the ship full of a compound of ground cork and castor oil; this, understandably, came to nothing.

Late in 1931 two Americans approached the L. & W. R. with a novel plan. They were Captain Hilton Railey and an inventor called Simon Lake who had achieved brief notoriety in 1908 with a plan to salvage bullion from the *Lutine*, wrecked off the Dutch coast in October 1799.

Their idea for the *Lutine* had been to lower a metal pipe down to the sand in which the ship was embedded and blast the sand away with compressed air. Their part-completed tube still lay at Stones' shipyard at Brightlingsea in Essex. They believed that if they built a larger tube some 300 feet long and filled it with compressed air, divers could then walk down a staircase to be built inside the tube, and direct blasting and grab operations from an observation chamber at the bottom. Incredible as it may seem they were granted permission and the vast tube with its integral staircase was built by the Dartmouth firm of Phillips and Son. During the building period, Railey and Lake made no fewer than seven separate trips to Kinsale, chartering boats with which to locate the wreck. They were unsuccessful. During their several searches they had the sense to mount an excellent public relations exercise. They obtained sponsorship from the B.B.C. and even hired former Junior Third Officer Albert Bestic, by now a lieutenant-commander in the Naval Reserve, to be their salvage master. Numerous American insurance companies and survivors gave them commissions to recover items from the wreck. However, unable to locate the wreck, they ran out of money and folding their tents stole quietly away to America, from where a somewhat chagrined Captain Railey said he doubted the position of the *Lusitania* and that there was gold in it anyway.

Railey's abandonment of his project left the field open to a remarkable Manchester-based engineer called Joseph Peress who had been working for years on what is called the 'Atmospheric' diving suit. Peress had been amongst the first to realize that as divers wished to go deeper and for longer they were liable to several physiological problems, of which the best-known symptom is called 'the bends'.

His research showed that nitrogen from the air divers breathed was absorbed into their bloodstream and body tissues whilst they were at depth. When a diver rose to the surface the pressure decreased and the nitrogen bubbled out of their blood solution mainly into their joints where it often caused paralysis or death. Most divers had learnt that the slower they ascended the less likely this was to occur. In a normal suit a diver could just get down to the *Lusitania* – assuming she could be found – but after just five minutes on the bottom it would take him more than an hour to rise to the surface without risking the bends. Even then, the risk of breathing oxygen at that depth led to a form of narcosis which destroyed the diver's sense of judgement. Peress decided to design a suit that was so strong that it would completely shield the diver from all pressure and enable him to work for long periods on the bottom and then surface without having to decompress. His principal patent was finally granted in 1933. Peress needed a sponsor to build his suit and a suitable ship on which to demonstrate its capabilities to the world. He found such a man in a Glasgow businessman called J. H. Demetrious. Demetrious thought logically and he thought big. He founded the Tritonia Corporation of Scotland which pulled off a blanket deal with the L. & W.R. to salvage all three hundred and eighty-six of its wrecks which lay deeper than 50 metres, which was the accepted maximum operational limit of commercial and ordinary suits. Included in this blanket deal was the *Lusitania*.

Having acquired the rights, Demetrious then analysed all the previous efforts and concluded quite accurately that the *Lusitania* was probably not where the Admiralty said she was. He adopted a two-part plan.

Firstly, he sent a former lighthouse supply boat called the *Orphir*, commanded by Captain Henry B. Russell of Glasgow, to search an area four miles square around the official Admiralty position. The *Orphir* was equipped with the first primitive echo-sounder hearing developed by the Hughes Company Ltd and after combing the sea bottom for 108 days found innumerable wrecks but not the *Lusitania*. Secondly, he hired Albert Bestic and two ex-navy navigators who formed a shore party. Their function was to visit as many lighthouse men, coastguards and fishermen along the Cork coast as they could find who had seen or been present at the sinking, and ask them for their own idea of where she lay. The result was remarkable. Without exception they placed her about 12 miles south of the Old Head. Finally, he heard that Captain Turner was dying at his cottage in Merseyside and sent Albert Bestic to see him. (This information was not known to me at the time of the first edition of this book.) Bestic explained what was happening and the dying Turner asked him to recover his sextant which he had left in his cabin. More importantly he produced the original chart on which he had been working as his officers took their four-point bearing whilst Schweiger's torpedo sped towards his ship. As he left the bridge, and in more of a reflex action than anything else, he had seized it and stuffed it inside his tunic.

The chart was stained and heavily watermarked, but Turner's courses were still visible. They showed that in fact he had been plotting his ship's position ever since receiving the first message that submarines were active. They also showed that at the time of the hit he was approximately 12 miles south of the Old Head. His radio signal 'Come at Once Big List 10 miles south of Old Head' was a fair approximation, as allowing for the ship's momentum that is where he would probably have gone down had he not had most of his bows blown off underwater.

The chart was examined by Peress and an American diver, Captain John D. Craig, who made a manuscript note at the time, which is reproduced with permission.

It was an invaluable and pathetic document. It bore faded pencil [?] jottings – Captain Turner's record of the progress of his ship during 6 and 7 May 1915. Amongst these jottings were notes of the signals that had been radioed to the ship . . . His marginal notes indicate that the ship was steering a zigzag course which was abandoned momentarily to get a four point bearing on the land. The Course had been S87E, then N67E until 1.40 p.m. when the Old Head was sighted. The Course was then changed to S87E magnetic which is in the direction of Queenstown. At 2.10 p.m. the course ends. There is a laconic observation 'struck' . . .

The chart was an important and historic discovery. Captain Craig is, I believe, in error when he implies Turner was zigzagging as a tactic. I subscribe to the view that he was on his original southeasterly course in order to keep well off the headlands during the morning fog. When the fog lifted around 11.30 he steered towards land until he sighted the Old Head and thence began to take a four-point bearing on his run to Queenstown. However it does confirm that he was right and Captain Webb was wrong in the distance that he was from the land. If he had been allowed to produce his chart in evidence, his exoneration would have been far greater.

On 6 October 1935 the *Orphir* positioned herself at the point where Turner recorded he had been 'struck'. Captain Russel was at the helm, and a naval officer on leave, Lieutenant-Commander D. H. Dring, ran the plot. Captain Craig and Joseph Peress watched the echo-sounder. Shortly before noon the recording graph showed a shape on the bottom that measured 769 feet long and 84 feet high. The depth at this point was 312 feet. The measurements could only be those of the *Lusitania* and some attendant wreckage. Her dimensions were 760 by 87 feet. The *Lusitania*'s exact position is 11.2 miles south and 3 degrees west of the Old Head. Peress was anxious to dive at once, but Captain Russel did not like the look of the weather, and was anxious to report to Demetrious in Glasgow. It was a sensible decision.

Within two weeks Demetrious transferred his rights in the *Lusitania* to a new company called the Argonaut Corporation, which also had a stake in what was called Scottish Film Productions Ltd. The feature film rights were offered for an advance of £50,000 and a further £12,000 for the newsreel options. Exclusive press coverage was purchased by the *Daily Sketch* newspaper for an undisclosed sum and, when the *Orphir* sailed again for the wreck, her crew were almost outnumbered by pressmen and film cameramen plus every

Lusitania survivor Demetrious could cajole, or pay to attend. Bestic was there, Chisholm the second-class steward, Grant the carpenter and a host of others.

Peress had chosen Jim Jarrett as the man to use his suit; he was probably the most experienced diver in the country. He commenced his dive at noon on Sunday 27 October 1935 and landed on her port side deck at 11 minutes past. Peress spoke to him on the radio telephone and noted what he said: 'I am standing on the plates of a ship; I can see her rivets. The hull is covered with slime, but under it is only a little corrosion. I will measure the rivets.' He did so, then telephoned. 'They are about two inches.' The rivets of the *Lusitania* are one and three quarter inches. That was almost Jarrett's last message. Captain Craig again takes over the account.

Hardly had he done this when the giant drag anchor which the *Orphir* had secured to the *Lusitania*'s hull tore loose. Jarrett did not know what had happened until he saw the hook swing past his glass mask, almost scraping it. He thought he had escaped when he realized it was swinging in ever-decreasing circles and that very shortly it would hit him. He was whisked up as quickly as possible and arrived pale and trembling. Then the weather closed in, and he never got down again.

One of the facts that Jarrett brought back was that even with his powerful light, visibility was bad and that plankton and other marine life reflected the glare of the lamp. It was, in his experience, totally unsuited for photography. Demetrious, pacifying the attendant press and cameramen, returned to his base and declared that operations were postponed until the following season.

Captain Craig was retained to go over to America and search for suitable lights and to regenerate interest amongst the film companies. He took his responsibilities rather further. He had lights, each of 5000 watts, developed by the Nela Parl Laboratories of the General Electric Company of Cleveland, Ohio. These were mounted in batteries of twelve and tested to a depth of 1500 feet. Once the lights were fixed, he turned his mind to the suit. He decided that the Peress suit was too cumbersome for the job and that the answer was to find a diving system that would mean less decompression time, less narcosis and much more manoeuvrability. Prophetically he opted for helium.

To explain briefly, helium is 40 per cent less soluble than nitrogen so will not dissolve into the body fluids so rapidly. It also has a lighter molecular weight, four as against twenty-eight for nitrogen, so that in decompression it will escape from the lungs more rapidly. Experiments with it had been attempted by the United States Navy and had been abandoned. With the assistance of the University of Milwaukee, Craig designed a dress and diving system that operated on an oxyhelium mixture and on 1 December 1937 a diver using it established a world record dive of 420 feet in the waters of Lake Michigan.

Now that Demetrious had the lights and the suit he had no difficulty securing the backing of Paramount Pictures. But as the 1938 series of dives were being planned and for the first time it appeared likely that at last someone would be able to thoroughly explore the *Lusitania*, two further factors gave the British government the understandable excuse to cancel their venture.

Hitler had marched into the Rhineland whilst Mussolini was in Ethiopia. Demetrious was summoned to London, ostensibly by the Department of Trade. The official he spoke to was polite but emphatic. 'Times,' Demetrious was told, 'are difficult ones. To salvage the *Lusitania* with all the attendant publicity would be rubbing salt into German wounds. The Germans would not like it. For the time being,' he was urged, 'let sleeping dogs lie.'

The Big Time

Paddy Allan lives at Sandy Cove, in a trim little house looking due south from the Old Head of Kinsale. Today he is probably the most respected underwater man in County Cork, though he retired from diving a few years ago. During an active life he was a local boat-owner and the Irish agent for the firm of Siebe Gorman, the famous designers and manufacturers of deep diving equipment. The *Lusitania* is his special interest. It has been since he was a youth of eighteen in 1946, when he heard a series of muffled explosions rolling in across the sea to his home. They came from the direction of the grave of the *Lusitania*.

He sailed out to investigate. Over the wreck were vessels of the Royal Navy, flying the danger flag that warned they were using explosives. Further inquiries showed that the ships were part of what were called 'disposal units'. Their task was to dispose of massive stocks of time-expired depth-charges used for submarine hunting. Someone in the Admiralty had decided that the disposals could be combined with naval training and each ship was making a series of dummy runs attacking an imaginary submarine. The target in question was the *Lusitania*.

The exercises went on for a week and were repeated each year until 1949. It became apparent that they were part of the annual training for naval reservists. The local inhabitants did not object, for the shore parties were welcome visitors to the bars and cafés of the town.

There was a second visitor to the wreck in June 1948, when the naval diving vessel, the *Reclaim*, moored over the wreck for three days, sheltering each evening behind the lee of the Old Head. No shore parties landed at Kinsale and the visit was shrouded in secrecy. Allan and other local seamen noticed that the *Reclaim* was flying the international signal to warn other vessels to keep clear as divers were working below.

During the early and mid fifties the Southampton firm of Risdon Beazley, who were the Admiralty salvage contractors, had at one time or another two vessels in the area whenever the weather was fine. These were a salvage vessel, the *Recovery*, and the 769 ton tug, *Lifeline*, which was fitted with a 'Peress'-style diving suit and a massive cargo grab. Risdon Beazley denied then and do to this day that they were working on the *Lusitania*, claiming they were concentrating on other wrecks close by. Few of the local seamen accepted these denials but reserved their judgement until some third party arrived on the scene with the funds and the technical ability to explore the *Lusitania* both in detail and in public. This happened in 1960 when an American diver called John F. Light took Kinsale by storm.

Light is a colourful, cantankerous character with a distinguished diving career. He learnt his trade in the United States Navy, and on demobilization joined the American television company N.B.C., specializing as an underwater cameraman. In this role he made a number of spectacular films and took part in several dives that established new records for their depths and duration. In 1960 he took severance pay from his employers and arrived in Kinsale with the idea of diving on the *Lusitania*. He had rather more skills and reputation than he had capital, but this did not deter him. He and a group of like-minded spirits persuaded a local trawlerman called Dan Griffin to put his ship, the *Resolution*, at their disposal.

The plan was to use the simplest type of scuba gear, utilizing compressed air. The maximum safe operating depth of this equipment is 150 feet. A dive to the *Lusitania* at 315 feet was almost suicidal, but was just possible provided strict discipline was maintained on decompression times. As Light had no decompression chamber, he had to stagger his return to the surface in order to avoid getting the bends. The timing was such that a few minutes on the bottom entailed a return to the surface that would take almost two hours, spent hanging on to a cable lowered from his mother ship. If the weather blew up whilst he was below there were two alternatives: to surface and risk almost certain death, or be marooned 11.2 miles offshore. There is no doubt that Light was and is brave beyond the point of foolhardiness.

On 20 July 1960 Light dived alone to the depth of 240 feet, landing on the same riveted plates as Jim Jarrett had done twenty-five years before. His return to the surface was an agonizing time for Dan Griffin and his crew. 'When we hauled him out of the water he looked like death itself,' recalled

Griffin. 'The pressure had taken a terrible toll of him. There was blood coming out of his ears, his eyes were popping out and a stream of blood and mucous hung two foot from his nose.' However, Light had made his point. He secured backing from the B.B.C. and a clutch of magazines. Three weeks later and assisted by two other divers and a B.B.C. film crew operating a remote camera suspended on a cable and guided by the divers, Light made a further seventeen dives, finishing on 12 October 1960.

The following year, Light's old employers N.B.C. joined the B.B.C. and between 12 May and 7 July made a further fourteen dives until bad weather led to the abandonment of the expedition. From the film shot over these two seasons, the B.B.C. made a film called *50 Fathoms Deep*, which was screened for the first time on the anniversary of the *Lusitania*'s sinking – 7 May 1962.

Light's final dives were made during the late summer of 1962 when he was sponsored by the German magazine *Bunte Illustrated* and the American *Sports Illustrated*. On these dives Light and his companion Charles Aquadro claimed that they had seen what they believed to have been a six-inch gun on the liner's foredeck. They also reported visual evidence that possibly someone else had been working on the wreck. Light and his colleagues have never been back to the ship.

It was the *Sports Illustrated* report that led to my own and my employer's – the *Sunday Times* – interest in the *Lusitania* affair, and our role is fully explained in the introduction.

Between 1962 and 1966 Light began to research the *Lusitania* in as much detail as he could and, using a copy of the B.B.C. film, endeavoured to find further financial backing for his venture. The dives for the TV companies and the magazines had not netted him sufficient money to cover his costs. For example, Dan Griffin and his crew made their boat available for three seasons of dives and by the summer of 1982, twenty years later, had still not been paid their bill of some £15,000 for charter fees, fuel, crew wages etc. There

278

were numerous other debts, but most of Kinsale believed that sooner or later John Light's ship would literally come in and then all would be the richer.

Light's problem was that he had no rights to the wreck. He had been down to it and photographed it, but no financier was going to advance monies to him when at any time the Liverpool and War Risks Company could grant a salvage licence to a salvor. It should be stressed that at this time Light was not selling a salvage-deal. He was trying to finance a book and a film about the mysteries of the ship. Was she carrying guns or contraband? At the back of his mind was the theory that if he pulled off the film that definitely answered these questions, then he could turn salvor. His answer was to buy the rights to try and salvage the ship.

In 1967 the L. & W.R. *sold* him the 'hull and machinery' of the wreck of the *Lusitania* for £1000 on the understanding that 'it will not be salved as a whole, repaired or put into commission again'. The contract specifically excluded all cargo or movable fittings. It involved simply the hull and the machinery. Once Light had this piece of paper, it should have been plain sailing. On 16 June the same year Light persuaded New York publishers Holt, Rinehart & Winston to advance him $136,000 for a book and photographic record of the *Lusitania*. The writer was to be Commander Ned Beach (Retd) of the U.S. Navy, a distinguished submariner, but Beach and Light had differences of opinion and Light decided to write the book himself.

On 10 January 1968 Light sold 60 per cent of his salvage rights to George Macomber of Boston for a sum which has been disputed as between $1 and other valuable considerations and $27,000. Shortly afterwards Macomber's share increased to 66 per cent in consideration of his advancing Light a further $18,000. Macomber in his turn introduced an acquaintance called Greg Bemis Jr, the president of an international firm called Oceanics Inc., who bought half of Macomber's share.

An intriguing point is that in all these contracts Light sold them not only a percentage of the rights to the hull and the machinery, but he also sold his non-existent rights to the cargo. Both Bemis and Macomber were aware of this at the time but the cargo clause was inserted on the advice of their American lawyers who argued that they could salvage the cargo first and argue later.

Bemis and Macomber then formed a Liberian company called Kinvarra Shipping in which they granted Light three shares in exchange for the sum of $45,000, which may well be the sum of $27,000 and $18,000 which Light received, at least on paper, from Macomber. The Liberian company paid $27,000 for an old French trawler called the *Kinvarra* in which Light returned, flush with money, to Kinsale.

What happened next is remembered by the people of Kinsale with awe and some indignation. Today they still call them the 'Light Years'. The *Kinvarra* was expensively converted into one of the most extensively-equipped diving vessels afloat, but it never made a voyage except to and from the shipyard which installed the equipment. Nor did it ever make a dive.

By the summer of 1969 the publishers' patience had expired and they sold the rights to the book that Light was to write and the film he was to make to Bemis and Macomber. Immediately they had acquired these rights, Kinvarra Shipping approached the United States Inland Revenue Service with a plea for special tax concessions. Some relevant extracts of their application are reproduced below because they show what was intended to happen and what will probably happen in a slightly varied form and using other vessels during 1983 and 1984. The key extract is in italics.

'The *Kinvarra* is a 151 foot diesel-powered motor vessel, a former fishing trawler. The vessel has subsequently been converted into a diving tender and salvage vessel equipped with the most advanced type of diving equipment and gear to constitute a 'Saturation Diving System'. The *Kinvarra* has a cruising speed of 12 knots and a cruising range of 40 days. She is equipped with central heating, deep freeze, washing-machine and hot and cold water pressure system. She has sleeping quarters for twenty-three. Her navigation equipment includes decca, radar, radio telephones and echosounders. Briefly, *Kinvarra* is a complete sea-going surface-oriented 'sea laboratory', providing a system which allows divers to live under pressure (to depths of 500 feet) for periods of time up to two weeks. Utilizing this system, as many as four divers can be placed on the *Lusitania* for from four to six hours per day per man. This enables the expedition to take the utmost advantage of whatever good weather is available to accumulate from twenty-four to thirty-two working man hours on the bottom in any twenty-four-hour period. In addition, the *Kinvarra* is fully equipped for underwater as well as surface photography, both black and white and colour, for still cameras, movie cameras and television cameras. A dark room has been installed for black and white development and printing of all still work.

Macomber, Light and Bemis will assign to Kinvarra Shipping, as contributions to the corporation's capital, all their respective rights and interest in the wreck of the *Lusitania*, free from any liabilities.

Kinvarra Shipping will qualify to do business in Ireland in branch form. It is expected that the activities of Kinvarra Shipping (described below) will constitute the manufacture of Irish products and thus qualify for certain tax concessions under the laws of Ireland when the manufactured and reprocessed product are sold for export. It is also expected that Kinvarra Shipping will qualify as a less developed country corporation within the meaning of Section 902(d) of the Internal Revenue Code of 1954.

Kinvarra Shipping will conduct a complete exploration of the wreck of the *Lusitania* to gather and record pertinent information in preparation for the salvage programme. Photographic records will be obtained on 16 mm colour film, 70 mm colour and black and white still film on 1 inch video tape being fed from two separate closed circuit TV camera systems.

Following the completion of the exploratory and photography phase, the salvage of the non-ferrous metals contained in the cargo and the hull of the *Lusitania* will be attempted. This involves the scrapping of the ship on the ocean bottom and the raising of the items of salvage to the surface for transport to Kinsale, Ireland, where the manufacturing process will take place.

Light has been and will continue to be Manager of Operations, supervising the entire working complex and personnel. Reporting to Light will be the Captain of the vessel whose responsibilities will include ship-handling and security, navigation, setting and handling of moorings and anchors, handling of the diving-bell, the TV chassis, pontoons, tools and all overboard equipment, the lifting and surface transfer of salvage and the maintenance and readiness of all equipment. There will also be a Salvage Master having daily supervision of the on-the-bottom salvage work and a Diving Master in charge of the operation and control of the entire diving complex and the assignment and direction of the diving complex personnel, their medical safety and decompression. In addition to the team of divers and technicians, there will be an engineer, a mechanic and an electrician and their assistants. The deck crew will consist of twelve men. The entire ship's crew will number approximately thirty.

Present plans contemplate that when the salvage has been raised to the surface, it will be towed, lot by lot, into Kinsale Harbour and beached at high tide at a location which will enable cranes to pick it up at low tide for transportation to the work site. Although timing of the actual salvage operations is completely dependent upon weather and diving conditions, it is hoped that the salvage operations can be completed within two diving seasons. Because of the long period of submersion, the lack of knowledge of the exact condition of the wreck and its contents, and the newness of the salvage techniques to be employed, it is impossible to estimate with any degree of certainty the amount of salvageable material which may be brought up or its composition. The project nevertheless is being planned on the basis of the expectation that there will be considerable valuable recoverable salvage capable of reprocessing for manufacture and sale. The items of salvageable materials anticipated include: the *Lusitania*'s four bronze propellers, each weighing 29,000 lb; boiler room piping, all copper and bronze, varying in diameter from 4 inches to 48 inches; condenser piping consisting of 4 inch bronze tubing in condenser units varying from 50 to 150 tons each; bronze valves and bronze pumps with overall outside dimensions ranging up to 6 feet by 10 feet; bronze and brass deck fittings, cleats, davits, blocks, portholes; shell casings; bars of ingot copper; sheet brass, brass tubes, copper tubes, brass rods, reels of copper; teak and mahogany furniture and fittings; andirons; sterling silver tableware and serving dishes and platters.

The recoverable salvage will have been under water at a depth of approximately 300 feet for fifty-four years and will be in no condition for immediate sale to third parties. Kinvarra Shipping will substantially transform the salvage from its bulk corroded state into material suitable for sale to third parties. Some portions of the material such as deck fittings, portholes, pipe sections and shell casings will be transformed into souvenir pieces, such as table lamps, coffee tables, umbrella stands, lamp stands, ash trays and the like. Other items such as valves will be retained in their original form as souvenirs. The mass of piping and tubing recovered from the *Lusitania*'s boiler and condensers will have to be cut into marketable sizes and shapes, cleaned of growth and oxidation, and formed into saleable scrap. All of the salvaged material will have to be cleaned, and those portions which will be used for souvenirs will, in addition, have to be polished, mounted and engraved. The teak and mahogany furniture and fixtures will have to be renovated and refinished.

The recovery and preparation of the salvage will require the removal of crustaceous marine growth and oxidation, both within and on the surface of the tubing, by acid washing, sand blasting, wire brushing and other suitable methods utilizing both machine and hand labour. To accomplish this programme will require facilities including a warehouse and a machine and power tool shop, fabrication and assembly space, and power cutting tools, power presses, reforging, stamping and engraving machines, branding and packing machines and equipment, and trucks, trailers and cranes.

After the reprocessing and manufacturing of the salvage, Kinvarra Shipping will undertake sales of the salvage to unrelated third parties. Sales in the United States, if any, will only be incidental, and the primary markets will be Western Europe, Japan and other metal-consuming countries.

The *Lusitania* programme will have served as a testing ground for the application of saturation diving as applied to a commercial undertaking of deep water, open ocean salvage. Following the completion of the *Lusitania* operations, Kinvarra Shipping will seek out other underwater projects.'

However, whilst the Inland Revenue Service were considering the application Bemis and Macomber, as the controlling shareholders, relieved Light of all his executive powers in the company. The I.R.S. looked on the project with disfavour. They had no objections as to Kinvarra's plans for the *Lusitania*, but decided that it should not be done at the Inland Revenue's expense. After a brief but fruitless search for further capital, Macomber and Bemis met in Boston on 26 June 1970 and voted Kinvarra into liquidation. Shortly before the meeting, their agents, unbeknown to Light, paid the outstanding harbour dues on the *Kinvarra* and removed her to Amsterdam where she was sold to the highest bidder; the sale was not enough to cover the debts of the venture.

John Light stayed on in Kinsale for a brief period until, hounded by debts, including the original hire charges due to Dan Griffin from the 1960 dives, he left at short notice for America.

Salvage programmes for the *Lusitania* appear to have a ten-year cycle. Early in 1982 a Mr John Pierce from Wrexham, North Wales, called me at the *Sunday Times* with a novel idea for salvaging the *Lusitania* and the *Titanic*. The *Sunday Times* is not in the salvage business but Pierce was sensible enough to realize that before anything could be done it would be essential to survey the wrecks concerned. His technique is a secret, but possibly it could work.

By a coincidence the *Sunday Times* had also been intimately concerned in writing about other salvage operations, such as that on H.M.S. *Edinburgh* which raised a fortune in bullion. We were aware of certain machines that could make a detailed photo survey at hitherto unheard-of depths, and of new diving techniques that would make the *Lusitania* a relatively easy operation. We introduced Pierce to U.M.E.L. Ltd of Bordon, Hampshire, with the result that six weeks later I sat in the cabin of the Irish-registered brigantine *Coos Bay* watching a TV screen as, far below, a sophisticated mini-submarine equipped with cine and still cameras scanned every inch of the great hulk below.

The first object I saw was the shattered condenser that had nearly decapitated Third Officer Lewis. The second was the open hatch through which the sack of registered mail presumably drifted. Altogether we shot 28½ hours of video film and these have been analysed over the last few months.

They show that the *Lusitania* lies on her starboard side, with much of her superstructure collapsed down on to the sea bed. They show that a determined attempt to salvage or at least work on the wreck has been made. For example, each of the great bronze letters on her bows which tell her name has been neatly burned off, and evidence left on the wreckage indicates that it was burned with a tool called a 'Seafire' cutting torch. There is also evidence that someone has been into the forward hold and there is a gaping hole in the bows, far forward of where the torpedo struck but exactly where the cargo was stored. On our last inspection we used the claw hand fitted to our submarine and located and recovered the great bronze ship's bell which at one time hung at the foremast.

Whilst we studied the video, it transpired that a share of U.M.E.L. belonged to an American company called Oceaneering Ltd of Houston, Texas. Oceaneering, who specialize in oil rig diving and maintenance, were about to take delivery of a brand new diving ship called the *Archimedes*, and for her trial-cruise proposed a dive on the *Lusitania*.

During September and October the *Archimedes* made several dives using the intensive helium technique originally developed by Captain Craig. Using controlled explosive charges they brought up three of the great manganese bronze propellers and thoroughly explored the specie room. They found no pictures, only picture frames. There was no bullion, but a considerable quantity of silver plate spoons and watch cases. There was also a box of 821 brass fulminate of mercury fuses for 6-inch shells. These were 'live'. They were photographed and then disposed off, though one is on my desk as a paperweight.

We also recovered an unexploded depth-charge, bearing the Admiralty's mark and dropped in 1946. We exploded it.

Elsewhere we recovered quantities of china, silver dishes from the butler's pantry, the foghorn and the telegraph from the bridge. We brought up the anchors and masses of items of bronze and brass and considerably more evidence that there had been other divers there before. Lastly, we located the area in which lies the purser's safe, but it is buried beneath about 200 tons of wreckage and will have to wait until next season's dive which should start at Easter 1983. Unhappily, as with anything connected with the *Lusitania*, there are problems. The prime one is legal.

When Kinvarra Shipping went into liquidation the rights to the *Lusitania* would normally have been available for the creditors. Unhappily for them Bemis, Macomber and Light never got around to vesting these into the company as they assured the American tax authorities they would. They kept them to themselves and are currently claiming that Oceaneering and its associates have no right to be on the wreck at all.

Provided this dispute can be resolved then next season should answer once and for all the remaining mysteries of what is still the most famous and mysterious ship of the century.

Acknowledgements

I owe a great deal to Harold Evans, the Editor of the *Sunday Times*, for his indulgence over the last few years, and to colleagues of mine on that newspaper who have helped in the research and advised on presentation: in particular to Arnold Field for his work in Liverpool; to Sheila Robinette, Bob Ducas and Stephen Fay for carrying out inquiries in the United States; to Phillip Knightley and David Leitch nearer home.

Lieutenant-Commander Godfrey R.N. (Retd), a former Keeper of the Rolls Room at the Public Record Office, and Miss Karen de Groot spent months on my behalf amongst the Admiralty and Foreign Office archives. Transcripts of Crown-copyright records in the Public Record Office appear by permission of the Controller of H.M. Stationery Office. I am grateful to Dr Gerd Sandhofer, keeper of the naval section of the Bundesarchiv, Koblenz, for assistance and for permission to quote from Bauer's and Schwieger's war diaries; to the University of Chicago Press for extracts from T. A. Bailey: 'German Documents Relating to the Lusitania', *Journal of Modern History*; and Mr Thomas A. Bailey for extracts from 'The Sinking of the Lusitania', *American Historical Review*; and the Edward M. House Collection, Yale University Library. Apart from those responsible for the libraries mentioned in the Sources, I am indebted to the librarians of the London Library, of the Norfolk and Norwich Public Libraries, and of the Middle Temple and the *Sunday Times*, especially the latter, where 'Pip' Yates and his staff never once lost their reason despite the most recherché requests.

Technical advice and assistance were given by Dan Wallace, formerly chief designer of Cunard and designer of the *QE2*, Professor Cedric Ridgely-Nevitt of the Webb Institute of Naval Architecture, New York, Noel Bonsor, the steamship historian, and

David Kahn the American cryptographer. Lord Mancroft and the Board of the Cunard Company, together with their solicitors, Messrs Hill, Dickinson & Co. of Liverpool (in particular Mr R. L. Adam), gave me every assistance; and my thanks are also due to Mr Kendrick Williams, a former Assistant Secretary of Cunard, who has devoted a great deal of time and trouble to searching the records of the Cunard company and assisting Mr Adam. I am also indebted to Mr J. S. M. Booth of Booth and Co. (International) Ltd. London, who allowed unlimited access to and use of his father's personal papers. The directors of Booth and Co. granted me unrestricted use of the business correspondence between George and Alfred Booth. I have been able to benefit from Miss Mabel Every's memories of Captain Turner. Lord Mersey allowed me to use his library to study his grandfather's 'Lusitania case notes', and Lady Mersey very kindly fed me between shifts.

There is a saying in the newspaper business that behind every *Sunday Times* reporter is a good lawyer. I am fortunate in having had the assistance of Mr John Calderan of Theodore Goddard & Co. and Mr James Evans the legal adviser to Times Newspapers Ltd.

I spent hours talking 'Lusitania' with John and Muriel Light of Kinsale, who know as much as anyone about the construction and history of the vessel, and while in Ireland I was excellently looked after by Niall and Patsy Caughley of Garrettstown. Miss Susan Dakins of the *Sunday Times* typed the manuscript. Lastly, my wife Jane not only allowed me to turn our home into a near replica of the *Sunday Times* features room on a rough Saturday night but also managed to remain as loyal and unruffled as she did when in 1966 I postponed our wedding a week so that I could go to New York to talk to a diver.

Notes

Chapter 1 (pp. 20–32)

1. Senate doc. 191, 66th Congress, 2nd session, paper 7670.
2. Hicks Beach, *Life of Sir Michael Hicks Beach*, ii, 153.
3. P.R.O., ADM/116/940/B.
4. Joseph Chamberlain papers, Box JC 14/4.
5. Letter from Hill, Dickinson to Lord Inverclyde 19 March 1903, Cunard archive.
6. Cunard archive, agreement with H.M. Government.
7. Swan Hunter originally tendered for the construction of the *Lusitania*, but their graving-dock would only permit a beam of 84 feet. Peskett advised against the Swan Hunter tender on the grounds that such a beam – a reduction of 3 feet 6 inches – could render the vessel 'dangerously unstable'.
8. U.S. District Court, Southern District of New York, 'Inquiry into the loss of the screw schooner Oregon', 17 April 1887.
9. Commissioner Wynne hearings 1917 (Peskett testimony), 1–29: Department of Justice archives.
10. Cunard archive, 'Instructions to Masters Lusitania and Mauretania'.
11. Scale plan of the *Lusitania*, John Brown Ltd, Clydebank.
12. Commissioner Wynne hearings, *loc. cit.*
13. National Maritime Museum, Greenwich, Box 556, 1359–62.
14. Hansard, 5th series, vol. lix, col. 1583.

Chapter 2 (pp. 33–42)

1. G. Booth to A. Booth 25 September 1914 (cf Ch. 3, n.1).
2. 'The oil engine and the submarine', Fisher papers.
3. W. S. Churchill, *The World Crisis*, rev. edn, 1931, 298.
4. *Ibid.*, 724–5.

5. Richmond diaries, 27 February 1915.
6. P.R.O., ADM/116/1359, 23 December 1914.
7. G. Booth to A. Booth 5 October 1914.
8. *Ibid.*

Chapter 3 (pp. 43–53)

1. George Booth left an uncompleted autobiography on his death in 1970. His son Mr J. S. M. Booth has given me unrestricted access to this MS. referred to hereunder as Booth Autobiog. There are three other important Booth sources: George Booth's private and commercial correspondence and his diaries, referred to hereafter respectively as Booth papers and Booth diaries; the correspondence between George and Alfred is preserved in the 'partnership letters' of Booth and Co. of St James's Street, London, SW1, to which reference is given as 'partnership letters', with the date. Additional sources on the Booth family are A. H. John, *A Liverpool Merchant House*, London, 1959, and certain charming elderly members and retainers of the Reform Club, Pall Mall, London.
2. This quotation and series of facts about mining is drawn from Marder, *From the Dreadnought to Scapa Flow*, ii, 77–84.
3. Booth partnership letters.
4. The details of the Morgan operation in this and succeeding chapters is largely taken from the volumes of the Nye Committee hearings into the American Munitions industry. Numerous files were subpoenaed and some 4000 letters between Morgan and Co. and suppliers to the Allies were scrutinized. These are condensed into Senate Report No. 944 submitted to the 74th Congress, 2nd session. The executors of the late Senator Gerald P. Nye and the late Mrs Stephen Raushenbush own holeographs of all relevant material and these are available to readers at the Library of Congress and Johns Hopkins University. References throughout are to 'Nye Committee'. The Booth Autobiography supplements these files and gives more 'personal' details.

Chapter 4 (pp. 54–63)

1. J. P. Morgan to Henry White 13 June 1914, White papers.
2. Banker Wharton Barker to Senator Underwood 14 August 1914: 'Of course every one knows that the Secretary of the

Treasury is almost without knowledge of credit and its use and many know that the President is a doctrinaire on such questions and therefore all who have knowledge of the use of credit are anxious beyond measure', Wharton Barker papers.

3. American State Papers. Foreign Relations 1914, Suppl., 580.
4. Lansing to Bryan 13 October 1914, Bryan papers.
5. Nye Committee Exhibit 2045; cf Baker, *Life and Letters of Woodrow Wilson*, v, 186–7. In relation to Lansing's activities as a spokesman for American financial interests it is instructive to study a document in the Lansing papers in the Library of Congress entitled 'Memorandum of a conversation with the President at 8.30 this evening relative to loans and credits to belligerent governments'. This paper which is still classified was an exhibit before the Nye Committee, No. 2047; the rest of the exhibits are not classified.
6. Lane, *Letters*, 164.
7. Lansing, *My War Memoirs*, 218.
8. *Ibid.*, 218–19.
9. P.R.O., ADM/137/1058, 71/A.
10. *Ibid.*, 167–70.
11. *Ibid.*, 150.
12. *Ibid.*, 199.
13. *Ibid.*, 198.
14. *Ibid.*, 196, 198, 199.

Chapter 5 (pp. 64–74)
1. Report by Rear Admiral Sir Reginald Hall to Amos Peaselee, the New York lawyer, 14 February 1930. The transcript of 'the Black Tom case' in the Library of the Department of Justice contains a full biography of Curt Thummel. He is also briefly mentioned by Admiral Sir William James in his short biography of Sir Reginald Hall, *The Eyes of the Navy*.
2. Hendrick, *Life and Letters of Walter Hines Page*, iii, 361.
3. State Department Archives, ref. 841.857.L97/74, declassified 29 April 1963.
4. P.R.O., ADM/137/1053/Oliver, 20 May 1915.
5. P.R.O., ADM/137/89/Oliver, 30 January 1915.
6. Bundesarchiv, Koblenz.
7. Fisher, *Memories and Records*, ii, 215.

Chapter 6 (pp. 75–85)

1. Tirpitz, *My Memoirs*, ii, 141.
2. This anecdote is related in a letter from Rear Admiral Arno Spindler, who was present at the time, to Charles Tansill, Albert Shaw Lecturer in diplomatic history at Johns Hopkins University, of 26 October 1936.
3. Scheer, *Germany's High Seas Fleet in the World War*, 230.
4. Foreign Relations, suppl. 1915, 94.
5. Baker, *Life and Letters of Woodrow Wilson*, v, 246.
6. *Ibid.*, v, 247.
7. Cranch, *Reports of the U.S. Supreme Court*, Washington, 1817, ix, 388, 430. A condensation of the Supreme Court decision in more digestible form is contained in Borchard and Lage, *Neutrality for the United States*, 111–12 and 119ff.
8. Evidence of John Bassett Moore to Senate Committee of Foreign Relations Hearings on S 3474: 74th Congress, 2nd session, 1936, 185.
9. Telegram from Wilson to House 3 February 1915, House papers.
10. Lord Morley to Andrew Carnegie 17 February 1915, Carnegie papers.
11. Foreign Relations, suppl. 1915, 98–9.
12. *Ibid.*, Ambassador Page to Bryan 20 February 1915.
13. Bryan to Sir Cecil Spring-Rice 9 September 1914. The British request to withdraw the last sentence is noted on the margin in Lansing's hand. Lansing papers.
14. *The Times*, London, 16 July 1914.
15. Quoted by Bluell, *The Washington Conference*, 221.
16. House to Wilson 5 May 1915, House papers. Also quoted in Seymour ed., *The Intimate Papers of Colonel House*, ii, 431–2.
17. This and the following narrative are drawn from Viereck's booklet *Spreading the Germs of Hate*, 60 and 61.

Chapter 7 (pp. 86–98)

1–4. These quotations are drawn from the Cunard archive. Details of the crew of the *Lusitania* and her operating expenses come from papers of Charles Sumner in the author's possession.
5. The details about Captain Turner come from Miss Mabel Every who first met him in 1908. During the war years Turner was

separated from his wife and at the request of Turner's sisters Miss Every looked after him when he was ashore; she stayed as his housekeeper until he died in 1933. Miss Every, who is 92 as this book goes to press, is still living on Merseyside.

6. The narrative of Georg Vierick's advertisement comes from his own account of the affair which he published in 1930 and from a series of papers he submitted to Bernstorff, the German Ambassador in Washington. Von Papen's memoirs briefly touch on this episode and there is an excellent and scholarly account by Admiral Spindler entitled 'Der Lusitania-Fall' published in 1935.

7. Fregattenkapitän Bauer's war diary is in the German marine archives at Koblenz. Approved translation from Bailey: 'German Documents Relating to the Lusitania'. A copy of the translation, omitting the reference to the leakage of information, is in the Navy Library at the Ministry of Defence, London.

8. Dr Ritter von Rettegh's affidavit and numerous supporting documents are to be found in the State Department archives under the reference 841.857 L.

Chapter 8 (pp. 99–109)

1. Curt Thummel, alias Charles Thorne and Chester Williams, features throughout 'the Black Tom case' which has already been referred to (ch. 5, n.1). Leach's personal history and movements are noted by Agent Bielaski in his report on 'Gustav Stahl', filed with the State Department *Lusitania* file (341.111 L97/37). This report also contains most of the material on Hardenburg, Paul Koenig and Captain Boy-Ed.

2. The original loading plan of the vessel is in the Cunard archive, and the details of the cargo are taken from the manifest in the F. D. Roosevelt papers. The Liverpool box number features on the original consignment notes which were exhibits at the New York inquiry, and the identity of the holder is stated on the Roosevelt manifest. The cables as to the location of the ammunition are in the Cunard archive, as is the statement prepared but not used at the New York inquiry that certain sections of F Deck were used for cargo stowage. The Bethlehem Steel Company shipping note is Exhibit No. 28, Records of the New York District Court, Southern District, filed 11 May 1918. Mr Fraser's fur shipments are confirmed by the manifests: all copies

of them. The Cunard archive shows the shipping rate at which they were carried and the State Department *Lusitania* file contains a series of letters relating to the 'furs' which are examined in a later chapter.

3. The trans-shipment of the *Queen Margaret* passengers and cargo is related in a memorandum to Cunard from Sumner and a statement he swore before Lord, Day and Lord in New York which was entered into evidence at the New York inquiry. The cabin allocation of Mr and Mrs Matthews was given by Cunard to Donald Macmaster, K.C., M.P., who appeared as counsel for the Canadian Government before Lord Mersey's Inquiry on 15 June 1915. The body reports are from the Cunard archive which also contains a letter from Sgt Phelan of the Royal Irish Constabulary asking for a reward for finding and delivering the bodies of, presumably, Mrs Matthews and her child.

4. The affidavit and clearance certificate are open for public inspection among the Roosevelt MSS., Hyde Park, New York.

Chapter 9 (pp. 110–120)

1. Senior Third Officer Lewis compiled a short outline narrative of the disaster which is in the author's possession. He eventually retired to California and for many years he was a courteous and authoritative correspondent to the numerous enquirers interested in the history of the *Lusitania*.

2. The details of Captain Turner's visit to Sir Courtenay Bennett come from Miss Mabel Every.

3. Lansing to Bryan 1 May 1915; missing from the Bryan papers but quoted by Carlton Savage in *Policy of the United States towards Maritime Commerce in War*, 303–4.

4. *New York Times Magazine*, 31 January 1937, 3–27.

5. Schwieger's actions are taken from the log of the U-20 and his diary.

Chapter 10 (pp. 121–133)

1. W. S. Churchill papers, quoted in Gilbert, *W. S. Churchill*, iii, 185.

2. Fisher to Jellicoe, Jellicoe papers, 186.

3. *Ibid.*

4. Asquith to his wife: 'It is all *vanity* – he is devoured by vanity.' Countess of Oxford and Asquith papers, quoted in Margot Asquith diary, 289.
5. Clementine Churchill to W. S. Churchill. 187. Spencer-Churchill papers.
6. Beatty to Ethel Beatty. 187. Beatty papers.
7. Kenworthy and Young, *The Freedom of the Seas*, 211.

Chapter 11 (pp. 134–148)
1. *Liverpool Post*, 8 May 1915.
2. Schwieger war diary, Bundesarchiv, Koblenz; approved translation from Bailey: 'The Sinking of the Lusitania'.
3. P.R.O., ADM/137/1058/3269 and Home Waters Telegrams and Instructions No. 17/8/2/15.
4. Hendrick ed., *The Life and Letters of Walter Hines Page*, i, 436.
5. *Ibid*.
6. Report of Wesley Frost to Secretary of State, State Department Archives 341.111.L97/61.
7. Seymour ed., *The Intimate Papers of Colonel House*, i, 435.
8. Booth Autobiog. 149.
9. Seymour, *op. cit.*, i, 435.
10. Log of U-20, Bundesarchiv, Koblenz; translation from Bailey: 'The Sinking of the Lusitania'.

Chapter 12 (pp. 149–158)
1. Log of U-20, Bundesarchiv, Koblenz; translation from Bailey: 'The Sinking of the Lusitania'.
2. Testimony of Thomas Madden, Mersey Inquiry, 47: P.R.O., Foreign Office 3711/773(579).
3. The private papers of the Director of Naval Intelligence and his staff are kept at the Navy Records Office, Bath, and are not available for inspection.
4. Testimony of Leslie Morton, Mersey Inquiry, 16–19: P.R.O., Foreign Office 3711/773(579).
5. All the narrative in this chapter is taken from statements under oath made by survivors within a week of the disaster.

Chapter 13 (pp. 159–169)

1. State Department Archives 841.857.L97/29. Judge Mayer's Transcript, 262–72 and 294–312.
2. Evidence of J. C. Morton, Mersey Inquiry 170–80: P.R.O., Foreign Office 3711/773(579).
3. State Department Archives 841.857.L97/80.
4. ADM/137/1058–x 1, 101. Duplicated in Bd. Trade docket M.T.9.

Chapter 14 (pp. 170–182)

1. Nicolson, *Dwight Morrow*, 188–9.
2. Carlton Savage, ed., *Policy of the United States towards Maritime Commerce in War*, 335–7.
3. J. J. Horgan, *Parnell to Pearse*, Dublin, 1948, 372–6.
4. P.R.O., ADM/137/1058.
5. P.R.O., Board of Trade MT/9/1128.16308/1915.9949.
6. The Webb memorandum in Lord Mersey's papers, duplicated in P.R.O., ADM/137/1058.
7. P.R.O., ADM/137/1058/3621, 129.
8. *Ibid.*, 130.
9. *Ibid.*, 143.
10. The best account is to be found in Gilbert, *W. S. Churchill*, iii, 438–42.
11. Mersey papers.

Chapter 15 (pp. 183–196)

1. Hendrick ed., *The Life and Letters of Walter Hines Page*, iii, 239.
2. *Ibid.*, 243.
3. *Ibid.*, 254.
4. *The Public Papers of Woodrow Wilson*, iii, 321.
5. Hendrick, *op. cit.*, ii, 6.
6. *Baltimore Sun*, 14 May 1915.
7. Bryan to Wilson 12 May 1915, Bryan papers.
8. Wilson to Bryan 13 May 1915, *ibid.*
9. Bryan to Wilson 13 May 1915, *ibid.*
10. Lansing's diary, 8 May 1915, Lansing papers.
11. Memorandum from L. M. Garrison to William J. Flynn, Department of Justice Archive; copy in Garrison papers.

12. William J. Flynn, 'Tapped wires', *Liberty*, 2 June 1928, 19.
13. Wilson to Bryan 13 May 1915, Bryan papers.
14. *Vossische Zeitung*, Berlin, evening edition of 18 May 1915.
15. Lansing papers.
16. Bernstorff, *My Three Years in America*, 156. A similar version of the incident is told by Dumba himself in his *Memoirs of a Diplomat*.
17. Wilson to Bryan 20 May 1915, Bryan papers.
18. Lansing to Wilson, copied to Bryan, Bryan papers.
19. Lansing to Ambassador Gerard 9 June 1915, *Senate Foreign Relations*, monthly supplement for June, 436–8.

Chapter 16 (pp. 197–214)

1. Quotations in this and the following chapter are taken from the published transcript of the proceedings, P.R.O., Foreign Office 3711/773(579); of the *in camera* proceedings, Cmd 381 1919; and the published Report of the Court, P.R.O., ADM/137/1058/9966.
2. Lord Mersey's papers, and stated by him in his *in camera* address to the counsel concerned. It is missing from the Admiralty file of the case but a copy is in the British Museum as it appeared in Cmd 381 1919, which is also in the P.R.O. with the Foreign Office papers.
3. *Ibid.*
4. State Department Archives 841.857.L97/encl.4. Sworn before U.S. Consul Wesley Frost and enclosed with consular despatch of 17 June 1915.
5. Statement in letter addressed to Lansing which accompanied Mr Adams' statement referred to in 4 above.
6. Mersey papers, Marichal to Mersey 3 July 1915.

Chapter 17 (pp. 215–232)

1. Lord Mersey's report, 7: P.R.O., ADM/137/1058/9966, sheet 81.
2. Booth partnership letters, A. Booth to G. Booth 21 June 1915.
3. Mersey papers.
4. The carbon of the letter dated 19 July 1915 is in the Mersey papers. The original is not in Asquith's papers in the Bodleian

Library, but a second, silent copy was sent to Lord Cromer whose acknowledgement dated 25 July is in the Mersey papers.

Chapter 18 (pp. 233–242)

1. Mrs —— to the President of the United States 12 June 1915, Lansing papers.
2. State Department Archive 841.857.L97/74; copy in Lansing papers.
3. *Ibid.*
4. P.R.O., Foreign Office 371/773(579) complete file.
5. *Ibid.*
6. *Ibid.*
7. These incidents are also covered by a telegram from Ambassador Page to Lansing 29 August 1915, quoted in *U.S. Foreign Relations*, supplement 1915, 528. Affidavits from several U.S. citizens also appear in *Foreign Relations*, supplement 1915, 527–9, 543, 577, 605–6, 651. Admiral Spindler details them in *La Guerre sousmarine*, ii, 326–7. The English author E. K. Chatterton's *Q-Ships and their Story* omits to mention the treatment of the crew of the U-27.
8. Lansing to Page 18 October 1915. *Foreign Relations*, supplement 1915, 576–7 should read: 'change its *lenient* attitude . . .'.
9. This dialogue is now declassified and available on U.S. National Archive microfilm roll 198/580. This warning is repeated on frames 0376-7-8.
10–12. This is covered in great detail on U.S. National Archive microfilm (M 367 roll 25 frames 0074–0449). It is also copied in the Lansing papers.
13. Lansing papers and desk diary.

Chapter 19 (pp. 243–256)

1. Cunard archive.
2. *Ibid.*
3. *Ibid.*; also exhibit A99/1, Mayer Trial.
4. Cunard archive.
5. Lucius Beers to Lansing, 19 May 1917, Lansing papers.
6. Cunard archive.
7. *Ibid.*
8. *Ibid.*

9. State Department personal file on D. F. Malone.

10. La Follette, *Robert M. La Follette*, ii, 376.

11. Mayer transcript, 8; Cunard archive.

12. Secretary of the Navy to Mayer, Department of Justice Lusitania file.

13. Mayer decision, Southern District Court of New York, 23 August 1918.

14. *Lusitania* manifest package, Naval MSS. collection of F. D. Roosevelt, Hyde Park, New York.

15. Anecdote recounted by Sir Edward Marsh, Churchill's former private secretary, and a friend of both Strachey and Keynes.

16. Miss Every, Captain Turner's housekeeper, to Arnold Field of the *Sunday Times*, January 1972.

17. Lt-Com. Godfrey R.N. (Retd) to the author November 1971.

18. Leslie Gardiner, *The British Admiralty*, Edinburgh, 1968, 371.

19. Naval MSS Collection, Franklin D. Roosevelt Museum, Hyde Park, New York. The President had its manifest bound in a leather case. It is of course the carbon copy of the original which went down with the ship.

Sources

OFFICIAL SOURCES
British

Unpublished
The British documents relating to the *Lusitania* are widely dispersed.
In the Public Record Office they are divided between (and occasion-
ally duplicated by) the Admiralty records under the general file
reference ADM/137, the Foreign Office records under some 300
separate files listed in the index, and the Board of Trade records
under the classification MT/9. The records of the Naval Intelligence
department which relate to the vessel and her cargo are still
embargoed and are kept in the Navy Records Office at Bath. Papers
relating to her design, construction and modification to Admiralty
requirements and to her conversion to an armed cruiser exist in
photocopy form in the National Maritime Museum, Greenwich.
The originals have been 'mislaid'. The movements of the numerous
ships mentioned in the story are drawn from the series of Naval
Staff monographs available for inspection in the Navy Library, Earls
Court, whilst most signals are taken from the volumes of Home
Waters Telegrams available in the Public Record Office. The page
which relates to the telegrams sent on the morning of 7 May 1915 has,
in the words of the official responsible, 'been missing for a long
time'. A certified copy of the relevant signals is in the archive of the
1st Viscount Mersey at Bignor Park, Sussex. A copy of the transcript of Lord Mersey's Inquiry is in the British Museum Library
(Lord Mersey retained the original himself). There are several minor
differences between the original and the published versions.

Published
British Documents on the Origin of the War, 1898–1914, ed. G. P.
    Gooch and H. Temperley, Vols i–xi. London, 1926–36.

British and Foreign State Papers 1914–17. Vols cvii–cxi. London, 1917–1921.

Command Papers:

Cd 7816	1915	Correspondence between H.M.G. and the United States Government respecting the rights of belligerents.
Cd 8022	1915	Report of a formal investigation into the circumstances attending the foundering of the British steamship Lusitania.
Cd 8145	1916	Statement of the measures adopted to intercept the seaborne commerce of Germany.
Cd 7223	1916	Memorandum by H.M.G. and the French Government to neutral Governments regarding the examination of parcels and letter mails.
Cd 8225	1916	Correspondence with the United States Ambassador respecting the Trading with the Enemy Act 1915.
Cd 8233–4	1916	Further correspondence between H.M.G. and the United States Government respecting the rights of belligerents.
Cd 8349	1916	Memorandum respecting the treatment of belligerent submarines in Neutral waters.

American

Unpublished

The United States National Archives contain a far fuller account of the *Lusitania* affair than their British counterpart. Mostly the papers are filed under the classification 341.111.L 97, whilst the index to the State Department 'decimal files' as they are known has some two thousand relevant entries, mostly under the heading Confidential Box 141. Almost all have been microfilmed and the retrieval system of the National Archives makes them available almost immediately. Wesley Frost's consular despatches from Queenstown contain the most accurate account of the disaster, whilst the transcript of Cunard's plea to limit their liability and of the evidence together with all exhibits presented to Judge Julius B. Mayer in the Southern District Court of New York is available from the Federal Records Bureau (reference nos. A61–169). Much of the State Department material is duplicated in the 'Proceedings of the Mixed Claims

Commission of 1924' available from the Federal Records Bureau, but the latter is also valuable as it throws some light on the postwar life of Gustav Stahl.

Published

Compilation of the Messages and Papers of the Presidents, ed. James D. Richardson. 20 vols. Washington, 1896–1927.

Congressional Records. 63rd and 64th Congress. Vols li–iv.

European War, iii. *Diplomatic Correspondence with Belligerent Governments relating to Neutral Rights and Duties.* Washington, 1916.

Federal Reporter. Vol. ccli. St Paul, 1918.

Federal Reserve Bulletin 1914–1917. 4 vols. Washington, 1915–18.

Hearings before the Special Senate Committee [Nye Committee] *on the investigation of the Munitions Industry. U.S. Senate, 74th Congress, 2nd session.* Parts 25–32. Washington, 1937.

Hearings on Senate Bill 3474. U.S. Senate, 74th Congress, 2nd session. Washington, 1936.

Monthly Summary of the Foreign Commerce of the United States. Washington, *1914–17.*

Papers relating to the Foreign Relations of the United States. Supplements. The World War, 1914–17. Washington, 1928–32.

Policy of the United States towards Maritime Commerce in War, ed. Carlton Savage. 2 vols. Washington, 1936.

Report of the Federal Trade Commission on War Time Profits and Costs of the Steel Industry. 25 June 1924.

The United States Naval War Code. Washington, 1900.

Senate documents:

63rd Congress, 3rd session, No. 660.
66th Congress, 1st session, No. 62.
66th Congress, 2nd session, No. 191.
67th Congress, 2nd session, No. 176.
74th Congress, 2nd session: *Special confidential document printed for the use of the Special Senate Committee on the investigation of the Munitions Industry.* Washington, 1936.

Senate Reports:

42nd Congress, 2nd session, No. 183. Washington, 1872.
74th Congress, 2nd session, No. 994. Washington, 1936.
Proceedings of the Democratic National Convention, St Louis, Missouri, June 14–16 1916. Chicago, 1916.

The Public Papers of Woodrow Wilson. Authorised edition, ed. W. E. Dodd and R. S. Baker. New York, 1925–27.

German

Unpublished

Fregattenkapitän Bauer's war diary and the log of the U-20 are in the Bundesarchiv, Koblenz. The marine section of this archive also provided correspondence and records of telephone conversations between the Chief of the Naval Cabinet, the Chief of Naval Staff, the Chancellor and the Ministry of Foreign Affairs, 1914–17; also Orders and Instructions from the Chief of Naval Staff to submarine commanders, 1914–17.

Published

German Official Documents relating to the World War. New York, 1923.
Die Grosse Politik der Europäischen Kabinette. Vol. xl.
The Kaiser's Speeches, ed. Wolf von Schierbrand. New York, 1923.

PRIVATE PAPERS

(unless otherwise stated, in the Manuscripts Division of the Library of Congress)

ARNOLD-FORSTER, H. O. British Museum.

ASQUITH, EARL OF OXFORD AND. Bodleian Library, Oxford, by permission of Mr Mark Bonham-Carter.

BALFOUR, A. J. British Museum.

BARKER, WHARTON.

BAYARD, THOMAS.

BOOTH, ALFRED and GEORGE. Mr J. S. M. Booth and Booth and Co., London.

BRYAN, WILLIAM JENNINGS.

CARNEGIE, ANDREW.

CHAMBERLAIN, JOSEPH and AUSTEN. University of Birmingham Library.

CHOATE, JOSEPH H.

CUNARD COMPANY. Chairman's letter file and Board minutes.

GARRISON, L. M.

FISHER, ADMIRAL OF THE FLEET LORD. The Duke of Hamilton.

GORE, THOMAS P.

GREY, SIR EDWARD. Foreign Office Library.

HALL, CAPTAIN REGINALD. Private possession.

HOUSE, EDWARD M. Yale University Library.

HILL, DICKINSON AND CO. Mr R. L. Adam, Liverpool.

KITCHIN, CLAUDE. University of North Carolina.

LANSING, ROBERT M.

MAYER, JULIUS B. Archives of Department of Justice, New York.

MERSEY, 1ST VISCOUNT. 3rd Viscount Mersey, Bignor Park, Sussex.

MORGAN, J. P., JR. His full correspondence is not available but some 4000 letters and files relating to the purchase of munitions were exhibits before Senator J. P. Nye's committee investigating the munitions industry (74th Congress, 2nd session. Published Washington, 1936).

MORLEY, JOHN. India Office Library.

PAGE, WALTER HINES. Johns Hopkins University.

RICHMOND, ADMIRAL SIR HERBERT. National Maritime Museum, Greenwich.

ROOSEVELT, FRANKLIN D. Naval MSS. collection, Hyde Park, New York.

ROOSEVELT, THEODORE.

ROOT, ELIHU.

SCHWIEGER, WALTER KURT. Bundesarchiv, Koblenz.

SPINDLER, ADMIRAL ARNO. Correspondence with Professor Charles Seymour, Yale University Library, and with Charles Tansill, Johns Hopkins University.

WHITE, HENRY.

MISCELLANEOUS LETTERS, DIARIES, AND AUTOBIOGRAPHIES

ASQUITH, HERBERT. *Memories and Reflections 1852–1927*. 2 vols. London, 1927.

BEAVERBROOK, LORD. *Politicians and the War*. London, 1928.

BERNSTORFF, COUNT JOHANN H. *Memoirs*, trans. Eric Sutton. New York, 1936.

——. *My Three Years in America*. New York, 1920.

BATHMANN-HOLLWEG, THEOBALD VON. *Reflections on the World War*, trans. George Young. London, 1920.

BROWNRIGG, SIR DOUGLAS. *Indiscretions of the Naval Censor*. London, 1920.

BRYAN, WILLIAM JENNINGS and MARY. *The Memoirs of William Jennings Bryan*. Philadelphia, 1925.

CHURCHILL, WINSTON S. *The World Crisis*. 4 vols. London, 1923–27.

DUMBA, CONSTANTIN. *Memoirs of a Diplomat*, trans. Ian Morrow. Boston, 1932.

FALKENHAYN, GENERAL ERICH GEORGE A. S. VON. *General Headquarters 1914–16*. London, 1920.

——. *The German General Staff and its Decisions 1914–18*. New York, 1920.

FISHER, LORD (JOHN A.) *Memories and Records*. 2 vols. New York, 1920.

GREY, VISCOUNT (EDWARD). *Twenty-five Years 1892–1916*. 2 vols. London, 1924.

GWYNN, STEPHEN ed. *The Letters and Friendships of Sir Cecil Spring-Rice*. 2 vols. Boston, 1929.

HALDANE, RICHARD B. *An Autobiography*. New York, 1929.

HOFFMAN, GENERAL MAX. *The War of Lost Opportunities*, trans. A. E. Chamot. New York, 1925.

HOUSTON, DAVID F. *Eight Years with Wilson's Cabinet 1913–20*. New York, 1926.

JUSSERAND, JEAN J. *Le Sentiment américain pendant la guerre*. Paris, 1931.

LANE, FRANKLIN K. *Letters*, ed. A. W. Lane and L. H. Wall. Boston, 1922.

LANSING, ROBERT M. 'Memorandum of Secretary Lansing', published by Allen Dulles in *New York Times* magazine, 31 January 1937.

——. *My War Memoirs*. Indianapolis, 1935.

LLOYD GEORGE, DAVID. *War Memoirs 1914–18*. London, 1932–33.

LODGE, HENRY CABOT. *Selections from the Correspondence of Theodore Roosevelt 1884–1918*. 2 vols. New York, 1925.

LUDENDORFF, ERICH. *The General Staff and its Problems*, trans. F. A. Holt. 2 vols. London, 1920.

MCADOO, WILLIAM G. *Crowded Years*. Boston, 1931.

PARKER, SIR GILBERT. 'The United States and the War', *Harper's Magazine*, March 1918, 521–31.

REDFIELD, WILLIAM C. *With Congress and Cabinet*. New York, 1924.

REPINGTON, CHARLES À COURT. *The First World War 1914–18.* 2 vols. London, 1920.

SCHEER, ADMIRAL REINHARD. *Germany's High Seas Fleet in the World War.* London, 1920.

SCHURZ, CARL. *Speeches, Correspondence and Political Papers,* ed. Frederick Bancroft. 6 vols. New York, 1913.

SEYMOUR, CHARLES ed. *The Intimate Papers of Colonel House.* 2 vols. Boston, 1926.

SHARP, WILLIAM G. *War Memoirs.* London, 1931.

TIRPITZ, GRAND ADMIRAL ALFRED VON. *My Memoirs.* 2 vols. London, 1919.

——. *Politische Dokumente.* 2 vols. Berlin, 1926.

TUMULTY, JOSEPH P. *Woodrow Wilson as I know him.* New York, 1921.

VORSE, MARY. *A Footnote to Folly.* New York, 1935.

WHITLOCK, BRAND. *The Letters and Journal,* ed. Allan Nevins. 2 vols. New York, 1936.

WILHELM II. *The Kaiser's Memoirs 1888–1918.* New York, 1922.

BIOGRAPHIES, HISTORIES, SPECIAL STUDIES, ARTICLES ETC.

ADAMS, JAMES T. 'Anglo-American Relations', *Landmark,* xvi, 629–33.

ALLISON, CHARLES R. ed. *Alien Enemies and Property Rights under the Trading with the Enemy Act.* New York, 1921.

ALPHAUD, GABRIEL. *L'Action allemande aux Etats Unis, de la mission Dernberg à l'incident Dumba.* Paris, 1915.

ANDERSON, CHANDLER P. 'The British prize court decision in the Chicago packing house case', *American Journal of International Law,* xi, 1917, 251–69.

APPUHN, CHARLES. 'L'Ambassade de Bernstorff à Washington', *Revue d'Histoire de la Guerre Mondiale,* iii, 1925, 297–329.

ARCHIBALD, JAMES F. J. 'New Light on Ambassador Dumba's Recall', *Current History,* xxxv, 1931, 210–15.

BAILEY, THOMAS A. 'German Documents Relating to the Lusitania', *Journal of Modern History,* viii, 1936, 320–37.

——. 'The Sinking of the Lusitania', *American Historical Review,* xli, 1935–36, 54–73.

——. 'The United States and the Blacklist During the Great War', *Journal of Modern History*, vi, 1934, 14–35.

——. 'World War Analogues of the Trent Affair', *American Historical Review*, xxxviii, 1932–33, 286–90.

BAKER, RAY S. *Woodrow Wilson: Life and Letters.* 5 vols. New York, 1927–35.

BASSETT, JOHN S. *Our War With Germany.* New York, 1919.

BATY, THOMAS. 'Neglected Fundamentals of Prize Law', *Yale Law Journal*, xxx, 1920–21, 34–47.

——. 'Danger Signals in International Law', *Yale Law Journal*, xxxiv, 1924–25, 457–79.

——. 'The Declaration of London', *Empire Review*, July 1911, 361ff.

——. 'Judge Betts and Prize Law', *Transactions of the Grotius Society*, xi, 1926, 21–6.

BEARD, CHARLES A. *The Devil Theory of War.* New York, 1936.

——. 'New Light on Bryan and War Policies', *New Republic*, 17 June 1936, 177–8.

BELL, EDWARD P. *The British Censorship.* London, 1915.

BELLOT, HUGH L. 'The Right of a Belligerent Merchantman to Attack', *Transactions of the Grotius Society*, viii, 1922, 43–58.

BEMIS, SAMUEL F. *A Diplomatic History of the United States.* New York, 1937.

BENTWICH, NORMAN D. *The Declaration of London.* London, 1911.

BISHOP, JOSEPH B. *Theodore Roosevelt and His Times.* 2 vols. New York, 1920.

BLUELL, R. L. *The Washington Conference.* New York, 1922.

BORCHARD. EDWIN. *Review of International Law and the World War* by James W. Garner, *The Nation*, 20 July 1921, 72–3.

BORCHARD, EDWIN, and LAGE, W. P. *Neutrality for the United States.* New Haven, 1937.

BRIERLY, JAMES L. 'International Law in England', *Law Quarterly Review*, li, 1935, 24–35.

BRIGGS, HERBERT W. *The Doctrine of Continuous Voyage.* Baltimore, 1926.

BROOKS, SIDNEY. 'America at the Cross-Roads', *The English Review*, xx, 1915, 356–66.

BRUNAUER, ESTHER C. 'The Peace Proposals of December 1916 – January 1917', *Journal of Modern History*, iv, 1932, 544–71.

BRUNTZ, GEORGE C. 'Propaganda as an Instrument of War', *Current History*, xxxii, 1930, 743–7.

BUELL, RAYMOND L. *The Washington Conference.* New York, 1922.

CAMPBELL, REAR-ADMIRAL GORDON. *My Mystery Ships.* London, n.d.

CECIL, SIR ALGERNON. *British Foreign Secretaries, 1807–1916.* London, 1927.

CHAMBERLAIN, JOSEPH. 'The Embargo Resolutions and Neutrality', *International Conciliation*, June 1929.

CHATTERTON, EDWARD K. *Q-Ships and Their Story.* London, 1922.

CHIROL, VALENTINE. *Cecil Spring-Rice: In Memoriam.* London, 1919.

CLAPP, EDWIN J. *Economic Aspects of the War.* New Haven, 1915.

COHEN, SIR ARTHUR. *The Declaration of London.* London, 1911.

COLE, SANFORD D. 'Belligerent Merchantmen in Neutral Ports', *Transactions of the Grotius Society*, iii, 1918, 23ff.

CONSETT, MONTAGUE W. W. P., and DANIEL, O. H. *The Triumph of Unarmed Forces, 1914–1918.* New York, 1923.

CORBETT, SIR JULIAN S. *Naval Operations.* 2 vols. London, 1920–1921.

COREY, LEWIS. *The House of Morgan.* New York, 1930.

CRECRAFT, EARL W. *Freedom of the Seas.* New York, 1935.

CROWELL, BENEDICT. *America's Munitions, 1917–1918.* Washington, 1919.

CURTI, MERLE E. *The American Peace Crusade.* Durham, 1929.

——. *Bryan and World Peace.* Northampton, 1931.

DANIELS, JOSEPHUS. *The Life of Woodrow Wilson, 1856–1924.* Philadelphia, 1924.

DAVIS, ELMER. *History of the New York Times.* New York, 1921.

DEMARTIAL, GEORGES. *Comment on mobilisa les consciences.* Paris, 1922.

DENNIS, ALFRED L. P. *Adventures in American Diplomacy.* New York, 1928.

DEWEY, DAVIS R. *Financial History of the United States.* New York, 1928.

DODD, WILLIAM E. *Woodrow Wilson and His Work.* New York, 1920.

DOYLE, SIR ARTHUR CONAN. 'Danger!', *Collier's Weekly*, 22 August 1914, 5ff, and 29 August 1914, 7ff.

ELLIOTT, CHARLES B. 'The Doctrine of Continuous Voyage', *American Journal of International Law*, i, 1907, 61–104.

FAY, SIDNEY B. *The Origins of the World War*. New York, 1928.

FAYLE, CHARLES E. *Seaborne Trade*. 3 vols. London, 1920–24.

FLYNN, WILLIAM J. 'Tapped Wires', *Liberty*, 2 June 1928, 19–22.

FRENCH, GERALD. *The Life of Field-Marshal Sir John French*, London, 1931.

FROST, WESLEY. *German Submarine Warfare*. New York, 1918.

FULLER, JOSEPH V. 'William Jennings Bryan' in *American Secretaries of State and Their Diplomacy*, x, 3–44. New York, 1929.

——. 'The Genesis of the Munitions Traffic', *Journal of Modern History*, vi, 1934, 280–93.

GANTENBEIN, JAMES W. *The Doctrine of Continuous Voyage*. Portland, 1929.

GARNER, JAMES W. *Prize Law During the World War*. New York, 1927.

——. *International Law and the World War*. 2 vols. New York, 1920.

GAYER, CAPT. ALBERT. 'Summary of German Submarine Operations in the Various Theaters of War from 1914 to 1918', *Proceedings of the United States Naval Institute*, li, 1926, 621–59.

——. *Die Deutschen U-Boote in ihrer Kriegführung, 1914–1918*. Berlin, 1920.

GILBERT, MARTIN. *W. S. Churchill*. Vol. iv. London, 1972.

GRAHAM, MALBONE W. *The Controversy Between the United States and the Allied Governments Respecting Neutral Rights and Commerce during the Period of American Neutrality, 1914–1917*. Austin, 1923.

GROOS, OTTO. *Der Krieg in der Nordsee*. 5 vols. Berlin, 1922–25.

GUICHARD, LT LOUIS. *The Naval Blockade*, trans. Christopher R. Turner. London, 1930.

HENDRICK, BURTON J. ed. *The Life and Letters of Walter Hines Page*. 3 vols. London, 1925.

HICKS BEACH, LADY VICTORIA. *Life of Sir Michael Hicks Beach*. 2 vols. 1932.

HIGGINS, A. PEARCE. *Studies in International Law and Relations*. Cambridge, 1928.

HOUGHTON, W. H. 'The Albert Portfolio', *Saturday Evening Post*, 17 August 1929, 117.

HOWDEN-SMITH, ARTHUR D. *The Real Colonel House*. New York, 1918.

HURD, SIR ARCHIBALD S. *The Merchant Navy.* 3 vols. London, 1921–29.

HYDE, CHARLES C. *International Law Chiefly as Interpreted and Applied by the United States.* 2 vols. Boston, 1922.

JAMES, ADMIRAL SIR WILLIAM. *The Eyes of the Navy.* London, n.d.

JANE, FRED T. *Fighting Ships.* London, 1914.

KEIM, JEANETTE. *Forty Years of German-American Political Relations.* Philadelphia, 1919.

KENWORTHY, JOSEPH M., and YOUNG, GEORGE. *Freedom of the Seas.* New York, 1929.

LA FOLLETTE, B. and F. *Robert M. La Follette.* 2 vols. New York, 1953.

LAMONT, THOMAS W. *Henry P. Davison.* New York, 1933.

——. Article in *Manchester Guardian*, 27 January 1920.

LAURENS, ADOLPHE. *Histoire de la guerre sous-marine Allemande.* Paris, 1939.

LAURIAT, CHARLES E. *The Lusitania's Last Voyage.* New York, 1915.

LAWRENCE, DAVID. *The True Story of Woodrow Wilson.* New York, 1924.

LINGELBACH, WILLIAM E. 'England and Neutral Trade', *The Military Historian and Economist*, ii, 1917, 153–78.

LINK, PROFESSOR A. S. *Woodrow Wilson.* Vols. i–iii. Princeton, 1947–1965.

LODGE, HENRY C. *Senate and the League of Nations.* New York, 1925.

LUETZOW, CAPT. FRIEDRICH. 'Der Lusitania-Fall', *Süddeutsche Monatshefte*, xviii, 1921, 391ff.

Lusitania-Fall, Der. Breslau, 1915. (A symposium of articles by German university professors relating to the sinking of the *Lusitania.*)

LUTZ, HERMANN. *Lord Grey and the World War.* New York, 1928.

MCMASTER, JOHN B. *The United States and the World War.* New York, 1918.

MARDER, A. J. *From the Dreadnought to Scapa Flow.* 4 vols. Oxford, 1964–70.

MATHEWS, JOHN M. *The Conduct of American Foreign Relations.* New York, 1928.

MICHELSEN, ANDREAS H. *Der U-Bootskrieg.* Leipzig, 1925.

MILLIS, WALTER. *Road to War.* Boston, 1935.

MONGER, J. W. *The End of Isolation*. London, 1964.

MONTAGUE, VICTOR A. 'For and Against the Declaration of London', *Nineteenth Century and After*, lxix, 1911, 414–16.

MONTGELAS, MAX. *British Foreign Policy under Sir Edward Grey*. New York, 1928.

MOORE, JOHN B. *Principles of American Diplomacy*, New York, 1918.

——. Statement during Hearings on Senate Bill, 3474, Senate Committee on Foreign Relations, 74th Cong., 2nd sess.

——. *Digest of International Law*. 8 vols. Washington, 1906.

MORLEY, JOHN. 'On the Eve of Catastrophe', *New Republic*, 10 October 1928, 194–200.

NICOLSON, HAROLD. *Dwight Morrow*. New York, 1935.

NOTTER, HARLEY. *The Origins of the Foreign Policy of Woodrow Wilson*. Baltimore, 1937.

NOYES, ALEXANDER D. *The War Period of American Finance*. New York, 1926.

OSUSKY, STEPHEN. 'The Secret Peace Negotiations Between Vienna and Washington', *Slavonic Review*, iv, 1926, 657–68.

OWSLEY, FRANK L. *King Cotton Diplomacy*. Chicago, 1931.

PARMELEE, MAURICE. *Blockade and Sea Power*. New York, 1924.

PAXSON, FREDERIC L. *The Pre-War Years, 1913–1917*. Boston, 1936.

PHILIPS, ETHEL C. 'American participation in belligerent commercial controls, 1914–1917', *American Journal of International Law*, xxiv, 1933, 675–93.

PIGGOTT, SIR FRANCIS. *The Neutral Merchant and Contraband of War and Blockade*. London, 1915.

POHL, HEINRICH. *Amerikas Waffenausfuhr und Neutralität*. Berlin, 1917.

POLLOCK, SIR FREDERICK. 'The Declaration of London', *Law Quarterly Review*, xxvii, 1911, 269–70.

PONSONBY, ARTHUR. *Falsehood in War-Time*. New York, 1928.

POTTER, PITMAN B. *Freedom of the Seas*. New York, 1924.

PRATT, JULIUS W. 'The British Blockade and American Precedent', *United States Naval Institute Proceedings*, xlvi, 1920, 1789–1802.

——. 'Robert Lansing', in Samuel F. Bemis, *American Secretaries of State and their Diplomacy*, x, 47–175. New York, 1929.

——. *Expansionists of 1898*. Baltimore, 1936.

PRENDERGAST, MAURICE, and R. H. GIBSON. *The German Sub-marine War, 1914–1918.* New York, 1931.

PYKE, HAROLD R. *The Law of Contraband of War.* London, 1915.

ROBINSON, EDGAR E., and WEST, V. J. *The Foreign Policy of Wood-row Wilson, 1913–1917.* New York, 1917.

ROOSEVELT, THEODORE. *America and the World War.* New York, 1914.

SALTER, SIR ARTHUR. *Allied Shipping Control.* Oxford, 1921.

SCOTT, JAMES B. *A Survey of International Relations between the United States and Germany.* New York, 1917.

SEYMOUR, CHARLES ed. *The Intimate Papers of Colonel House.* 2 vols, Boston, 1926.

——. *Woodrow Wilson and the World War.* New Haven, 1921.

——. *American Diplomacy during the World War.* Baltimore, 1934.

——. *American Neutrality, 1914–1917.* New Haven, 1935.

SIMS, ADMIRAL WILLIAM S. 'The truth about German sub-marine atrocities', *Current History*, xviii, 1923, 355–63.

SKAGGS, WILLIAM H. *The German Conspiracies in America.* London, 1915.

SNOW, FREEMAN. *International Law.* Washington, 1888.

SPENDER, JOHN A. and ASQUITH, CYRIL. *Life of Herbert Henry Asquith, Lord Oxford and Asquith.* 2 vols. London, 1932.

SPERRY, EARL E., and WEST, W. M. *German Plots and Intrigues in the United States during the Period of Our Neutrality.* Washington, 1918.

SPINDLER, REAR-ADMIRAL ARNO. 'Der Lusitania Fall', *Berliner Monatshefte*, May 1935, 402–10.

——. 'Der Eintritt der Vereinigten Staaten in den Weltkrieg', *Berliner Monatshefte*, April 1937, 281–321.

——. 'The Value of the Submarine in Naval Warfare', *Proceedings of the United States Naval Institute*, li, 1926, 835–54.

——. *La Guerre sous-marine*, trans. Captain René Jouan. 3 vols. Paris, 1933–35.

SQUIRES, JAMES D. *British Propaganda at Home and in the United States, 1914–1917.* Cambridge, 1935.

STOLBERG-WERNIGERODE, COUNT OTTO. *Deutschland und die Vere-inigten Staaten von Amerika im Zeitalter Bismarcks.* Berlin, 1933.

STRAUS, OSCAR S. *Under Four Administrations.* Boston, 1922.

STREET, CECIL J. S. *Lord Reading.* London, 1928.

STROTHER, FRENCH. *Fighting Germany's Spies*. New York, 1918.

——. 'America, a New World Arsenal', *World's Work*, xxxi, 1916, 321–33.

TANSILL, C. C. *'America Goes to War'*. Boston, 1938.

THUILLIER, SIR HENRY F. 'Can Methods of Warfare be Restricted?', *Journal of the Royal United Service Institution*, lxxxi, 1936, 264–76.

TREVELYAN, GEORGE M. *Grey of Fallodon*. Boston, 1937.

TRIMBLE, E. G. 'Violations of Maritime Law by the Allied Powers during the World War', *American Journal of International Law*, xxiv, 1930, 79–99.

TURLINGTON, EDGAR. *Neutrality: Its History, Economics and Law*. Vol. viii.

VAGTS, ALFRED. *Deutschland und die Vereinigten Staaten in der Weltpolitik*. 2 vols. London, 1925.

——. 'Colonel House', *Europäische Gespräche*, vii, 1929, 430–42.

VALENTIN, VEIT. *Deutschlands Aussenpolitik von Bismarcks Abgang bis zum Ende des Weltkrieges*. Berlin, 1921.

VAN ALSTYNE, RICHARD. 'The Policy of the United States Regarding the Declaration of London, at the Outbreak of the Great War', *Journal of Modern History*, vii, 1935, 434–47.

——. 'Private American Loans to the Allies, 1914–1916', *Pacific Historical Review*, ii, 1933, 180–93.

VIALLATE, ACHILLE. *Les Etats-Unis et le Conflit Européen*, 4 Août 1914–6 Avril 1917. Paris, 1919.

VIERICK, GEORGE S. *Spreading the Germs of Hate*. New York, 1930.

——. *The Strangest Friendship in History*. New York, 1932.

WARREN, CHARLES. 'Troubles of a Neutral', *Foreign Affairs*, xii, 1934, 377–95.

——. 'Safeguards to Neutrality', *Foreign Affairs*, xiv, 1936, 199–215.

WHITE, WILLIAM A. *Woodrow Wilson*. Boston, 1924.

WHITNEY, EDSON L. *The American Peace Society*. Washington, 1928.

WILLIAMS, BENJAMIN H. *Economic Foreign Policy of the United States*. New York, 1929.

WINKLER, JOHN K. *Morgan the Magnificent*. New York, 1931.

WOOLSEY, LESTER H. 'The Personal Diplomacy of Colonel House', *American Journal of International Law*, xxl, 1927, 706–15.

WRIGHT, QUINCY. *The Control of American Foreign Relations*. New York, 1922.

Index

National City Bank, 54, 56

National Maritime Museum, 11, 31

National Sailors' and Firemen's Union, 204

Naval Annual, 1914, 72, 137

Naval Operations, 115

Nereide, 77–8

New England Steamship Company, 109

New York, Austro-Hungarian Embassy, 69, 96; British Consulate, 59; Customs, 11, 51; district court inquiry, 18, 253–254; German Embassy, 64, 92–3, 101; Harbour, 65, 72; port of, 64, 70

New York Sun, 91, 93, 111

New York Times, 57, 118, 171, 172, 194, 233

New York Tribune, 30–1, 110, 118–9

Nicolson, Sir Arthur, 230

Nicolson, Harold, 172

Nicosian, 238

Nolan, Friedland and Digby, 251

Norddeutscher Lloyd Company, 20, 62

Nolan, John M., 251, 253

North Atlantic, shipping trade, 20–1

North Sea, British blockade of, 39, 58–9; minefields, 57; war zone, 74, 75–7, 83

Official Secrets Act, 10

Old Head of Kinsale, 9, 14, 109, 130, 133, 147, 168, 175, 177, 254

Oliver, F. S., 45

Oliver, Vice-Admiral, Henry, as Chief of Naval War Staff, 66,

123–8, 141; at Loch Ewe, 33n; concealment of facts, 173, 175–6, 179, 202; and *Juno*, 169; and message interception, 67; and mine-laying, 47; and munition and troop cargoes, 70–1

Olympic, 234

Orduna, 52

Oregon, 26

Orion, 127

Osborne Naval Training College, 34

Oysterhaven, 168

Page, Walter Hines, and American intervention, 183–4; and Captain Hall, 66–7; and Colonel House, 141–2; and news of the sinking, 170–1

Paish, Sir George, 53

Papen, Franz von, 64–6, 69, 91, 99, 100, 256

Parmour, 1st Baron, 44

Peaslee, Amos, 100

Pershouse, Mr, 247–8

Peskett, Leonard, 23–7, 34, 205, 247–9, 251

Phelan, Sergeant, 109

Pinkerton Detective Agency, 62

Pinto, Manuel, 78

Pitney, Vance, 118–9

Pohl, Vice-Admiral von, 75

Poole, 38

Post Office, censorship, 67

Powell, Mr, 237

Providence Journal, 111

Public Record Office, 11, 119

Queen Margaret, 103, 108

Queen Mary, 66, 256

FIND OUT MORE ABOUT
PENGUIN BOOKS

We publish the largest range of titles of any English language paperback publisher. As well as novels, crime and science fiction, humour, biography and large-format illustrated books, Penguin series include *Pelican Books* (on the arts, sciences and current affairs), *Penguin Reference Books*, *Penguin Classics*, *Penguin Modern Classics*, *Penguin English Library* and *Penguin Handbooks* (on subjects from cookery and gardening to sport), as well as *Puffin Books* for children. Other series cover a wide variety of interests from poetry to crosswords, and there are also several newly formed series – *King Penguin*, *Penguin American Library*, *Penguin Diaries and Letters* and *Penguin Travel Library*.

We are an international publishing house, but for copyright reasons not every Penguin title is available in every country. To find out more about the Penguins available in your country please write to our U.K. office – Dept EP, Penguin Books Ltd, Harmondsworth, Middlesex UB7 ODA – unless you live in one of the following areas:

In the U.S.A.: Dept DG, Penguin Books, 299 Murray Hill Parkway, East Rutherford, New Jersey 07073.

In Canada: Penguin Books Canada Ltd, 2801 John Street, Markham, Ontario L3R 1B4.

In Australia: Marketing Department, Penguin Books Australia Ltd, P.O. Box 257, Ringwood, Victoria 3134.

In New Zealand: Marketing Department, Penguin Books (N.Z.) Ltd, P.O. Box 4019, Auckland 10.

In India: Penguin Overseas Ltd, 706 Eros Apartments, 56 Nehru Place, New Delhi 110019.

Also by Colin Simpson in Penguins

THE SHIP THAT HUNTED ITSELF

At the beginning of World War 1, the captains of British ocean liner *Carmania* and the German liner *Cap Trafalgar* were ordered to convert their ships into armed merchant cruisers. Neither was particularly strong, so both resorted to disguise.

By coincidence, each disguised herself as the other. By an even greater coincidence, they met in the south Atlantic – and fought one of the most curious and heroic engagements in naval history.

VOICES FROM THE GREAT WAR
Peter Vansittart

'This stupendous and kaleidoscopic book takes the lid off the Great War of 1914–18 and reveals . . . the sight, sound and smell of Armageddon' – *London Magazine*

Bringing together Freud, Mandelstam, Lloyd George, Bertrand Russell, Rosenberg, Sassoon, Vera Brittain – voices famous and unknown, Peter Vansittart takes us through the course of the Great War, juxtaposing letters from the trenches with music-hall songs, the words of poets and politicians. Linking the public and the personal, the history with the myth, his rich and unorthodox anthology forms a moving image of everything that went into the War, and culminated in its 'scalding waste of spirit'.

'A historical echo chamber, agog with eye-witnesses, news-paper headlines, memoirs, massacres and maniacs. He arranges his relics with moving irony' – *Sunday Times*

'This valuable and entertaining anthology . . . does not set out to demythologize the War . . . But it goes a long way towards decosmeticizing it, showing the savage realities in which the myth had its roots' – *Observer*

THE PENGUIN BOOK OF
FIRST WORLD WAR POETRY
Edited by John Silkin

This volume offers the best work by the best poets of the war. A few of them, like Kipling, Hardy and Flint, were not com-batants yet wrote poetry concerned with the War: others, like Edward Thomas, did not survive long enough for the experience of combat to enter into their work. But most of the poets were also soldiers and the representatives of a crucial period in the development of English poetry.

DEATH'S MEN
Soldiers of the Great War
Denis Winter

'I would say that it is by a long way the best general book I have read on this war. It tells me a great deal about it that I did not know before and there is nothing in it I would question. I find it amazing that someone who did not experience it should write so vividly and movingly and accurately about it. Certainly every survivor of that distant holocaust should read it' – Gerald Brenan in a letter to the author.

THE FIRST OF THE FEW:
Fighter Pilots of the First World War
Denis Winter

'We had scarcely more than begun to know what living meant but we all knew about dying . . .'

Author of the highly acclaimed *Death's Men*, in which he memorably distilled the dark and terrible experiences of the men in the trenches, Denis Winter examines here the world of the fighter pilot, from enlistment to demobilization. A fascinating and accurate reconstruction of tactics, machines and procedures, a penetrating assessment of psychological behaviour, a brilliant evocation of the excitements, dangers and dream-like unrealities of the time, he has once again written a book which rises above the purely military and technical to say something important about people and war.

'A very good book indeed' – *Guardian*

'Fascinating reading' – *Aviation News*

'An excellent book which will be widely read' – *Book Choice*

THE PRICE OF GLORY
Verdun 1916
Alistair Horne

'Brilliantly written . . . almost like a historical novel – except that it is true' – Field Marshal Viscount Montgomery.

Verdun was the battle that lasted ten months; the battle where at least 700,000 men died, along a front of fifteen miles; the battle which aimed less to defeat the enemy than to bleed him to death; the battle whose once fertile terrain is even now 'the nearest thing to desert in Europe'. Alistair Horne's profoundly moving study shows it to be also the key to an understanding of the First World War.

IN FLANDERS FIELDS
Leon Wolff

Passchendaele 1917. There is no name more evocative of the 'mud and blood' of the gallant and inglorious trench warfare on the Western Front. Leon Wolff's classic account of the Flanders campaign was described by Major-General J. F. C. Fuller as 'an outstanding book . . . much more than a military history, rather an invocation which summons from out of the depths of the past the catastrophic year of 1917 . . . Here is brought to light again all its many facets, its antagonisms, its blunders, its horrors and its heroism'.

THE SPANISH FARM TRILOGY
R. H. *Mottram*

As the line of the Western Front ebbs and flows across Flanders, the Spanish Farm – built to withstand the wars of an earlier century – faces this one with the same imperturbable stolidity. And to the men who come to know the farm, the rough comfort of its buildings, Jerome Vanderlynden's persistent preoccupation with his crops, and his daughter Madeleine's bourgeois practicality offer an oasis of enduring sanity to which they turn with relief.

The Spanish Farm, Sixty-Four, Ninety-Four and *The Crime at Vanderlynden's* were first published as a trilogy in 1927, when *The Times Literary Supplement* acclaimed it as 'perhaps the most significant work of its kind in English that the War has yet occasioned'.

THE WARS
Timothy Findley

Winner of Canada's Governor-General Award and of the City of Toronto Book Award.

A book about war that illuminates all wars. A book with the immediacy – and impact – of a film. The story of a young Canadian officer in 1915, drawn into the most traumatic war of all time.

'It is a book that demands superlatives and that stands comparison with any fiction being produced in the English language. I doubt if any reader will think that statement too sweeping' – *Toronto Star*

Penguin Travel Library

A selection

THE WORST JOURNEY IN THE WORLD
ANTARCTIC 1910–13
Apsley Cherry-Garrard

Comparable to any story of adventure in the world, Scott's last Antarctic expedition is unforgettably described by a survivor whose book is a record of the faith and courage of his friends. The author was in the party which found the bodies of Scott, Wilson and Bowers on 12 November 1912 and buried them 'in a grave which kings must envy'.

'It is told without the slightest literary affectation or artificiality, and is thus – what few travellers' tales are – absolutely and convincingly credible' – George Bernard Shaw

THE HILL OF DEVI
E. M. Forster

An account of two visits E. M. Forster made to the state of Dawas Senior, where he was secretary to the Maharajah – 'certainly a genius, and possibly a saint, and he had to be king'. Consisting largely of letters written home, *The Hill of Devi* portrays as vivid and immediate impressions many of the details which were to recur in *A Passage to India*.

'A classic account of a vanished side of India that has never before been so graphically painted' – Raymond Mortimer in the *Sunday Times*

Penguin Travel Library

A selection

A REED SHAKEN BY THE WIND
Gavin Maxwell

Between Baghdad and Basra lies 2,000 square miles of un-explored marshland waste, inhabited by the Ma'dan, a tribe whose primitive way of life has remained unchanged for thousands of years. Gavin Maxwell went to live among these people and describes their strange existence in this classic travel book.

'He writes so well and effortlessly that his experiences become our own' – *Sunday Times*

'A work of art' – *Spectator*

AFRICA DANCES
Geoffrey Gorer

Describing his travels through French West Africa, Senegal, French Guinea, the Ivory Coast, Dahomey, the Gold Coast and Nigeria, Geoffrey Gorer's marvellous book vividly recreates an Africa on the point of transition.

'He has made one of the most singular journeys of modern times . . . There are no reservations in this astonishing book. Sex, religion, politics, the negro conception of life contrasted with the white man's, the place of fetish and magic, wrestling, dancing and marriage . . . The result is a book I could not put down' – *Daily Telegraph*

Penguin Travel Library

A selection

PASSAGES FROM ARABIA DESERTA
C. M. Doughty
Selected by Edward Garnett

Eccentric, redolent with sharply observed life, anecdote, local colour and telling detail, *Arabia Deserta* is not only a Victorian traveller's interpretation of a mysterious – and largely unfathomed – Orient, but also a daring experiment in the use of language at its richest.

'A book so majestic, so vital, of such incomparable beauty of thought, of observation, and of diction as to occupy a place apart' – *Observer*

ONE'S COMPANY
Peter Fleming

Packed with classic incidents – brake-failure on the Trans-Siberian Express, the Eton Boating Song singing lesson in Manchuria – *One's Company* is Peter Fleming's account of his journey to China as Special Correspondent to *The Times* in 1933.

'Original and impressive . . . As a journalist he is modernity itself; as a traveller he has about him an Elizabethan aroma, being both cruel and amused' – Harold Nicolson in the *Daily Telegraph*